RETROCOGNITIONS

AN INVESTIGATION INTO MEMORIES OF PAST LIVES AND THE PERIODS BETWEEN LIVES

Wagner Alegretti

RETROCOGNITIONS

An investigation into memories of past lives and the periods between lives

1st Edition in English

Miami, USA
International Academy of Consciousness
2004

First Edition in English – 2004
Copyright © 2004 by Wagner Alegretti

Notes:
The author's rights to this edition have been graciously transferred to the
International Academy of Consciousness (IAC)
The original pages of this edition were produced and revised using elec-
tronic desktop publishing and laser printing (text in Baskerville
Regular/Medium: 225,769 characters, 39,951 words, 3,802 lines and
1,242 paragraphs)

Cover: Valesca Ferreira
Photography: IAC – Florida Office
Translation into English: Luis Minero
Proofreaders: Jeffrey Lloyd, Liliana Alexandre, Bruce Samuels, Cecilia
Calderon, David Lindsay, Ikam Acosta, William Bliss, Jack Grabon, Mike
Lydon
Electronic typesetting: David Lindsay, Jane Lloyd
Printing: Innova Books. Miami, USA.

Alegretti, Wagner, 1961 -

A366r   Retrocognitions: an investigation into memories of past lives and the
         periods between lives/
         Wagner Alegretti
            1st Edition in English – Miami, USA: International Academy of
            Consciousness   2004.
314 p.

         1. Projectiology. 2. Conscientiology. 3. Mnemosomatics. I. Title

    ISBN 0-9702131-6-6   CDD 132.221

Card Catalog Information prepared by the Center of Information and
Documentation of the IAC

International Academy of Consciousness (IAC)
7800 SW 57th Ave, Suite 207D
Miami, FL 33143
USA
E-mail: florida@iacworld.org

Internet: www.iacworld.org

ACKNOWLEDGMENTS

I consider it a privilege to be able to leave an imprint, a permanent and public thosenic signature, of sincere gratitude to those of our evolutionary group who have helped us, in one way or another, in the execution of our existential program.

I thank my parents - Jeovah and Anizia Alegretti - who made every effort so that, among many other things, I could study in favorable circumstances. It was possible for me to dedicate myself to university, full-time for 5 years, without having to work; which facilitated the beginning of my study of multidimensionality and the practice of conscious projection. I recognize their encouragement and support of my eagerness for scientific exploration, research and experimentation, and also the proffering of total freedom of thought, without the imposition of ideas or values that could have inhibited my intermissive course.

I dedicate all thosenes of sincere and honest gratitude to the old-friend consciousness, in this life called Waldo Vieira, who since our first contact by telephone in 1982, adopted me and offered me his friendship, energy, knowledge, patience and, mainly, many hours, days, months and years of discussions and summations of ideas. His presence has been so profound that this book is permeated with his influence.

To my past and present evolutionary companions, colleagues from IAC, ARACE, Assinvexis, CHSC, IIPC and IOC, who have added so many ideas and experiences and have helped me begin to overcome certain deep-rooted weak traits from the past. I am convinced that I was never, in the last centuries, surrounded by so many good people. Thanks, obrigado, grazie, kiitos, dank and gracias to you, and I hope all of you become existential completists so that we can continue together in the next intraphysical existence.

I would like to enumerate everybody; nonetheless it would be impossible to include everyone. To diminish the list of those not mentioned here, I also thank these important people, for their support and inspiration: Wilson Alegretti, Jandira Vianna, Luis Minero, *and* Umberto Silva.

And, mainly, my affectionate holosomatic gratitude to my evolutionary partner, Nanci Trivellato. Much beyond the revision of this work and her opportune suggestions, I thank her for her companionship and support during the most critical phase of this physical life, for her inexhaustible affection and patience with this consciousness in evolution. Our reencounter occurred in the context of the end of the preparatory phase of my existential program and the beginning of the executive phase, with new recycling and maturing that allowed the integration of several more theoretical concepts and information into a more practical and assistential body of knowledge, including the present book.

After intraphysical consciousnesses, I remember those that do not need nor wait for gratitude: the extraphysical helpers. Today, more than ever, I understand that without their permanent, subtle, but intense performance, I would not be here typing these acknowledgments.

I dedicate this book to an intraphysical consciousness who is still in the preparatory phase of his existential program. I hope that this book can serve as one of the elements that contribute to the discovery and materialization of his existential program: to my son Allan Alegretti.

To all of you, readers, my sincere wishes of existential completism.

Wagner Alegretti
London, March 9, 2004

CONTENTS

PREFACE

The Value of Retrocognitions

Consciential epicenter. With unusual pleasure we present this opportune book, the author's first broader work, a person with professional level of high capacity, whom we admire and with whom we have coexisted since 1982. We have followed his trajectory closely, since he chose to execute his existential program making an evolutionary career in conscientiology, giving up economic-financial independence where he was very well established in an international company, to his current condition as a *self-conscious multidimensional epicenter*, beyond the limits of neuropsychic circuits.

Search. We observed throughout that entire period the carefulness of the extremely disciplined personality of Wagner Alegretti in monitoring infantile or infantilizing enthusiasms in his search for lucid self-evolution. We now see one more of the durable results of all that personal and continued effort of his indelible *thosenic signatures* in being in the counterflow of the clarification task.

Cosmo-vision. The relevance, seriousness and depth of the subjects in question in these pages offer a wide cosmo-vision of the intimate problems of the intraphysical consciousness; starting from the convention of time − *the measurement of the movement of matter* − and personal memories, up to the valuing of self-induced and healthy retrocognitions.

Self guinea pigs. The past supplies examples and irreplaceable formulas for avoiding the repetition of errors and spurious acts generated by inexperience. Retrocognitions expose us as *explicit self guinea pigs*.

Mnemosomatics. This technical volume demonstrates permanent rigidity in the observation and interpretation of facts, filling in the holes in the universe of studies regarding Mnemosomatics, with a didactic, clear and accessible composition, logical explanations regarding the multiple investigations of our day-to-day lives, based on the most complete intellectual honesty with science and conscience.

Therapy. Here we conclude that the memory can act as a vigorous therapeutic process inside the consciential micro-universe, leaving aside the *uncontrolled pharmaco-mania*. Memory is capable of self-healing varied disturbances including *retroactive jealousies* that interfere in our present-future, starting from this consciential attribute connected with others, and by accentuating the capacity of self-regeneration of human personalities.

Opening. The methodological analyses of the panorama yielded by this text uncover an opening in the resistance, which hinders scientific and multidimensional progress, to revolutionary discoveries that are giving critical jolts to the *everestiarian egos* of the sub-reptilian elite, *anesthetists of consciousnesses* and defenders of the decadent culture of the materialistic, theological and dogmatic institutions inside this schemed and noxious *establishment* to the collective health.

Prophylaxis. This book clarifies and indicates the effective prophylaxis regarding theories that are apocalyptic or about the end of the world − one of the most common suicidal manias in our tumultuous time of the rush for economic survival that renders billionary dividends to the *businessmen of chaos*.

Emphasis. We cannot forget to emphasize in this work, beyond its clarifications about consciousness-time interaction, the specialized filmography with tabulated analyses, with the evident intention of expanding the leading-edge artifacts of knowledge.

Information. As it is observed, the book − profound in content and simple in form − surpasses the myopic vision of those intraphysical consciousnesses that lack gray matter, processing unquestionably useful and prioritary information for our personal and group evolution, exhibiting data of the highest order of cosmoethical significance.

Laboratory. It is pertinent to recommend the readers of this specialized work that they technically or practically complement the knowledge acquired here by using the *Retrocognitions Laboratory* at the Center for Higher Studies of Conscientiology (CHSC or CEAEC) in Iguassu Falls, Paraná, Brazil.

Discernment. In the context, the impressive results of discernment are observed that personal and participative studies can lead to, when the researcher is dedicated to parapsychism and to intrapsychic exploration of the human mind, in relation to multidimensional realities, without the influences of *catatonic banalities*.

Metabolism. Let us metabolize the precious reports of the author's text while we await his next works, of the same heftiness and competence that, we are sure, will come in short time for the macro-public of the International Academy of Consciousness (IAC) interested in the deepening of their self-consientiality.

Waldo Vieira

FOREWORD

*In conscientiology, as well as in archaeology,
we do not excavate the past with pickaxes or explosives,
but with tweezers, a brush and patience.*

The basic objective of this work is to act as a retrocognitive agent, motivating its readers to invest more in their evolution, utilizing healthy and self-provoked retrocognitions as an instrument for the study of their selves.

Furthermore, this is intended to demystify retrocognition by approaching it from the perspective of conscientiology and to give it proper evolutionary value while integrating it in the present and future.

This book was born from specific research initiated in 1990, through the consultation of a specialized bibliography, study of cases discussed by students during courses of projectiology given by me since 1987, study of remembrances that occurred – including those in group – inside the IAC and IIPC, and from personal occurrences of retrocognition experienced by the author.

The result of this compilation of information was transformed, in 1996, into an extracurricular course called 'Retrocognition: remembering past experiences,' which has been given in several cities (Los Angeles, Miami and New York - in the USA; London - in England; Barcelona, Madrid and Seville - in Spain; Lisbon and Porto - in Portugal; Rotterdam - in Holland; Geneva - in Switzerland; and in numerous cities in Brazil).

The experience acquired in giving the course - in different localities, cultures and languages - permitted constant renewal and enrichment. The reactions of students, their stories, doubts, and questions were noted and analyzed resulting in the further advancement of the research.

The results of this compilation of theory and practice were condensed into this book. However, before beginning to write, it was necessary to decide the style and target audience. My choices were to write either a small technical book, directed towards the people already familiar with the concepts of conscientiology and projectiology, or a larger and more accessible book, aimed at those interested in the subject who may or may not have participated in courses of conscientiology or read its books.

Due to the current level of dissemination on the subject and the world-wide interest of people in this subject, this author decided on the 2nd option. In this case, it was necessary to touch on various concepts already approached in other conscientiology books, primarily those authored by Waldo Vieira, so that this work was complete and self-explanatory.

Despite the option for a more accessible work, conscientiological terminology has been used. Normally, a term is explained when it is introduced in the text and, in some cases, synonyms are supplied. Also included, at the end of the book, is a glossary for consultation. Another resource that can be used to better comprehend the technical terms of conscientiology is the index.

Experience with the 'Retrocognition' course showed which concepts would have to be prioritized and which sequence would have to be used so that this work would be as clear as possible to the largest number of readers.

Another relevant point is that this work is not primarily composed of case studies of regressions and their interpretations, as is with the majority of books on the subject. This is a more objective and theorical (theoretical and practical) study of the mechanisms, implications, benefits and techniques involved in the phenomena of precognition, simulcognition and, principally, retrocognition.

To evolve is not easy. Therefore, there is no one technical approach contained in this book that will allow you to have instantaneous retrocognitions, a desire very common today in this pay and receive, click and connect, swallow and be cured culture. The approach of this book is consciential and evolutionary, and does not try to pander to the curious, motivated by in-vogue fashions.

In this spirit, important basic concepts for the study of consciousness are first presented, which will give the reader precise information to more deeply understand retrocognition, its role in consciential evolution, and the mechanisms of the relationship between consciousnesses and time (Section I).

With this theoretical base, a detailed study of the phenomenon of retrocognition - its mechanisms, characteristics, types and benefits, follows. This leads to more practical approaches, through the discussion of blocking and triggering factors of the phenomenon and of specific technical procedures for the attainment of self-retrocognitions (Section II).

Finally, this work is concluded with an examination of the evolutionary aspects of retrocognition and its relationship to lucidity in the present moment - the simulcognition - and the perception of the most likely future - the precognition (Section III).

Individuals with a greater predisposition will be able to obtain retrocognitions in a short time; do not, however, expect immediate results. We do not remember all of our past at one time. We do not even have the neurological or psychological capacity for this.

Normally, we recuperate the memories of our past little by little, fragment by fragment, put together in a great jigsaw puzzle. As in archaeology, we do not excavate the past with pickaxes or explosives, but with tweezers, a brush and patience.

Another delicate point to be discussed is that, despite the undeniable therapeutic value of the retrocognition, this cannot be seen as a universal panacea - an infallible remedy for all ills. The true panacea is evolution, which is only obtained step by step, through personal effort and lucidity, and which can only be accelerated with hard work.

Author's Note:

This author acts as a researcher and instructor of the IAC - International Academy of Consciousness, and, currently, is also the president of this organization, and does not perform therapy or sessions of past experience regression, individual or in group.

If you should judge that you need assistance from a therapist, I suggest you look for a specialist in conscientiotherapy by contacting the IOC - International Organization of Conscientiotherapy (E-Mail: oic@consciencioterapia.org.br).

If you have had retrocognitions, of any type, and want to contribute to the author's data bank of cases, please send your stories to the email address indicated below. Such stories will be used to generate statistics and for analyses of patterns, which will enrich future editions of this work. In the case that any story is used as an example, names will remain undisclosed.

I am thankful in anticipation of the criticisms, suggestions and commentaries on this work, which will be used for its improvement.

Wagner Alegretti

walegretti@iacworld.org

SECTION I:
CONCEPTUAL BASIS

1
INTRODUCTION

*We grow much more remembering
our last period between lives, than
recovering the memories of several
of our previous physical lives.*

Probably everyone has thought, at least once in their life,
how good it would be if it were possible for us to return to
our youth, but having all the maturity that we possess
today. More than a simple lamentation or regret for certain decisions we have made, this attitude reflects our current awareness and intimate level of maturity, resulting
from the accumulation of multiple and different experiences.

Since it is not possible to return to the past in order to
change it, let us be more lucid and pragmatic and think
about what is possible to do in a practical and effective
manner, in the multidimensional here-and-now. With this
objective, conscientiology and projectiology propose techniques such as conscious projections and the control of our
own bioenergies, among many others.

This book discusses another extensively studied, complementary approach used within these scientific fields to
achieve this objective: retrocognition or, as it is popularly
known, regression to previous existences.

Retrocognition, when healthy and assisted by evolved
extraphysical consciousnesses, allows the individual to
recover, in time, the memory of previous intraphysical
lives or extraphysical existences. This increase in our
library of experiences would be analogous, albeit inverse-
ly, to a return to the past with the entire repository of accumulated experiences. In other words, we could bring the
experiences and lessons of the past to the here-and-now,
thereby increasing our level of manifested consciential
maturity.

The profound theorice (the conjugation of theory and practice) of multidimensionality shows us that we grow much more by remembering our last period between lives than by recovering the memories of several previous, repetitive and semiconscious lives. This can, and should, be the main goal of retrocognition.

Conscientiology and projectiology view retrocognition as an important evolutionary instrument for developing self-research and self-knowledge, and not just as a therapeutic medium. Actually, retrocognitions are inevitable in the process of evolution of the consciousness. The more the consciousness matures, the more it remembers its previous experiences, and the more it remembers the more it can mature.

It is important to emphasize that, contrary to what many people believe, hypnosis is not the only means of accessing this reality. There are several other techniques in which the self-researcher does not need the presence of any other consciousness besides its (extraphysical) helpers. As is discussed throughout this book, the practice of hypnotic suggestion should be seen as *exception-conduct* and not as *standard-conduct.*

CONSCIENTIOLOGY AND PROJECTIOLOGY

Waldo Vieira, a doctor, dentist, and independent researcher from Brazil, proposed conscientiology and projectiology, the sciences upon which the present work is based. He was president of the IIPC - International Institute of Projectiology and Conscientiology from its inception in January of 1988, in Rio de Janeiro, Brazil, until 1999.

Stimulated since his youth by experiences of conscious projections and several other parapsychic phenomena; enriched by decades of study, autodidactic and multidisciplinary research with his personal library of more than sixty thousand works; and, matured by interaction with the public in countless lectures, courses and conferences, Dr. Waldo Vieira subsequently published his three main works - *Projectiology: A Panorama of Experiences of the Consciousness Outside the Human Body*, in 1986; *700 Experiments in Conscientiology*, in 1994; and *Homo sapiens reurbanisatus*, in 2003.

The first two treatises introduced the sciences of projectiology and conscientiology to the public and scientific communities. These sciences have been gaining international prominence as non-conventional leading-edge sciences that are reinserting the consciousness into the scientific paradigm. Consciousness was discarded from scientific endeavor approximately 300 years ago, when science assumed the materialistic paradigm, a paradigm now considered by many to be exhausted.

Conscientiology, as the expression indicates, studies the consciousness in itself, but in an integral manner, multidimensionally and multiexistentially. It tries to analyze in the most systematic and logical way possible, all of the states, capacities, aspects, attributes and manifestations of consciousness.

It has a broader approach than those of medicine, psychology or physics, as it goes beyond the consciousness's cerebral and material intraphysical manifestation. Conscientiology moves forward in areas such as the classification of evolutionary levels, consciential types, cosmoethics, and the best strategies for the obtainment of consciential maturity, the permanent-total-intrusion-free condition and the condition of serenism.

While conscientiology studies a wider area of activity, in projectiology the experiential and phenomenological focus of multidimensionality prevails. In this fashion, the basic objective of projectiology is to study the techniques related to discoincidence, or manifestations of the consciousness when totally or partially out of alignment with the human body, as well as all of its bioenergetic manifestations.

In spite of having been conceived before conscientiology, projectiology is, along with several other areas of study, a subfield of the first - more or less what physiology is to biology.

Projectiology defends the hypothesis of the Objective Body, meaning that the lucid projection (projection of the consciousness, out-of-body experience, astral projection) is a manifestation of the consciousness outside of the physical body through a subtle, yet very real body (the psychosoma). It is not mere oneiric activity, coming from a dream or hallucination, as claimed by many researchers who are not conscious projectors.

In this way, conscientiology also includes holosomatics, the study of the constitution and mechanisms of the holosoma – the set of bodies consisting of the soma (physical body), holochakra (energetic body, etheric double), psychosoma (astral body) and mentalsoma (mental body).

In agreement with this approach, a wide array of typically human phenomena, and so-called paranormal, are included within conscientiological and projectiological fields. In all, there are approximately 54 basic phenomena, some of which are well worth mentioning. These include: death or final projection; NDE or near-death experience, reported by people who have come back to life after some accident, illness or trauma; autoscopy or seeing your own body; clairvoyance or the capacity to see extraphysical realities or distant scenes; the cosmoconsciousness state; physical bilocation or tangible manifestation in two places at the same time; among many others. Precognition, or premonition, and retrocognition, or the remembrance of past intra or extraphysical experiences, are the basic themes of this present work.

THE CONSCIENTIAL PARADIGM

Conscientiology and projectiology, as any other science, have their philosophical basis or paradigm. In this case it is the Consciential Paradigm.

There is a current consensus that the human brain is the most complex object known. The consciousness, for those who experience lucid projections, is obviously an entity independent of the physical brain, because the projector perceives himself or herself awake and active outside of the physical body. Therefore, to study the consciousness (exactly what a science should be capable of doing), which is beyond the brain and actually controls it, is an endeavor truly worthy of the scientific spirit.

In this way, we can conclude that new methodologies and techniques are necessary to study the consciousness. Even the most sophisticated biomedical technology does not prove sufficient to study the consciousness. At best, all that the current conventional materialistic paradigm (Newtonian, Cartesian, positivistic, reductionist, physicalist) can yield are insights into the physiological and psychological alterations that are but manifestations of a specific consciousness.

The obvious conclusion is that in order to study the consciousness it is necessary to use the consciousness itself. This unavoidably leads to participative research, where the researcher is, in most cases, also the subject, while his or her daily existence, inside and outside of the body, is the laboratory.

This is the Consciential Paradigm's essence, which provides a starting point for the studies of conscientiology and projectiology.

SUBDISCIPLINES OF CONSCIENTIOLOGY

With a basis in the proposed specialties and subfields of conscientiology presented by Dr. Waldo Vieira, and aimed at technical researchers of the consciousness, the topics of this book can best be classified within the following disciplines, in this order:

- **Mnemosomatics** - the study of the memory and its systems.

- **Evolutiology** - the science of the evolution of the consciousness.

- **Intermissiology** - the science of the intermissive periods.

- **Resomatics** - the study of the somatic reactivation, or rebirth, and physical life.

- **Proexology** - the science of the existential program and its implications.

- **Desomatics** - the study of the somatic deactivation or death. Thanatology expanded by the consciential paradigm.

- **Experimentology** - the study and application of techniques, experiments, formulas, and optimizations seeking evolutionary acceleration.

- **Parachronology** - the registration and measure of time and its events from a multidimensional point of view.

- **Parahistory** - the history of other dimensions and the study of multidimensional events and their influence in the physical dimension.

- **Conscientiotherapy** - the therapy of the consciousness in an integral way.

- **Paratherapeutics** - therapeutics through the subtle vehicles of the consciousness.

2
THE CONSCIOUSNESS
AND ITS ATTRIBUTES

*With a series of existences, countless attributes,
many memories, several intelligences, some egos,
and four vehicles of manifestation, it is inevitable
to conclude that the consciousness is the most
complex object of study that one can conceive
of at this point in our evolution.*

CONCEPTUALIZATION

The central object studied in the sciences of conscientiology and projectiology is the consciousness and, unavoidably, its different manifestations.

In these sciences, the *consciousness* is understood not only as the conscious state or the internal voice of reason and personal ethics (superego), but as the entity that is capable of being conscious. This way, as the basis or substratum of intelligent individuality, well beyond matter and energy, consciousness can be understood by many as spirit, soul, *I,* essence, *atman,* self, or even with some approximation, ego and personality.

In this meaning, it is understood that we *are consciousnesses* and not that we *have a consciousness.* Many times you hear people saying: "My consciousness (or soul, or spirit) left me last night." In this case it is easy to notice the misinterpretation. They are identifying themselves with the body and think that they possess a consciousness, when what is correct is exactly the opposite: all of us are consciousnesses who possess bodies.

Many times the consciousness is identified as being a form of subtle energy. This is another serious conceptual mistake, since it is known that matter and energy are the same thing, and that one can be transformed into the other. Following this line of thought, if (the) consciousness were some type of energy, it could be transformed into matter. This makes absolutely no sense.

Similarly, it is difficult to precisely define, in short sentences, what matter, energy or life are - even though everyone understands quite well what is meant by these words. It is still quite difficult to conceptualize consciousness in an objective and academic way. Often, to overcome this difficulty, a list of characteristics, properties or attributes of such concepts is presented. This may allow us to associate previous ideas and experiences in order to conceive and understand such concepts.

Following this line of thought, such concepts can be explained using the following lists of properties, which are by no means assumed to be complete:

Matter:

- Possesses mass;
- Manifests the force known as weight when submitted to a gravitational field (masses attract each other);
- Composed of molecules, atoms and sub-particles, organized in many different forms;
- Presents volume, that is, it occupies a certain portion of space;
- Can be transformed into energy (according to $E=mc^2$).

Energy:

- Can accomplish work;
- Cannot be created or destroyed, but only transformed;
- Presents itself under multiple forms, as it is convertible; *

- In its transformations it affects the entropy of a system, which tends to increase;
- Can be transformed into matter (according to $E=mc^2$).

Life:

- Metabolic;
- Manifests growth;
- Reproductive (maintenance of the species);
- Presents a survival instinct (individual preservation);
- Based on the carbon element (at least in known life forms).

CONSCIENTIAL ATTRIBUTES

As was the case with matter, energy and life, we can get closer to an explanation of the concept of (the) consciousness by enumerating its main characteristics, properties or attributes:

- **Self-consciousness** - The capacity of the consciousness to recognize itself as such; to know it exists; to be aware of itself. This is the basis of lucidity.

- **Individuality** - The property of existing, being, acting and deciding, up to a certain point, as an autonomous and independent individual. Coupled with rationality, this composes free will.

- **Evolution** - The potential for evolving and maturing, each time being or becoming more capable, adaptable, complex, sophisticated, skilled, and powerful. It is based on learning, which is itself a function of memory.

- **Multidimensionality** - The intrinsic characteristic of the consciousness that allows it to manifest, present itself, perceive, and act in different dimensions, realities or parallel universes.

•**Rationality** - The individual's attribute that allows him or her to think, compute, compare, ponder, analyze and process data, impressions, or perceptions. This encompasses several forms of intelligence. Combined with hyperacuity, it forms discernment.

•**Hyperacuity** - Also known as lucidity (derived from the Latin *lux*: light, clarity), it is the capacity of the consciousness to be awake, alert, attentive, concentrated and connected to all of its perceptions, its moment and place, and to the antecedents (previous causes) and consequences (future effects) of its thosenes, that is (to say), its acts, decisions, intentions and thoughts. Coupled with multidimensionality, hyperacuity results in Multidimensional Self-awareness (MS), which is the capacity to be lucid in any dimension, perceiving it and changing the focus or tuning of the consciousness to different dimensional ranges with efficiency and continuity.

•**Will** - The basic, essential, primary driving impulse of the consciousness. It corresponds to the magnitude and applicability (where, when, how, why) of the thosenes. Associated with rationality, it forms intentionality.

•**Attention** - The concentration mechanism, focalization, and zoom (in and out) of the perceptions (inputs) or manifestations (outputs) of the individual.

•**Perceptions** - This indicates the capacity of the consciousness to capture, perceive, feel, *scan*, and sense itself, its vehicles of manifestation, other consciousnesses or the external environment. It is the set of input channels of the individual. The consciousness does not live isolated from the environment (autistic), but reacts to the external environment and its stimuli. Intraphysically it manifests itself as the conventional physical senses. In conjunction with multidimensionality, it results in paraperceptions.

•**Sentimentality** - The attribute that generates the individual's emotional, affective, or sentimental processes. When there is a predominance of the mentalsoma, it manifests as advanced sentiments (fraternity, respect for life, motivation to help, evolution, altruism). In cases where the psychosoma predominates, it is manifested as emotions (happiness, sadness, hate, fear, passion, among many others). Combined with discernment, it results in assistentiality.

• **Bioenergeticity** - The capacity of the consciousness to use bioenergies as a tool for performance or as a channel of perception. Actually, every action of the consciousness, at least when external to it, is accomplished through the application of several forms of bioenergy, which are transferred and transformed, through the holosoma, from the consciousness to the soma and vice-versa. Together with intentionality and sentimentality, they compose thosenity.

• **Holosomaticity** - The property of the consciousness that allows the use of numerous vehicles of manifestation, each expressing specific capacities that are adapted to distinct dimensions.

• **Memory** - The ability to store and recover information in the form of experiences, perceptions and even internal processes of the consciousness. It is impossible to imagine or to conceive of a consciousness without any type of memory, because, as one of the main and most complex attributes of the consciousness, it is the basis for evolution. Without memory, consciousnesses would always be the same.

• **Seriality** - The set or series of resomas (*somatic* reactivations), physical lives, deaths (desomas - *somatic deactivations*) and intermissions (periods in-between-lives) of the consciousness, in several planets, civilizations, cultures and dimensions, for evolution, learning, and resolving problems of the past.

• **Complexity** (Also called multiplicity) - With a series of existences, countless attributes, many memories, several intelligences, some egos, and four vehicles of manifestation, in consciential terms it is inevitable to conclude that the consciousness is very complex, multiple, polymorphic and multifaceted. It is, in fact, the most complex object of study that one can conceive of at this point in evolution.

The consciousness exists and cannot be destroyed, it does not stop and cannot be stopped, it is never silent and cannot be silenced, it manifests and cannot be isolated. Its mere existence, as limited and *autistic* as it may be, disturbs the universe and other consciousnesses, creating and maintaining energetic links with everything and everyone. *Simply by existing, the consciousness acts.*

3
MEMORY

It is supposed that even the most remote experiences of the consciousness, from when it was some kind of unicellular being, vegetable (being), or subhuman animal, as well as its experiences as a self-conscious being on other planets, before transmigration to Earth, are included in the memory of the consciousness.

DEFINITION

The word 'memory' can be explained in several different ways. For the objectives of this work the following meanings are most relevant:

1. The ability or mental capacity of retention, registration, preservation and storage, and posterior evocation, access or recuperation of experiences, facts and past events, as well as ideas, impressions, sensations, emotions and knowledge acquired previously.
2. The act or instance of retaining and recovering experiences, images, etc. Example: "sketching from memory."
3. The sum total of what can be remembered.
4. This ability as manifested by a particular individual. Example: to have a photographic memory.
5. Specific recollection, reminiscence, or remembrance. Person, fact, or impression brought back. Something remembered. Example: "pleasant memories of childhood."
6. The period of time covered by the memories of a person or group. Example: "understood in the memory of humankind."
7. The state or condition of being remembered. Example: "dedicated to his father's memory."

8. Vestiges, remainder, signal.
9. That which serves as a reminder.
10. The lasting modification of behavior resulting from an experience of an animal (Biology).
11. The ability of cells of the immune system to answer to previously encountered antigens (Immunology).

In spite of not being directly linked to the consciential processes, the following definitions, used as analogies, help with the association of ideas and enrich the context of this study:

- The fame or renown of a person or thing, especially after death.

- Relation, account, narration.

- The property of certain materials, usually metals and plastics, of returning to their original shape or original state after deformation (Physics of the Solid State).

- A group of past events that affect a given event in stochastic processes (Statistics).

- A device in which information can be introduced and stored, and from which it can later be recovered; accumulator; storage device (Computing).

Memory is from the Latin root memor, meaning mindful, from which we also get: memorable; remembering; memo; to commemorate; memorial and memento.

RELATED CONCEPTS

Mnemonic - The art and technique of developing and strengthening the memory by means of auxiliary artificial processes, for example: the association of what should be memorized with information already known or experienced; combinations and arrangements; images; etc. Synonym: mnemotechnique.

Engram - Unit of memory; memory trace; physical alteration or code that is thought to occur in the live neural tissues in response to stimuli, which is used as a possible explanation for the physical basis of memory and its permanency. Engrams possibly manifest as neurosynaptic circuits specific for each memory.

Mnemosyne - In Greek mythology, the goddess of memory. She and Zeus, father of the gods, were the progenitors of the nine muses. Mnemosyne was one of the pre-Olympic Titans, children of the god of the sky, Uranus, and of the goddess of the Earth, Gaia.

MECHANISMS AND CHARACTERISTICS

Memory is one of the main evolutionary acquisitions of superior living beings, and in the case of human beings, it plays a central role in the processes of learning, cognition, and intelligent behavior. Even so, it is one of the less understood processes of the human body. Many theories, some of them antagonistic, have been proposed to explain its mechanisms.

Some researchers theorize that memories are stored in specific and specialized areas of the brain, while others affirm that several different areas of the brain work together in expressing a certain memory. As each of these propositions can be checked by specific experiments, and based on the fact of the existence of multiple types of memory, it is thus probable that both types of processes are involved. At any rate, the areas of the brain considered to be strictly associated with memory are the cerebral cortex, the thalamus and the hippocampus.

A general consensus exists, however, stating that the storage of memory requires changes in the physiochemical structure of neurons and synapses. It is also assumed that the limbic system and its structures (particularly the hippocampus) act as a command center, playing a central role in the control and organization of memory. Some studies support the theory that neuronal circuits between the amygdala and the thalamus participate in the processes of emotional memories, while other circuits between the hippocampus and the thalamus are involved in spatial memory.

Human beings have, on average, 20 billion neurons in their encephalon. Each one of the neurons is connected to other (from 100 to 100,000) neurons by synapses. Human beings are born with approximately 30% of their synapses ready, and the remainder will be established, in a dynamic way, throughout life.

All biological functions, motor actions, physical perceptions, thoughts, or memories use a certain group of neuronal circuits. Each nervous pulse, transmitted through each one of these circuits, passes sequentially along many neurons. This pulse is transmitted in the form of electric conduction (depolarization) when passing through the neuron, and in the form of chemical transmission (neurotransmitter - receptor) when crossing the interval (synapse) to the next neuron.

The conduction of nervous pulses alters the chemical, electrical and structural characteristics of the neurons (dendrites and axons). Such alteration can be momentary, brief, of long duration or even permanent. Such alterations usually become permanent with repetition in the use of that circuit.

In this way, memories would be related to specific circuits that were already formed by previous sensorial perceptions or experiences. Such circuits can be reactivated in a given moment, reproducing the type of information or perception that created it, resulting in neurological processes that we call memory.

A new memory is more easily registered and maintained if it can be associated with other preexisting ones. The retention of memory is usually better when different types of stimuli converge and are added to the record of the same experience. For example, it is easier to memorize information obtained in the form of computerized multimedia (text, sound, photos, graphs, animation, and film - presented at the same time) than with text alone. The larger the number of circuits that are stimulated, the more stable that record will tend to be. For that same reason, interest, since it involves emotion, reinforces memories.

Due to the fact that the area of the brain that deals with emotions is also involved in the mechanism of memory processing (limbic system), a close and powerful relationship between emotion and memory can be observed. There is a tendency for memories of situations that involved intense emotions to be more stable and durable. Equally, certain emotions can evoke specific memories. Besides emotional events, pain or physical suffering can awaken the survival instinct mechanism, stimulating the production of hormones (one of which is adrenaline) that increase the level of attentiveness of the individual and stimulate the specialized receptors in the dendrites of the neurons, causing their activation. That is to say that throughout biological evolution, several living beings developed a prioritization in the registration of certain events that can be critical to their survival. However, long-term stress causes the saturation of the neurons and their circuits, leading to hypomnesia (impaired memory).

The emotion-memory relationship is used extensively in mnemonics with the objective of intensifying memorization by associating new information with pleasant or entertaining situations or images.

When studying the mechanisms of memory, we come across an interesting observation: there seems to exist a hierarchy among memories. The more complex forms of memory - acquired more recently in terms of genetic evolution - would be above simpler and older memories (also in terms of biological evolution). The more sophisticated memories - based on the cerebral cortex - are in general more fragile and subject to being forgotten, while the most primitive - based on the limbic system - are more stable and permanent. The nominative memory - complex - would be at the top of the hierarchy, and it is one of the first to suffer in cases of hypomnesia, in contrast to procedural skill memory - more primitive - which is rarely affected. This hypothesis fits with the modern theory of the brain, which states that it has developed in layers throughout evolution, the most external layers being the newest.

STAGES OF MEMORY

The processing of memory, as a whole, can be divided into 5 stages:

1. **Perception** - The process of reception of information or stimulus, usually originating in some sensory organ;
2. **Encoding** - The process by which the perceived information is introduced to the memory. The initial codification seems to occur in the limbic system;
3. **Storage** - The process through which the coded information is maintained in the memory;
4. **Retrieval** - The process of addressing, locating, recovering and using stored information;
5. **Forgetfulness** - The process of losing or distorting the stored information.

MECHANISMS OF MEMORY

Technically, four different forms or mechanisms are recognized for re-accessing or recalling memories:

1. **Recollection** – The reconstruction of events or facts starting from clues or stimuli that serve as reminders or hooks;
2. **Recall** – The active and unaided remembering of something from the past;

3. **Recognition** – The ability to correctly identify, as familiar, certain previously perceived stimuli;

4. **Relearning** – The mechanism that makes it easier to learn, for a second time, something previously learned and seemingly forgotten (reminiscence of memory), than to learn something totally new.

These mechanisms do not always work equally, as in the case of being able to recognize a person's face (active recognition), but unable to remember the person's name (recovery fails). Many times, a memory can also be partial or imprecise, as in the case of someone making an effort to remember a word, and only being able to recall the first letter and the number of syllables.

In other situations, a certain memory can only be recovered under conditions (environmental and emotional, for example) similar to the ones that existed when it was stored. When a memory is recovered or remembered during the same situation that existed when it was originally coded, this is called a *context-dependent recovery*. When a memory is evoked under the same psychological or physiological state that existed in the moment of its registration, it is called a *state-dependent recovery*.

In any one of these processes above, the re-accessed memory is subject to alteration, depending on the individual's tendencies, values, needs, or expectations. Sometimes, however, the recollection is accurate.

An example that can well illustrate some of the mechanisms involved in the evocation of memories is the case of attempting to remember a list of information in sequence. In this case, there is a tendency to remember the initial and final items more easily than the middle ones.

The relearning mechanism evidences that a memory is not lost, but simply loses its intensity, or the brain loses its address or index and consequently does not know how to locate it.

Further evidence in favor of this hypothesis is the evocation of seemingly forgotten or unconscious memories - namely those that are obtained through external resources, such as hypnosis. Experiments with this objective have shown that one could remember, under hypnosis, the number of lampposts on their route from home to work, despite the individual having never counted them, and, prior to entering a state of hypnosis, being unable to recollect how many there were. Hypnosis has also been used in police investigations to help passive witnesses remember details of a crime not immediately accessible to their recall. These facts lead us to believe that it is possible to memorize absolutely everything that is perceived by us through our physical senses. In time, only priority memories (those regularly reactivated) are maintained as recoverable, and the remaining memories are stored in a less accessible database, such as the so-called subconscious or unconscious.

If this is correct, we can infer the unimaginable amount of information that is stored every day. The process of dreaming seems to play an essential role in the screening, prioritization, organization, and dynamic restoration of this enormous mass of data.

Mechanisms of Forgetfulness

The forgetfulness curve (amount of data forgotten over time) is generally logarithmic, meaning there is a higher rate of loss of data soon after its storage and, with time, this rate decreases.

Different mechanisms participate in the apparent loss of (or inability to recover) information. They are:

1. **Attenuation** - With the passing of time, in the case of lack of use, a certain neuronal circuit disconnects (itself) through the natural deactivation of the physiochemical modifications installed when it was stored. Other forms of cerebral deterioration compete with

the above, such as arteriosclerosis and Alzheimer's disease.

2. **Distortion** - The initial memory loses its precision with time; even its content is capable of being altered.

3. **Interference**

   - *Retroactive inhibition* - new memories, when sharing certain neurons and synapses with other preexistent circuits, interfere with older memories, or in some cases replace them.

   - *Proactive inhibition* - old memories, when more stable and intense, interfere with the retention of new ones.

4. **Repression** - Some blockages can be motivated by desires or necessities of the individual, generally in the form of a semiconscious ego-defense mechanism.

Even though it seems undesirable, forgetfulness represents an important process for the individual, because it allows: the discarding of information that is no longer useful; the formation of new memories, most of the time of more importance; and the focalization of the individual on the present time.

LEVELS OF MEMORY

In terms of life span and respective retention mechanisms, memories are classified into 3 levels:

1. **Immediate** (or sensorial) - *1st level of storage*. Very short-term memory (in the order of a few seconds), corresponding to the ability to retain information for enough time to maintain a sequence of thoughts to accomplish a task in a coherent way; or so that sensorial stimuli can be registered. It is limited in the amount of information that can be stored in one specific moment and also in its duration. The more intense the original stimulus is, the longer (time) it

remains. Not all the information stored at this level is transferred to the short-term level.

2. **Short-term** - *2nd level of storage.* Transitional memory, basically bioelectric, that is maintained accessible during a period of time in the order of, at maximum, a few minutes. It works as an interface between immediate memory (new perception) and long-term memory (engram). These memories are retained while a certain neurosynaptic circuit is maintained active, temporarily, through the conduction of nervous pulses. Example: a telephone number that is read in the phone book and is forgotten soon after the conclusion of the call. Some studies point to the fact that, on average, a maximum of seven items of information can be kept in short-term memory in any specific moment, and that there is a natural tendency to group isolated information into larger groups. Training and techniques can increase the amount of stored information and its time of retention. Not all the information stored at this level is transferred to long-term memory.

3. **Long-term** - *3rd level of storage.* More permanent memory, sometimes indelible, based on the structuring of stable neurosynaptic architectures. Beginning with short-term memory, it becomes long-term memory with the repetition or intensification of the pulses driven through that specific circuit. The more a certain circuit is used, the higher its tendency or predisposition for nervous conduction. In this sense, each specific circuit can be considered an engram of memory. This memory seems to be limitless in terms of capacity and duration.

A natural tendency exists for memories to be *promoted* to the next highest level. If a piece of data does not undergo long-term memory encoding, it will be forgotten.

Some researchers speculate that each one of these levels operates through different mechanisms, and that their respective information is stored in different areas of the encephalon.

TYPES OF MEMORIES

The soma, or physical body, when studied as the consciousness's system of memories, is called the mnemosoma. But there are memories and memory processing in other subtle bodies, as classified below:

• **PHYSICAL** - or somatic. Stored memory, processed and recovered by the soma:

- *Encephalic* - Memory based on the central nervous system. In terms of encephalic memory, the following types can be recognized today:

- **Procedural Skill** - Memory of motor abilities and coordination of movements; memory of psychomotricity. A more primitive and stable memory of longer retention, it is a fundamentally cerebellar memory that allows us to walk or, for example, allows someone to ride a bicycle again after several decades. This type of memory allows the individual to accomplish routine motor activities without great participation of its conscious processes, facilitating, inclusively, the simultaneous accomplishment of one or more intellectual tasks (for example, reading a book while walking on the treadmill, or knitting while speaking with someone).

- **Factual** - Memory of experiences, facts, events, occurrences and their contexts. It is more complex than procedural skill memory, and is technically subdivided into the following types:

• *Visual* - The ability to retain and recall people, things, or facts seen before. It is based on the visual area of the cerebral cortex. For the human being, an essentially diurnal animal, the sense of vision and its respective memory plays an important role in the development of the consciousness. This supremacy of vision can be illustrated by the natural rapid eye movements that occur during sleep. As in the waking state the eyes scan the physical landscape, so in the dream state the eyes move to scan the virtual scenery. Visual memory is the basis of so-called photographic memory.

• *Auditory* - The capacity to remember what has been heard - simple or complex sounds, words and sentences. Based on the respective sensory area in the cerebral cortex. Example: Individuals that tend to study reading aloud can be demonstrating a better auditory memory than a visual one.

• *Tactile* - The memory of previously perceived tactile perceptions. Based on the respective sensory area in the cerebral cortex. It allows the blind to read Braille.

• *Smell* - The memory of scents already experienced. It seems that the limbic system plays an essential role in olfactory memory. Allows the identification of someone by his or her usual perfume or scent. Not as active in human beings, but especially well developed in several animals, like the dog for example (there is evidence that the beagle has a sense of smell 1,000 times more acute than that of *Homo sapiens*).

• *Taste* - The memory of flavors previously tasted. Based on the respective sensory area in the cerebral cortex. Allows the discovery of the ingredients of a specific meal.

- *Space* - The memory of the relative positioning of objects in space, as well as of distances and dimensions. The internal three-dimensional hologram, which allows a person to walk in the darkness through a well-known place without colliding with furniture.

- *Musical* - The capacity of storing rhythms, melodies and musical harmonies. It is different from the pure auditory memory, as many times we can remember the melody of a song but not its lyrics, or vice-versa.

- *Affective* - Used by actors in exercises according to the Stanislavski method (theater), by which they evoke the memories of previous experiences in their life, in order to build and play characters with the maximum of authenticity and psychological truth.

- *Numeric* - Memory of numbers and amounts.

- *Nominative* - Memory of names, titles, classifications, concepts, associations, or qualifications. It is the memory of internal connections that associates different memories and indexes them through symbols (mostly names). It is probably centered in the frontal lobes. This has a certain similarity with projective and retrocognitive memories, since it is not being stimulated directly or fed by any sensory circuit. Generally, when this memory declines, it can indicate or anticipate difficulties in recalling conscious projections.

a- *Subcerebral* – Instinctive memory associated with the abdominal sub-brain, containing the programs that allow maintenance of the basic vegetative functions performed by the autonomic nervous system of that region. We have more neurons in our abdomen than certain animals have in their brains.

- *Biochemical* - Several current studies point to the hypothesis that some simple memories are stored in the form of specific chemical substances, which can be spread throughout the entire body and flow through the blood. Cases of transference of learning have been observed among simple animals (the aquatic planaria flatworm - genus Dugesia, for example) after the transfusion of certain body fluids. Another example of this is immunological memory, which enables a cell of the immune system to respond to antigens that have been previously encountered, and thus allows the body to provide antibodies prepared as defenses against certain substances or pathogenic agents.

- *Genetics* – Memory based on the genes or DNA. It allows cellular reproduction, the production of proteins, and the control of the cell's metabolism, according to stable and suitable patterns, for the survival of the individual and the species. In embryogenesis, the soma being formed reviews the evolution of life on this planet, presenting fish, reptile, bird and mammal characteristics, until reaching a well constituted human shape.

•**EXTRAPHYSICAL** - or psychosomatic. This is the memory stored, processed and recalled by the psychosoma:

- *Paracerebral* - Memory based in the parabrain. This is called extracerebral memory by some researchers of memory regression through hypnotic induction, since it resides beyond the physical brain. The physiology of the brain of the psychosoma is still unknown, but it is presumed to be based on a matrix of thosenes (mnemothosenes, retrothosenes), holothosenes, and morphothosenes maintained by the flow of consciential energy. It is the memory used primarily in conscious projections and must later be transferred to the physical brain to facilitate post-projective recollection. Paracerebral memory constitutes the basis for learning during the intermissive courses. It allows retrocognitions, as well as the recollection of previous conscious projections not recalled while inside the physical body. The nature of specialization of the two hemispheres of the parabrain and its relationship to the mechanisms of extraphysical memory is still unknown.

- *Paragenetics* - One way in which the individual holothosene manifests is through information presented by the very constitution of the psychosoma as a result of the summation of the influences received from countless previous somas with their respective genetics (*retrogenetics*), plus extraphysical existences and, sometimes, intra or extraphysical affective-emotional traumas. The appearance of the psychosoma is evidence of paragenetics. The most serious cases of paragenetic pathology known are extraphysical mutants, extraphysical human consciousnesses that have reached their highest degree of intimate disorganization, to the point of being unable to sustain a stable extraphysical form. While in this state, they are incapable of assuming a soma that is being formed and of catalyzing the normal development of that new body.

• **HOLOMEMORY** - also called the integral memory. This is the largest or ultimate database of the consciousness. Stored in the mentalsoma, it contains the entire patrimony of accumulated existences wrought by its evolution. It is supposed that the most remote experiences of the consciousness, from unicellular, vegetable or subhuman being to experiences as a self-conscious being on other planets, before transmigration to Earth, are included in this great multiexistential consciential curriculum. In this fashion, all manifestation and perception of the consciousness permanently integrates with the holomemory, the primary base for the personal holothosene.

VARIATIONS

Memory can vary in intensity, reach, depth and accuracy. There are cases in which these variations are connected to pathological or traumatic processes:

• **Hypermnesia** - Great capacity for memorization and recovery of information; exceptional memory. This can be the result of training, genetic predisposition, a macrosoma, or even the influence of certain drugs (temporary effect). It is popularly called elephant's memory.

• **Hypomnesia** - Impaired memorization capacity; weak or failing memory. Some of the main causes of hypomnesia are:

- *Senility* - Reduction of memory due to advanced age or degeneration of nervous tissues. The individual has access to old memories (long-term), however, they have great difficulty or find it impossible to remember recent events (short-term). This is common in cases of Alzheimer's disease or arteriosclerosis.

- *Stress* - Reduction in memory performance caused by nervous tension and the permanent presence of high concentrations of adrenaline in the blood. Stress also drains the physical body's supply of important substances such as certain vitamins and minerals (oligoelements).

- *Lack of Sleep* - As a result of periods of insufficient sleep, in quality or duration, the memory is affected by a decrease in the likelihood of organic detoxification and the natural reorganization of information (defragmentation) performed during *dreaming*.

- *Intoxication* - The contamination of the soma by specific substances, legal or illegal, can directly affect the brain, and consequently the memory. Some prescription drugs, certain illegal controlled substances, heavy metals (most commonly, lead) and aluminum, common in cooking utensils and in the majority of modern antiperspirants have been implicated in the impairment of short-term memory.

- *Psychological Traumas* - Memory blocks resulting from ego-defense mechanisms, such as the repression of traumatic memories.

• **Amnesia** - Loss of the ability to recall. This is present in severe cases of hypomnesia, in which the individual can lose, for a short period of time, a great part of his or her capacity to recall memories, or be incapable for the rest of this physical existence of remembering certain specific periods of his or her current life. There are partial specific amnesias such as auditory, visual, and tactile amnesia. This is usually caused by serious trauma such as: severe cranial concussions; electric shock; general anesthesia; drug or alcohol intoxication; extended cerebral hypoxia, common in cases of drowning and cardio-respiratory arrest; degenerative diseases of the nervous tissues; and cerebral tumors. It can also be caused by emotional trauma, as is the case with hysterical amnesia, or by hypnosis.

• **Paramnesia** - Also known as false or mistaken memory, manifests as a natural and ordinary recollection of scenes, facts or events, which after deeper analysis, supported by objective testimony, have never been seen, witnessed or lived. In the least serious cases this may happen when dreams, fantasies or hallucinations are later remembered as real events. In the most serious cases, this may be caused by deep stress, mental exhaustion caused by lack of sleep, or often by consciential intrusion. In the latter case this happens when the extraneous memories of the intruder are mixed with the intrudee's memories, as an effect of intense intertransfusion of consciential energy and consequent thosenes (unconscious pathological telepathy). When paramnesia occurs in a sporadic and superficial way, it can be considered benign; however, if it occurs frequently and profoundly (known in psychiatry as confabulation), it can indicate serious cerebral lesions.

4
HOLOSOMA

*The consciousness exists and cannot be destroyed, it
does not stop and cannot be stopped, it manifests
and cannot be isolated. Just by existing,
the consciousness acts.*

Consciousness itself is neither matter nor energy, being
beyond the limits of space, time and forms. However, in
order for the consciousness to manifest itself in denser
dimensions like the intraphysical dimension, it utilizes
energy-matter vehicles.

Each vehicle manifests specific attributes of the consciousness, with each adapted to its specific dimensional
layer. As a group, these vehicles are called the holosoma
and, in the case of intraphysical consciousness, is composed of the following bodies:

SOMA

Also called the physical body, biological body, dense body
or cellular vehicle, it is the densest body of all and the one
that allows the consciousness to manifest in the intraphysical dimension. It is the vehicle that imposes the largest
degree of restriction on the consciousness, being the most
primitive of the bodies.

Its nobler part is the central nervous system, the headquarters of the consciousness and direct interface for the
commands of the consciousness to the body and of the
body's perceptions to the consciousness. Despite being the
most rudimentary body of all, we do not use the brain,
lungs and perceptions in their totality.

The consciousness changes somas each intraphysical
life, needing to dominate and domesticate each new animal body. In each life we inherit new genetics, and this

information integrates into the paragenetics of the psychosoma.

In previous lives, we clearly have had several very different bodies, that is, of different races, physical constitutions, and sexes. We can go even further, affirming that in an even more distant past, when we lived on other planets, our bodies were probably different, adapted to different atmospheric compositions and gravitational and climactic conditions. The previously used somas can be called retrosomas.

HOLOCHAKRA

It is the vehicle responsible for the energetic vitalization of the soma, its tissues and cells, enabling the psychosoma to control the soma. The holochakra, popularly known as the energetic body, etheric double or vital body, is the interface between the psychosoma and the soma.

Like the soma, it presents a para-anatomy, paraphysiology, and parapathologies. As part of its para-anatomy, we can mention the energetic structures known as chakras or energetic vortexes, which work as organs of the holochakra, responsible for the absorption, metabolization, and exteriorization of bioenergy.

These chakras interact closely with the central nervous system, the autonomic nervous system, and the endocrine system. The channels that circulate these energies are popularly known as nadis or, from acupuncture, meridians.

Being the vehicle that couples the consciousness to the physical body, it is responsible for the process of reactivation of the soma or rebirth, popularly known as reincarnation. In concordance with the quality of its energies, a consciousness can have a freer and more extraphysical life, or a more material and intraphysical life.

The holochakra is basically sustained by the permanent absorption of natural or immanent energies coming from the ground (geoenergy), water (hydroenergy), air (aeroenergy), the universe (cosmoenergy), plants (phytoenergy), food (phytoenergy and zooenergy), as well as the consciential energies exchanged with other people.

PSYCHOSOMA

The vehicle used primarily by the consciousness during the intermissive period, that is, in the interval between lives, and in most conscious projections, it is also known as the astral body, or emotional body.

Usually, the psychosoma presents the same visual characteristics of the current soma (in the case of a projected intraphysical consciousness), or of the last or one of the last somas (in the case of an extraphysical consciousness).

However, the psychosoma manifests characteristics radically different from the soma, such as light emission, absence of weight, invisibility, inaudibility, the capacity to pass through material objects, invulnerability to any and all physical influence and, mainly, the capacity to assume different forms. This last capacity is coherent with the fact that we have a different soma in each life and that the psychosoma adapts to each of them.

The psychosoma is the basic matrix or mold for the formation of the physical body. Through its paragenetics it contributes to determining the general characteristics of the soma. In a certain way, it can be affirmed that the psychosoma is a morphothosene (popularly known as: thought-form) maintained by the mentalsoma. Memories, traumas, and old events, mainly concerning emotions and affectivity, are registered in the structure of the psychosoma.

The consciousness, through the mentalsoma, acts on the parabrain or brain of the psychosoma, which is the primary location for memories from previous experiences, since this same parabrain has participated in each of the previous lives and intermissive periods.

MENTALSOMA

The mentalsoma is the vehicle of manifestation, that at our evolutionary level, seems to be inextricably bound with the consciousness itself, since, at this point, no projection in which the consciousness has left the mentalsoma, or any other form of perception or manifestation beyond the mentalsoma has been observed. Theosophy, one of the Oriental schools of thought that has studied this vehicle, calls this the "mental body."

The mentalsoma is the primordial seat of the consciousness, where the consciential attributes of discernment, lucidity, rationality and holomemory originate. It is the central, primary repository of all our evolutionary experiences.

This vehicle completely transcends the human notions of space, time, form, emotion, and sex. It is not a body in itself, because it does not have size or limits. However, it hosts the consciousness during mentalsomatic projections, in which the individual may feel himself or herself in a condition of expanded consciousness (cosmoconsciousness, *samadhi*, *satori*, *nirvana*), deeply connected with everything and everyone, omniscient and completely free of restrictions.

In our pathological human society, very little evidence of the mentalsoma operating at its highest level is observed. The evolutionary limitations most common on this planet - reduced level of lucidity or multidimensional self-awareness, materialism, egocentrism, lack of universalism, absence of cosmoethics, etc. - are actually indications of the degree of immaturity of the mentalsoma.

5
CONSCIENTIAL ENERGY

As conscious beings, we significantly disturb the ocean of immanent energies in which we are immersed, creating waves and broadcasting information. We leave the thosenic trace of our personality in whichever place or dimension we go, throughout our existences.

BASIS

It is impossible to understand the vast range of manifestations of the consciousness and its paraperceptions without understanding its primary agent, bioenergy.

An extensive list of synonyms bespeaks the universality of bioenergy. Known since ancient times, bioenergy is, in general terms, the same as the following: *acasa* (Hindu), *axé* (African), bioplasma (V. S. Grischenko), *chi/qi* (acupuncture, China), astral energy, biopsychic energy, cosmic energy, vital energy, negative entropy (Erwin Schrodinger), magnetic fluid (Franz A. Mesmer), psychic fluid, vital fluid (Allan Kardec), etheric force (radiestesists), vital force (C. F. S. Hahnemann), libido (Sigmund Freud), astral light (Helena P. Blavatsky), animal magnetism (Franz A. Mesmer), *od* (K. L. von Reichenbach), orgone (Wilhelm Reich), prana (yogis, India) and synchronicity (C. G. Jung).

This energy is the common key to projectiological phenomena as a whole, and specifically for conscious projection. It has also been related to paranormal phenomena, extrasensory perceptions such as parapsychic cure, *poltergeist* and telekinesis, among many others.

In conventional physics, energy is defined as the capacity of a system to accomplish *work*, and in a free analysis, *work* can be understood as change, dynamism, or transformation. In a similar way, bioenergy, which is also neither created nor destroyed, but only transformed, can be understood as the means through which the consciousness manifests in its dimension of activity or, in other words, how it accomplishes consciential work.

It is known that matter and energy are essentially the same thing manifesting themselves as two states of the same "substance" or universal property. In a certain way, all vehicles of the consciousness are formed from a specific spectra of energy (or matter), obtained from the respective dimensions of manifestation of those same vehicles.

In the schema of conscientiology, the consciousness is never reborn in the exact sense of the word. What actually occurs is an 'energetic resoma' (somatic reactivation); meaning that the consciousness, through its mentalsoma and psychosoma, links itself indirectly to the soma through the holochakra. The direct conclusion is that for us to live better in the physical dimension, developing our more advanced attributes and overcoming genetic and environmental influences in order to accomplish our existential program, we have to learn to fully and consciously control our bioenergies.

IMMANENT ENERGY AND CONSCIENTIAL ENERGY

In conscientiology, bioenergy is classified, for didactic purposes, into two groups: immanent energy (IE) and consciential energy (CE).

IE is the natural, primary energy, virgin, basic, impersonal, multiform and original, not altered or processed by more complex consciousnesses such as animals and human beings. It is dispersed and omnipresent in the entire physical universe and in all extraphysical dimensions. Being multiform, it can present itself in the form of immanent extraphysical energy (existent in other dimensions), cosmoenergy (energy from interstellar space or the universe - cosmic energy), aeroenergy (energy from the atmosphere and its meteorological phenomena), hydroenergy (energy from water in its several forms and natural sources), geoenergy (coming from the Earth and its geological formations), and phytoenergy (from plants).

CE is immanent energy that is qualified, polarized, or receives information when absorbed, metabolized, and applied by a consciousness in any of its manifestations. In the case of human beings, the information being added to the energy corresponds to thoughts, ideas, intentions, and memories, as well as feelings, emotions, affection, and certain instincts.

Therefore, in our evolutionary level, we are capable of absorbing both forms of energy, even though we mobilize and exteriorize only CEs.

THOSENES AND HOLOTHOSENES

It is impossible for the consciousness to separate or isolate the manifestations of thoughts, feelings and energy. While thinking, we maintain some emotion in the background and process a certain quantum of energy. When we express some emotion, it is impossible to silence ideas and memories and impossible to prevent the flow of energy. In addition, when working with energy, it is impossible to cease our mental and emotional processes.

Based on this fact, Waldo Vieira proposed the concept of thosene, where 'tho' represents mental manifestations, 'sen' indicates emotional manifestations, and 'ene' represents the energy.

In this context, the thosene can be defined as the minimum, indivisible unit of manifestation of the consciousness. We generate specific thosenes with any intention, manifestation, action, reaction, attitude, creation, posture, imagination or communication.

However, it is quite difficult to study or recognize isolated thosenes due to the great activity and mutability of the consciousness. In practice, the concept of the holotho-sene is used more, which is the result of the aggregation, accumulation and synergetic reinforcement of similar tho-senes.

An individual, alone, in a short period of time is able to create a certain, less intense, holothosene. On the other hand, a large group during a long period of time, thinking and feeling similar ideas and emotions, will create a much more powerful and durable holothosene.

When holothosenes possess characteristics that present or manifest extraphysical shapes, real to extraphysical or projected consciousnesses, they are called morphothosenes (popular: thought-forms).

Thosenes and holothosenes are the elements responsible for the mechanism of several paranormal phenomena, among which are: telepathy, psychometry, rapport, and retrocognition.

Human beings exchange thosenes all the time, establishing - to a greater or lesser degree, according to the level of thosenic affinity - auric couplings or energetic interfusions with other people, animals, plants, objects, environments and extraphysical consciousnesses. In certain cases, when the coupling is deeper and accomplished with more lucidity, a condition of sympathetic assimilation can be established, a process in which one or more of the participants of the coupling can perceive or feel in him or herself the physical sensations, emotional states, memories, or thoughts of the other.

Through studying and understanding the general context of bioenergies, we come to the conclusion that we live immersed in a great *ocean of energies* (energetic dimension). Energy can manifest itself in an infinite number of forms, frequencies, or degrees of density.

As conscious beings, we significantly disturb this ocean of energies, creating waves and broadcasting information. We leave the thosenic trace of our multiexistential personality in whichever places and dimensions we go, (intraphysical or extraphysical), throughout our existences. We generate thosenes that are exteriorized and will integrate with this *great ocean* (universal collective unconscious), and we also accumulate or record thosenes inside our consciousness's vehicles of manifestation.

From the specific point of view of retrocognitions and our memories, thosenes can be classified as:

- **Mnemothosenes** - units or minimum blocks that compose the holomemory, or the thosenes related to memories stored inside the consciousness.

- **Retrothosenes** - units of measure of retrocognitions. They are the specific mnemothosenes recalled in a retrocognition.

- **Traumatothosenes** - mnemothosenes associated to traumas of the past.

- **Omegathosenes** - the last thosene, normally quite intense, generated by the consciousness immediately before somatic deactivation (biological death), even when this process is a lucid one.

THE VIBRATIONAL STATE

The vibrational state (VS) is an energy regime of deep and intense activation of the whole structure of the holochakra, through the synchronized resonance of the chakras (energy vortexes), meridians (nadis) and energy points (acupuncture points). This resonance may reach other vehicles such as the psychosoma and mentalsoma, resulting in a vibrational state enriched by a pleasant euphoria and expansion of the consciousness.

In spite of being very exotic and intense, the sensation of vibration is quite pleasant, and sometimes through its intensification a sort of *energetic climax* is reached.

The VS can occur spontaneously, under different conditions, or it can be provoked voluntarily through a specific technique (see Chapter 17).

The basic uses of the vibrational state are: energetic self-defense against external energy; the removal or clearing of energetic blocks or decompensations; obtaining holosomatic homeostasis (the integral soundness of all manifestation vehicles); increase in holochakral flexibility; the installation of non-alignments (disconnection of the vehicles of manifestation of the consciousness) that can lead to conscious projections; development of paraperceptions in general; improvement in the exchange of energy and thosenes among the vehicles of manifestation; and an increase in the level of lucidity of the intraphysical consciousness.

6
EXISTENTIAL SERIALITY

As in a fossil, the past is present in us today.

To avoid mystical or romantic approaches and to encourage understanding retrocognitions in depth, as well as their interrelation with the evolutionary process of the consciousness, it is essential for us to study in more detail one of the previously mentioned consciential attributes: seriality.

A synthesis of factors relating to chronological time, retrocognitions and paraperceptions of the consciousness is presented here. For a more in depth study of this topic, refer to the works of Waldo Vieira, particularly *Our Evolution* and *Existential Program Manual* (see bibliography).

As already mentioned, the consciousness evolves through the accumulation of experiences in a very lengthy series of successive lives in different bodies, species, planets, and dimensions. This succession or series of interconnected existences is known as consciential seriality.

In this current level of lucidity we still do not have access to all of our seriality. That is to say, we do not reach the eternity of our past or the eternity of our future. We can remember lives that occurred 5,000 years ago, yet we do not access our existences as subhuman animals. It is possible to have precognitions regarding the next physical life, however we can not foretell our future as free consciousnesses.

Bodies, cultures, and names change, yet the consciousness that goes through this entire seriality is the same. Throughout this series of existences, the consciousness becomes more sophisticated, increasing its hyperacuity, expanding its universalism, and each time better and more cosmoethically controlling its holosoma and the dimensions in which it manifests itself.

Today we are a living summary of our past, the result of the addition of genetic and environmental characteristics, as well as the expression of everything that we have already lived, thought, felt, and done.

CONSCIENTIAL STATES

From the perspective of multidimensionality, the consciousness can manifest itself in four basic states:

- **Intraphysical** – The consciousness manifests itself through the soma, presenting a more stable and permanent energetic connection with the soma (silver cord). In popular language, this is the same as 'incarnated' or 'alive.' The consciousness is then called an intraphysical consciousness.

- **Extraphysical** – The condition in which the holosoma no longer includes the soma (physical body). It is the state assumed after the first somatic deactivation. In this state, the individual basically manifests through the psychosoma and is called an extraphysical consciousness. Popular: 'disincar-nated,' 'spirit,' 'entity.'

- **Projected** – A less permanent state than the others. In the case of the intraphysical consciousness this condition is manifested when the consciousness is out of its soma; maintaining the psychosoma-soma connection called the silver cord. In the case of the extraphysical consciousness, it is manifested when the consciousness is out of its psychosoma; maintaining the mental-soma-psychosoma connection called the golden cord.

- **Free** – The condition of the consciousness following the third somatic deactivation, in which it has reached a state of evolution and holomaturity such that it is no longer born (somatic rebirth) into a physical body. It no longer possesses any karmic links in the manner we understand them. With the third somatic deactivation, possibly manifesting a holosoma composed of only a matured mentalsoma, the consciousness completes its seriality as we understand it.

PHYSICAL LIVES OR SERIATE LIVES

At each new somatic rebirth, the consciousness has the challenge of controlling a new soma, which is basically the result of the *genetics* inherited from its progenitors, and *paragenetics*, accumulated and cultivated along the path of its seriality. Both can present positive and negative points.

During its physical life, a third deterministic factor grows in importance in the formation of the personality: nurture or environmental influences. In practice, these manifest in: culture, language, religion, social labels, family education, formal education, morals, codes of law, socially accepted or rejected behaviors, and ideological, philosophical, and scientific conditioning.

What can be observed is that for most intraphysical consciousnesses genetics and environmental influences override the programming of paragenetics.

The process of somatic rebirth (or reincarnation) is developed gradually, beginning before fecundation and prolonged for more than two decades after birth.

A fact that most people are unaware of, essentially due to social and religious conditioning plus a lack of extraphysical experience, is that for the most lucid consciousnesses the shock or trauma of somatic rebirth is much more intense than that of somatic deactivation (death).

There is no fixed pattern for this process, because each consciousness develops its somatic rebirth in a very individual way. However, a basic profile can be developed that fits most people on this planet.

The process of returning to a new soma begins in the extraphysical phase when, consciously or unconsciously, the consciousness prepares for its new life. This preparation can be lucid and participatory, as is the case in less immature and less unconscious individuals (in the form of intermissive courses, for example, as we will see later); or in the case of less lucid consciousnesses it can be natural, almost automatic, and is promoted by more mature and assistential consciousnesses. In some circumstances, somatic rebirth occurs against the will of the consciousness being born.

In any one of these situations, the consciousness that is to have a somatic rebirth begins to approach the physical dimension, increasing the density of its psychosoma by absorbing denser energy, which in practice is the beginning of the formation of the holochakra (pre-somatic rebirth) for those who have undergone the second somatic deactivation (death).

Parallel to this process, the coupling and rapport with the parents' energy becomes stronger, primarily with the future mother. This energetic connection, with its inevitable interfusion of consciential energy, completes the formation of the pre-holochakra, which will create the first and subtle connections with the ovule, when fecundated. In this manner, at the moment of conception, with the extreme vitalization of the intracellular processes of the cell-matter, the consciousness, already extremely unconscious in most cases, establishes the primordial silver cord connecting its energies to the recently fertilized ovule.

As the embryo becomes a fetus and matures in preparation for birth, these energetic connections are reinforced and become more complete with time. During this process paragenetics combine with genetics in programming the basic, initial characteristics of the new body.

While inside the maternal body, the juxtaposition or perfect coincidence of the other vehicles of manifestation of the consciousness is not possible. The consciousness being reborn remains, practically the entire time, unconscious and semi-projected.

At the moment of birth, while becoming an independent biological being, after the first inhalation of breath and severance of the umbilical cord, the psychosoma properly aligns itself, for the first time, with its new physical body.

From this point on, during the gradual maturation of the soma, primarily that of the central nervous system, the psychosoma connects, aligns and unites with greater intensity and stability to the biological body, by means of the growing connections of the silver cord.

According to the leading-edge relative truths of today, it is known that the body continues growing, on average, up to approximately 26 years of age (the moment in which the extremities or epiphyses of the long bones continue to grow due to local cellular multiplication). It can be said that the somatic rebirth process concludes at this age.

During these two and a half decades of progressive somatic rebirth, another important consciential process develops: the recovery of cons.

A 'con' is the theoretical unit of lucidity or hyperacuity of the consciousness. The more lucid the individual, the greater is their number of cons. While undergoing somatic, or physical rebirth, an individual suffers a dramatic reduction in the level of their lucidity. While an individual might manifest a large degree of lucidity (we will use the figure: 1000 cons) during their intermissive period, upon rebirth this level is greatly reduced, for example to 10. As an individual starts growing and maturing, they begin recovering their cons, part of their consciential patrimony.

Theoretically, we should be recovering cons until the last moment of our physical life, yet the majority of intraphysical consciousnesses stop recovering cons when they reach the age at which they begin manifesting signs of senility. In these cases, the individual again progressively loses his or her cons, many times as a form of pre-adaptation for the transition of somatic deactivation that approaches.

In a general estimate, it could be said that the average human being manifests around 200 to 250 cons during the highest phase of intraphysical lucidity. More lucid individuals, aware of multidimensional reality, can manifest approximately 400 cons. It is quite difficult to surpass this mark while in the soma. Retrocognition can help in this important process of recovering extra cons, beyond humanity's average.

One of the important points in this process of reacquisition of units of lucidity is that not all the cons present the same ease, possibility, probability, or readiness for being recovered. Usually, the first cons to be recovered are the oldest ones, related to survival, repeated life after life, and for that reason easier and more immediate. The newer cons, recently conquered during our last period or intermissive course, will be the most difficult, or least likely, to manifest here in the physical dimension. Thus, as a way of expanding our multidimensional self-awareness the effort in obtaining lucid projections and retrocognitions of the intermissive period is worthwhile.

The first layer or package of cons recovered from infancy through the end of adolescence is known in conscientiology as the consciential basement. These are the most instinctive, atavistic and primitive cons, and thus the most used, reinforced and repeated cons throughout seriality.

Children, in general, manifest frank egocentrism and aggressiveness, a sign of the consciential basement. A major problem is that many adults have yet to leave their phase of the consciential basement, as is the case with sport hunters or very selfish individuals.

During the consciential basement phase, some children who are more predisposed or parapsychic spontaneously report events and data regarding possible previous existences. This is especially so because, concurrent to the recovery of cons, a retrothosenic reflux unavoidably occurs. The absence of conditioning and mechanisms of repression and intellectualization facilitate this process even more.

Many people wonder or openly ask themselves the reason or need for somatic rebirth and, therefore, for physical life. We cannot say that we understand all of the reasons completely, yet we can present some initial ideas:

Perhaps the main reason is that the intraphysical dimension allows consciousnesses of very different evolutionary levels, while inside the body, to coexist within the same environment and to interrelate, as a means of catalyzing their maturation. Otherwise, in the extraphysical state, these consciousnesses would be dispersed throughout several different consciential dimensions that would permit, at maximum, short visits or periods of time together. If a more lucid extraphysical consciousness goes to a denser dimension, it needs to be attentive so as not to let itself be affected by the holothosenic pressure of that extraphysical dimension. This means that somatic rebirth acts in a democratic way, propitiating a larger interaction and imposing the same basic 'ground rules' for everyone. Without this possibility, less mature and lucid extraphysical consciousnesses would not have the opportunity of coexisting with healthier, more balanced consciousnesses. This would decrease the possibilities and incentives for growth.

Another reason for seriality is that it keeps the consciousness on track. If on the one hand, somatic rebirth restricts the consciousness and the freedom of its manifestation; on the other hand, for the same reasons, it specifies certain experiences, tasks, conditions and opportunities in a more rigid and efficient way. The comparison with a school is here inevitable. What gets lost in freedom, is won in efficiency and learning effectiveness.

The inertia of physical matter and this biological body allows the consciousness to think before accomplishing something; to have a destructive impulse and to moderate it before acting; to have a strong emotion without losing the structure of its vehicle of manifestation; or even, to feel something towards someone and hide these same feelings. In the extraphysical state, to generate a certain thosene is to act: everything is immediate and public.

The loss of memories due to rebirth, natural for the absolute majority of intraphysical consciousnesses, represents a new opportunity for the improvement of certain groupkarmic relationships, because it allows us to reacquaint with consciousnesses and to face situations again without strong emotions or traumas hindering the perfecting of these energetic links. For example, due to the reduced consciential maturity in humanity, the complete recollection of the past would impair overcoming enmities and passions. Besides, the process of forgetting results, inevitably, in a certain radical type of mental hygiene, preventing obsession, such as feelings of guilt.

1st, 2ND, AND 3RD SOMATIC DEACTIVATION

A somatic deactivation is defined as the discarding of a certain vehicle of manifestation. The consciousness itself does not die, yet it abandons one or more of its bodies, causing their disintegration or dissipation. Therefore, if we have at least four bodies, we can expect several types of somatic deactivations or deaths.

1st somatic deactivation - the common observed death of the soma. It is also the legal death that establishes the end of the physical person or citizen. It corresponds to a disconnection of the energies of the silver cord - which until that moment have kept the physical body alive - with the concurrent detachment of the psychosoma and the mentalsoma. Summarizing, it is when the deactivation of the soma and silver cord occurs. In general, helpers aid the individual who is undergoing this transition.

2nd somatic deactivation - the process of dissipation of the remnants of holochakral energy that are present in the structure of the psychosoma after the 1st somatic deactivation. The interval of time between the first and the second somatic deactivation varies greatly from consciousness to consciousness, and can range from a few hours to decades, in conformity with its evolutionary level and holosomatic homeostasis. Similar to the condition of a loaded (dense) projection, the extraphysical consciousness that has not gone through the second somatic deactivation has difficulties with changing dimension, flying, maintaining its lucidity, among other things. For some consciousnesses, the second somatic deactivation has yet to ever occur. These individuals go through somatic rebirth with almost exactly the same physical energies of their last physical life (or several previous lives). In this case, the intraphysical consciousness will have a more greatly restricted life, exhibiting blocked parapsychism, and very materialistic thosenes (locked existence) due to the presence of a *fossilized holochakra*. On average, for healthier and more lucid consciousnesses, the period of passing through the second somatic deactivation, after having passed through the first one, is approximately three days. Consciousnesses that pass through this second somatic deactivation exhibit, during their next physical life, a greater holochakral looseness, a greater understanding of life and its mechanisms, a larger predisposition to parapsychic experiences, sensibility to bioenergy, and conscious projections (alternating existential seriality). While helpers aid the first somatic deactivation, the evolutionary orientor acts more during the second.

3rd **somatic deactivation** - known in some oriental cultures as *moksha* (the liberation); it is the definitive and permanent exit of the mentalsoma from the other known bodies of manifestation through the deactivation of the psychosoma. In certain situations, it is supposed that the third desoma occurs together with the first and second somatic deactivations, the condition in which the consciousness dematerializes all of its other vehicles. After the third somatic deactivation, the consciousness is free from intraphysical commitments and from the long cycle of somatic rebirths, free from seriality as we know it. This state is called, in conscientiology, the Free Consciousness, when the individual begins another phase or evolutionary course in the mental dimension, a stage that is still poorly understood.

EVOLUTIONARY GROUP

Along its series of existences that surely surpass the limits of known history on this planet and even extend well beyond the planet's geological age, the consciousness experiences and develops contacts, encounters, experiences, and relationships with several other consciousnesses, mostly human. With the repetition of encounters and co-existences, the exchange of energy begins a process whereby the individuals' holothosenes contribute to establishing a holothosene for that specific relationship. The more intense the feelings, emotions, and energies of the shared and common ideas, the more powerful the holothosene will become. Since we end up living a greater number of existences together with certain individuals, more intense connections are developed with them than with the other members of the group.

After countless lives a condition is created that is called, in conscientiology, *groupkarmic inseparability*. This explains the condition in which individuals progressively create stronger links that enable them to evolve together, establishing the mechanism for the synchronicities of successive encounters, existence after existence.

During this process, the preponderance of *groupkarma* will begin to approximate the level of *egokarma* (personal or individual karma) due to the accumulation of conflicts, passions, revenge, assistances, commitments, criminal complicities, and evolutionary societies. For that reason, the evolutionary group of similar consciousnesses is also called the *karmic group*.

The nuclear family, second or third-tier extended families, circles of friends and work colleagues form only the tip of the *iceberg* of the evolutionary group as a whole, which includes millions of intraphysical and extraphysical consciousness. In practice, each large evolutionary group is composed of successive subgroups of consciousnesses that have a greater affinity with others in that particular subgroup. At the other end of the scale, we can say that the entire population of Earth forms an immense karmic group.

As in the case of terrorists and criminal groups, certain subgroups may become involved in anticosmoethical activities. In such cases, the holothosene created is not one of natural groupkarmic inseparability, but rather one of an *interprison*, in that they share the temporary and relative benefits of their destructive actions. Situations arise in which a member, upon becoming aware of this condition, decides to leave such a liaison - perhaps having lasted for many lives. This consciousness may well become a victim of its own group and holothosene in which it has participated and profited.

After a long period of *victimization*, the consciousness enters the *recomposition* phase, in which it begins to have the minimum lucidity and balance required to try to help the ones that stayed behind, still stuck in the interprison and victimization phases.

Knowing and understanding these first phases of the groupkarmic process, as proposed by conscientiology, is very important for understanding several types of recollections of previous existences, common to most retrocognitors, and to avoid the occurrence of *pathological retrocognitions*.

INTERMISSIVE PERIODS

After the first somatic deactivation, the consciousness exists and manifests outside the intraphysical dimension, during the intermissive period (also called the intermission or period between lives). It is a big mistake to assume that the consciousness only evolves during the intraphysical phase and that the periods between lives are ones of inactivity or of unconsciousness.

The intermissive period plays a fundamental role in evolution and, because of this, many of its characteristics determine several possibilities for accelerating the maturation process.

The duration of the intermissive period fluctuates within a very wide range, from hours to centuries (in rare cases). For most people the duration of the intermission, obviously measured in reference to the physical dimension, is of the same order as the duration of an average human life.

Another important factor, dependent on each individual and their evolutionary level, is the dimensional layer and consequent extraphysical colony that they will more permanently inhabit during the intermission. Outside the transitional periods of somatic deactivation and somatic rebirth, extraphysical consciousnesses have as an extraphysical base a specific consciential community, called their *extraphysical origin*. It is usually to this *general headquarters* or *native extraphysical city* that the consciousness returns following the somatic deactivation that occurs subsequent to each of its intraphysical lives.

The extraphysical origins of some consciousnesses are evolved, transcendental and subtle colonies, closer to the mental dimension and having practically no interaction with the physical dimension. Yet, unfortunately, most of humanity and para-humanity are still linked to dense extraphysical communities, communities very much connected to the physical environment. Even during the intermissive periods, regardless of the dimension, we live together with other individuals from our evolutionary group.

The primary criterion that defines the basic characteristics of each individual's intermissive period is whether the consciousness has passed through the second somatic deactivation. More than this, what matters is the percentage of holochakral energy dissipated, relative to somatic deactivation. If it does not go through the second somatic deactivation or passes only partially through it (not being able to release the totality of dense energies from the former holochakra), the holosoma of the extraphysical consciousness will be denser and energetically blocked, restricting the range or maximum level of subtler dimensions that can be reached, while limiting its residence in those subtler dimensions to shorter periods of time.

The materialistic paradigm as well as the dogmas of most religions (which end up being materialistic) induce the person to believe that its most basic and essential state is intraphysical. This is a serious error in the understanding of consciential processes. The consciousness is essentially extraphysical, while physical life is a temporary, artificial phase, in the advanced framework of the multidimensional universe. One of the many evidences that can corroborate such a statement is the disconnection or natural semiprojection - almost always unconscious - that most superior types of life (animals and human beings) exhibit during sleep. At the first possible opportunity, the consciousness leaves the physical dimension to recover in the extraphysical, its more natural state.

The intermission can be quite active and productive for more lucid consciousnesses. They take advantage of the opportunities that present themselves in the form of restructuring of consciential attributes, learning, assistance to other less lucid consciousnesses, as well as preparation for the next intraphysical life.

EXISTENTIAL PROGRAMMING

Everyone is born with the purpose of evolving primarily by helping others to evolve, so that the entire group will evolve together. Even subhuman consciousnesses are in this same condition. What is important to study is the quality of this objective, whether it is indefinite and of a personal nature, or more specific, planned, and with a greater collective reach.

During the intermission, parallel to the intermissive course, the existential program (existential plan, intraphysical task; popularly known as life mission) is planned and perfected. The type of existential program dictates the basic characteristics of the intermissive course.

In accordance with the capacity and level of maturity of each intraphysical consciousness, a *mini-existential program* or a *maxi-existential program* is established. The mini-existential program is a simpler mediocre program, like a life summarized by being born, growing, and generating some more bodies to give opportunities to other consciousnesses. The maxi-existential program is established as a plan pursuing tasks that will have a greater impact on humanity's general evolution, as in the historical example of Gandhi, who freed a country without recourse to violence.

Who decides or plans our existential program? A collegial collaboration of extraphysical helpers (popularly known as: protectors, spiritual guides) plan the dominant themes of the existential program, mapping the flight plan of the future life. Acting as a moderator and consultant to this collaboration is the evolutionary orientor or *evolutionologist*, a helper to the helpers. This consciousness provides a lucid and final word in relation to the plan that has been developed.

The existential program is not completely decided immediately at the beginning of the intermission, because information brought from the *intraphysical front* forces continual adjustments to the initial plan.

The participation of each future intraphysical consciousness in that programming will depend on its degree of lucidity. The more lucid, the more it can suggest, participate, and ask. The less lucid, the more it is helped in the logical planning and optimization of its next physical existence. In situations where the consciousness has no lucidity, certain decisions can and must be made that may be against its will or without its direct consent.

It is common to see many people uncomfortable with the possibility of not being able to decide 100% of their existential program, as they consider this an insult to their free will. Such observations generally come from more rebellious and egocentric individuals with little multidimensional experience. However, this is a very logical approach. Can a somnambulized consciousness, or even one in a state of extraphysical parapsychosis, plan their own incredibly complex and immediate destiny? Can a reasonably lucid consciousness decide alone, without intervention, several details of its future life, for which it will need so many others to achieve the desired conclusion? If someone intends to return to life and be an intraphysical helper, acting as a mini-cog in the maximechanism, can it do so without the help of more lucid mentalsomas, who have a wider and deeper vision?

From the point of view of the existential program, a typical life can be divided into two periods: the preparatory and the executive. In our modern society, most individuals spend the first half of their lives building and stabilizing the body, maturing psychologically and emotionally, studying and graduating in some specialty, conquering economic and financial independence, and establishing a mature and stable sexual-affective relationship. Without these minimum stipulations it is more difficult to begin to undertake the existential program.

At this point in the discussion of the process of seriality, memory, and access to our past, pertinent questions arise: why do we not remember our existential program? And how can we recall it?

Let us begin by understanding the rhythm of physical life and the level of immaturity of the human masses, as well as appreciating the helpers' point of view on the subject; generally it is understood that it is not ideal to remember the totality and depth of the existential program. If this recollection did occur, the intraphysical consciousness could experience a 'state of shock,' frustration, or aborting of its own existential program. As an analogy, imagine a small child asking what their future will bring. Depending on the realism and depth of our answer, in describing dramas, difficulties, and very typical human problems of this intraphysical life, we could be creating a counter-productive trauma that works against the maturation of the child.

It is not easy to remember our existential program for reasons we will discuss in Chapter 12, when we discuss potential blocks to having retrocognitions. One of the methods to recall the existential program is to have a retrocognition of the last intermissive period. Unfortunately, this is one of the least common types of retrocognition. The way to provoke this type of rare experience is discussed later in this book.

The mechanisms involved in the planning of intraphysical life presented here have the objective of aiding those who desire retrocognitions to direct their efforts towards memories that have a higher priority for their life goal. Retrocognitions are interesting as a means of increasing our lucidity in respect to data pertinent to the execution of the existential program.

Even without a clear recollection, people can discover their existential program, or at least the general themes, through the following technical approaches:

1. **Evolutionologist** - conscious projection and an interview with the evolutionary advisor.
2. **Helper** - conscious projection and an interview with a more experienced helper.
3. **Extraphysical Origin** - conscious projection with a visit to our extraphysical origin or the campus of the intermissive course.
4. **Strong and Weak traits** - analysis of one's profile – Strong and Weak traits (Chapter 17).

5. **Polykarma** - analysis of what life has offered to and demanded from the individual, or an analysis of polykarmic credits and debits (karmic reciprocation).

INTERMISSIVE COURSES

If the extraphysical personality has passed through the second somatic deactivation and is not the subject of interplanetary transmigrations, and, when applicable, has recovered its extraphysical adulthood, it will have met the basic pre-requisites to attend an intermissive course.

Several more advanced extraphysical colonies maintain infrastructures and personnel dedicated to training capable consciousnesses during their preparation for the new intraphysical life and associated tasks. The basic goal of these courses is to increase the chances that the intraphysical consciousness will complete its existential program, preventing the consciousness from being completely sedated by genetics or swallowed by environmental influences.

To create an analogy with the existential program and its preparation and in order to clarify these ideas, let us use a didactic parallel, where we can discuss the main and probable characteristics for a future manned mission to Mars:

- Astrophysicists associated with this mission will analyze all the information that is available for that planet and its physical conditions.

- Physicians and psychologists will establish ideal profiles, and will analyze all possible characteristics of the future astronauts, selecting the most capable among the many candidates.

- Engineers, physicists and other technicians will study all the characteristics and variables of the mission, in order to, as best they are able, foresee any potential problems, thus planning strategies to avoid or correct them.

- Specific clothes for each team member will be made according to their biometric characteristics and functional specialties.

- Roles, functions and hierarchy will be established based on skills, experience, and a certain consensus.

- The latest generation of computers will simulate several possible scenarios of how the mission might develop, taking into account accidents and other possible unexpected occurrences.

- Astronaut candidates will spend months or even years living in and training with many and distinct simulations of the conditions that will or might be encountered during the mission.

- Although the number of astronauts is small, the number of individuals involved in the project, in the most varied of tasks and specialties, is enormous.

- In spite of the small number of astronauts, the investment will be astronomical and the implications and results of the mission will be significant for humanity.

- However, despite all this planning, no one will be capable of categorically affirming that the mission will transpire as planned or whether it will be a success.

In quite a similar way, with regards to the process of intermission-existential program-somatic rebirth, the following can be pointed out:

- The future intraphysical consciousness receives information, classes, training and simulations to increase its chances of success here in the intraphysical life.

- Equivalent to the space suits, its future body will be planned, as far as possible, to facilitate the success of the mission.

- As in the case of the command center on Earth, the helpers accompany us throughout the mission, being able to reprogram, change routes and even substitute personnel, within certain limits.

- The intraphysical consciousness does not come alone to this dimension; but in a group of similar consciousnesses, trained and committed to a common task.

- The failure of an element of the team can compromise the entire mission.

- Often, to abort the mission at the *halfway* point means *total* failure.

- Without loyalty, balance, and camaraderie, failure is imminent.

- Analogous to the Mars mission, the consciousness might be lost, straying from the previously planned 'ideal' course (ectopy – see Chapter 6).

- The existential moratorium (see Chapter 6) is analogous to the re-planning of the mission and the shipping of extra supplies of fuel, oxygen, and provisions.

- For the advanced extraphysical consciousness at the end of its intermission, lucidly aware of its future life task or existential program, the expectations and reflections on its immediate future are analogous to the ones the astronauts and their partners have on Earth hours before take-off. This is a critical, risky, challenging, unpredictable, and important trip with profound collective meaning, and after all has been said and done it is a positive and calculated *adventure*.

• In a certain way, it can be said that we are now on Mars, in the midst of a red sand storm, without communication links to the command center on Earth.

The curriculum of the intermissive course for each extraphysical consciousness is decided based on the needs of its future existential program, the existential program of its group and of the personal characteristics of each consciousness (strong and weak traits).

The curriculum studied covers a wide range of topics essential for the future existential program, consisting of basic disciplines, common to all, as well as individually specific disciplines, especially developed for the need of the individual or group existential program. Among the basic disciplines we find the study of seriality, (the theme of this section), holosomatics and bioenergetics. With a specific future profession in mind, several projects and studies can be developed extraphysically, to saturate the consciousness. This serves to facilitate the recovery and materialization of the associated cons, when the consciousness manifests within a physical brain. And so it is considered that some cases of prodigies are more the result of learning obtained in intermissive courses than the result of past life experience.

In practice, the intermissive course is administered in extraphysical colonies that resemble a university campus, with classrooms, auditoriums, open spaces, laboratories, multimedia libraries, housing, and centers of cohabitation.

An interesting point is that intermissive courses in this *karmic jurisdiction* that we call Earth have been given for approximately 350 years and continue to be improved and developed. This coincides with the intensification of the transmigration (in this case immigration) of consciousnesses from other planets to Earth and with the observable surge in modern sciences and several other changes in human society.

During this period, the bilateral exchange of intermissive course students among planets also intensified. In other words, extraphysical consciousnesses more closely linked to Earth embarked on brief trips as well as longer sojourns in order to attend courses on other inhabited planets, as a way to enrich their ideas and increase their sense of universalism. The reverse also occurs, that is to say, extraterrestrial consciousnesses come here to do the same.

There is even the hypothesis that some more capable consciousnesses can serve an intraphysical apprenticeship, that is, a somatic rebirth on another planet, to live a typical life in that society, learn, go through somatic deactivation and then return to their planet. Logically we can assume that this might occur with visiting teachers of intermissive courses who come from other planets.

Another reality still not much studied or understood with respect to the intermission and its courses is that of dimensional pouches. These self-contained mini-dimensions, more closed and isolated from others, present a flow of time completely different from the physical dimension and other extraphysical dimensions. In these pouches, an intermissive course equivalent to years or decades (virtual time measured by the amount of experience or volume of learning acquired) inside that dimensional pouch can correspond to very short periods of intraphysical time. It is not known who creates and maintains these pouches and how this is done.

This fact has already been experienced in a limited way by conscious projectors, including this author. In such cases, during a projection that lasts some minutes (measured by calculating the difference between the arrival and departure time on a physical clock), the experience corresponds to an extraphysical duration that resembled years of existences, contacts, events and teachings. Upon returning to the body, a real perception of having been traveling for a very long period of time can be experienced. This can cause a benign though short-lived confusion.

EXISTENTIAL INCOMPLETISM

If we admit the existence of the existential program, the next logical step would be to consider to what level or degree someone completes his or her existential program. In other words, at the time of somatic deactivation, how much of its original existential program was that consciousness able to complete?

Unfortunately, what can be observed is that most individuals do not achieve the totality, and some do not even attain a reasonable percentage of success in the execution of their life program - this condition is called existential incompletism. Some of the basic reasons for such failures are genetic and environmental influences, lack of lucidity and self-corruption. By living outside the previously optimized and planned route, the consciousness lives an ectopic, inefficient, and ineffective life. It is striking to observe how many believe they suffer from depression, while actually suffering from intraphysical melancholy. They may feel useless, empty and feel that things have no meaning, even when, by all conventional measures they seem to be good examples of economic and social success.

The most serious and regretful condition is that of a consciousness already in an extraphysical existence, recovering, little by little, memories of the previous intermissive period and comparing the initially drafted existential program with the images and memories from its recent panoramic vision of its just completed intraphysical period. The result of the discovery that it did not accomplish most of the original plan is the aptly named condition of extraphysical melancholy.

A pertinent question that begs to be asked is: if you were to die this instant while reading this book, would you be satisfied and have a clear conscience concerning the life just concluded? Or would there still be unfinished projects, postponed commitments, unresolved enmities, badly finished passionate liaisons, dependent people or karmic debts?

In practice, cases of people who are obsessive about their responsibilities can also be observed. These people never relax nor allow themselves the right to enjoy certain good things in life, not even at a level reasonable and necessary for physical health. Many times these types of personality can be the result of a deep trauma in the consciousness, caused by extraphysical melancholy during the last intermissive period.

In rare cases, depending on the magnitude of the melancholy, the depth of the despair, and the amount of evolutionary deficit in question, a consciousness may enter a state of intimate war or destructive impulse against everything and everyone, as a kind of transference mechanism. Much the way that a person throws an object against the wall while having eruptions of immaturity or a lack of emotional control (disarray), the extraphysical consciousness riots against the cosmos. Some extraphysical mega-intruders are created in this struggle, and they take centuries or millennia to recover their holosomatic homeostasis.

SELF-MIMICRY

The intraphysical consciousness has a strong tendency to repeat patterns of thought, values, ethics and behaviors of its past. Such repetition is in fact inevitable and natural, being both simultaneously cause and effect of that consciousness's individual holothosene.

However, most of the time, the majority of the population on the planet repeats the worst parts of their previous physical experiences, an occurrence called negative or avoidable self-mimicry.

As in an old movie remade several times, the individual repeats dramas of the past, with the same characters, emotions, passions, and disappointments, losing evolutionary opportunities and wasting time. The intraphysical consciousness lives materialistically as a sleepwalker, not knowing why they are here or what they should be doing. They lose one third of their life sleeping, have no paraperceptions and follow the trends and fashions of the human masses. In brief, the individual manifests itself as a robot, a condition called existential robotization.

One of the main causes for incompletism is this very self-mimicry syndrome, catalyzed by social, familiar, and environmental (cultural) pressure.

In some cases, certain levels of self-mimicry are positive or planned. In these situations, certain formulas or combinations of factors that worked well in previous lives are repeated. The best example is self-relay, which is explained further on.

EXISTENTIAL COMPLETISM

Having accomplished the totality or a significant percentage of one's programmed task, the consciousness attains the condition of existential completism.

Existential completism remains a rare condition in this school-hospital planet called Earth. Nevertheless, with the improvement and generalization of intermissive courses, cases of existential completism will become more and more common.

When the consciousness becomes lucid of its completist status, the extraphysical consciousness enters into a condition of extraphysical euphoria, the opposite of the aforementioned extraphysical melancholy. Aware of existential completism while still in the physical life, the intraphysical consciousness manifests intraphysical euphoria.

On an unconscious or semiconscious level this may explain why some old people or seniors behave like the calm and benevolent grandparents of everyone (intraphysical euphoria) or, the opposite, as grouchy, conflicted, antisocial people (intraphysical melancholy).

In the same way that the best university students (honor students – as denominated in the USA) receive rewards and privileges, such as grants, financial aid, and priority in choosing disciplines or classes, existential completists earn the possibility of having an improved body in their next physical life.

A *customized*, extraordinary superbody - the macrosoma - will present one or more characteristics well beyond the possibilities of mediocre human genetics such as: excellent memory, high projectability, a strong immunological system resistant to any microorganism, predisposition to the production of ectoplasmy, among many others.

In addition, the completist will probably be invited to serve as an instructor (to a greater or lesser degree) of an intermissive course, sharing with others the manner in which they obtained success in their recently concluded life.

Something to think about: is it preferable to be a completist (100%) of a mini existential program or an incompletist (50%) of a maxi existential program?

EXISTENTIAL MORATORIUM

The existential program is not a rigid chronogram, nor is life governed by a pre-determined destiny. During intraphysical life, according to each personal decision and depending on collective events, or events within the evolutionary group (premature death of one of the key people, for example), corrections and re-planning need to be performed.

Possibly, one of the greatest examples of such replanning is the existential moratorium, which, just as the name implies, is an extension or prolongation of the life period originally planned for a given intraphysical consciousness. The existential moratorium can be of two types; one occurring because of an existential deficit (mini existential moratorium or 'for arrears') and the other because of an existential surplus (maxi existential moratorium or 'over-accomplishment'). In the majority of cases both occur in conjunction with the process of a near-death experience, or with some deep life crisis, and are the result of a direct intervention from the evolutionary orientor. Existential moratorium brings with it a recharging of the energies of the holochakra of the intraphysical consciousness.

A deficit moratorium occurs when the intraphysical consciousness has a near-death experience or deep crisis, which in many cases was planned to be its final projection. In meeting with its helpers, or even the evolutionary orientor, the consciousness understands that it has not accomplished a sufficient percentage of its previously planned existential program. In this case it can receive a life extension of some years, sponsored by the extraphysical team, so as to have a second chance.

Usually, in these situations, when the mini existential moratorium is accepted, the individual returns to the body and feels an intense urge to neither lose time nor waste opportunities. Many times the individual behaves as if they were on parole and might manifest a certain intraphysical melancholy.

A consciousness who qualifies as a completist, upon meeting its extraphysical colleagues, receives thosenes of congratulations, and in some cases the suggestion of the possibility of returning to physical life in order to transcend what has already been accomplished, producing more than was planned. The helpers and evolutionary orientor present this possibility when the physical life (physical health, financial stability, etc.) of the completist is compatible with the proposed extension of time and with the larger needs of its evolutionary group or community as a whole.

Normally, the intraphysical consciousness who is a maximoratorist, exhibits no stress, anxiety or existential crises, acting only with care not to make a mistake, and to avoid losing what has already been accomplished.

SELF-RELAY

It is easy to understand the inevitable relay that occurs among consciousnesses from the same evolutionary group. A generation arrives to give continuity to what was started by the previous one. Yet, what calls more attention because of its challenge and evolutionary effectiveness is the relay that the consciousness establishes with itself (self-relay).

Certain existential tasks are excessively complex and long to be concluded in a single intraphysical existence. In these cases, it is necessary to divide the respective mega-existential program into two, three or more smaller existential programs, compatible with conditions in the same number of intraphysical lives. In this case, the consciousness performing the self-relay, through each of these lives, leaves its work ready to be resumed in the next life, at the exact point where it was left; that is, it passes the baton (drawing an analogy with the relay race in athletics) to itself. Obviously this is not an easy task, since it is based on the completism of each one of these lives, and depends on a much more constant monitoring by the helpers.

Successful self-relay is the first step in stimulating lucidity and invigorating the existential continuum and in so doing beginning to fill in the blanks and blackouts between lives and dimensions, ultimately leading towards the state of continuous consciousness.

EVOLUTIONARY CYCLES

For didactic purposes, we have been discussing seriate lives (physical lives) almost as separate units or mutually exclusive entities. However, to complete this discussion, and to give the true magnitude and transcendence of our seriality, it is important to understand that, for the lucid extraphysical consciousness, each one of the physical lives is like a second in the great multimillenary sequence of physical and extraphysical existences. The existential program of each existence is planned without losing sight of the roots of the remote past, or the goals of the very distant future. In this context, individuals and karmic groups evolve in cycles, some of which may last thousands of years and involve numerous seriate lives.

In simpler terms, a comparison with the period of "life" of a certain culture can be made. A culture is born, reaches its apex, sows seeds for other new and younger cultures, and disappears (Egyptians, Romans, Celts and Cathars, for example). For many consciousnesses, the entire course of such civilizations can coincide with a well-determined evolutionary cycle for them, both personally and as a group.

On a wider time scale we can understand that we are in an evolutionary cycle linked to the period of intelligent life on this planet. Earth will not sustain life forever. One day, its quantum of vital energy be exhausted and consciousnesses will transmigrate to other planets - a process that will be set in motion hundreds of years in advance.

At this evolutionary moment, it is more interesting and pragmatic for us to study the current cycle of our karmic group as a whole. The need for reaching completism in this life is more critical today than in previous lives. The last life of a specific cycle, a critical life, or closing of the cycle, resembles the final examinations of a school year. There is no time left for procrastination or frolicking.

Whoever is able to meet the minimum requirements proceeds ahead with the group's best, towards new challenges, possibilities, and knowledge. Anyone who does not pass stays behind and resumes another cycle with evolutionary freshmen - the worst or repetitious part of our evolutionary group. For the consciousness left behind, this process is very obvious; they feel like a stranger in a nest or an abandoned E.T. on an alien planet. So, despite involution or absolute evolutionary regression not existing, it is clear that in this case there is a relative setback.

If in normal lives incompletism is acknowledged as consciential defeat, in times of critical lives it acquires the magnitude of a catastrophe.

Sometimes, when closing a cycle, the completist portion of the evolutionary group returns to their origins on this planet where they inhabited the first bodies of this simian that we now call *Homo sapiens sapiens*, to restart another cycle at a higher consciential level.

We cannot forget that the leading-edge relative truths of anthropology and history affirm that human civilization (not the human being itself) began with the Agricultural Revolution, approximately 10,000 years ago, which corresponds to 100 centuries, or a mere 100 physical lives, which is not that many when compared to cosmic rhythms.

One day there will be historians and archaeologists specialized in retrocognition and psychometry, able to complement or even rewrite human history (primarily those gaps that exist due to a lack of documentation) and thereby trace the general lines of humanity's parahistory and its origins.

7
EXTRAPHYSICAL SOCIETY

*Some people consider sociology a particularly
complex science. That is because they have not
yet awoken to the even greater complexity of
extraphysical society.*

It is not possible to understand many of the manifestations
of the consciousness and its evolutionary effects without
discussing para-humanity, also called extraphysical society.

For the veteran conscious projector, the permanent
and increasing migratory flow of consciousnesses to and
from the intraphysical dimension is very clear and natural.

Waldo Vieira, in his extraphysical research, offers an
approximate and initial estimate that the extraphysical
society is nine times greater than intraphysical society
(humanity). That is to say, if the *breathing* terrestrial population is today around 6.4 billion intraphysical consciousnesses, there must be approximately 57.6 billion extraphysical consciousnesses in the extraphysical dimensions
linked to a greater or lesser degree with this planet. In
other words, 64 billion consciousnesses exist in this multidimensional metropolitan zone called Earth.

Many opponents of the theory of seriality argue that
humanity has been growing inexorably since the Middle
Ages. From where then would the consciousnesses be
coming? Such a point of view is a relic of religious geocen-
trism, the same ideology that almost killed Galileo Galilei,
and which is not based on the theorice of
multidimensionality.

The consensus of many veteran projectors is that a
permanent transmigration exists among planets (karmic
jurisdictions) and that the immigration towards Earth has
accelerated heavily in the last four centuries. This coincides, approximately, with the Renaissance, the expansion
of global navigation, the beginning of modern science, the

decline of human mortality, religious reforms, the improvement and expansion of extraphysical intermissive courses, and the acceleration of extraphysical reurbanization on this planet.

Section II:
Retrocognition

8
THE PHENOMENON OF RETROCOGNITION

Retrocognition operates as a change of focus for consciousness, from the physical to the extraphysical memory – a movement from the brain to the parabrain.

DEFINITION

Retrocognition - Latin: *retro* = backward, behind + *cognoscere* = to know, to learn - paraperception of the consciousness that allows the recovery of and access to memories of facts, scenes, people, places, objects, events, feelings, emotions and experiences belonging to its previous intraphysical existences or to its past intermissive periods.

Other consciential phenomena related to chronological time, studied in greater detail in other chapters, are:

1. **Precognition** - Capacity or consciential ability of perceiving, seeing, capturing or intuiting future events (see Chapter 21).
2. **Simulcognition** - Parapsychic or paranormal sensing that allows the consciousness to capture or to become lucid of facts or situations that are occurring in the moment of perception (simultaneously), yet are outside the reach of its conventional intraphysical perceptions, either due to distance or the dimensional difference (see Chapter 19).

SYNONYMS

1. Recollection of past lives
2. Pre-uterine recollection

3. Extracerebral memory
4. Regression to past lives
5. Regression of memory
6. *Retromnesia*

When used as a therapeutic technique:
1. Past-lives therapy
2. Past experiences therapy
3. *Retrogression*

HISTORICAL

The hypothesis of existential seriality, popularly known as the Theory of Reincarnation, obviously is not new. On the contrary, it is older than many of the great religions (Christianity, Judaism and Islam), which, incidentally, do not admit this hypothesis.

In certain ancient civilizations - Egyptian (with references to ka or soul), Greek (in the philosophies of Pythagoras and Plato), Celtic (Druids), and Chinese - there was belief in the transmigration of souls or a succession of lives, and as a consequence in the possibility of remembering previous existences.

In the recent centuries of human history, the knowledge of seriality was largely maintained and spread by the eastern hemisphere (China, Japan, India, and Tibet, among many others). It also formed part of a few western cultures such as the Celtic and Cathar cultures. Today, three of the largest oriental religions support reincarnation: Hinduism, Buddhism, and Jainism.

Beginning in the 19th century, the Theory of Seriality gained renewed strength in the western hemisphere, mainly through Allan Kardec's Spiritism and Helena P. Blavatsky's Theosophy.

In the last three decades, largely as a result of the expansion in the use of hypnosis (after a long period of discrimination that first arose at the end of the 18th century in response to the works of Franz Anton Mesmer), the subject of seriality has been invading psychiatric and psychological clinics, and the general media.

In the same way that progress in the techniques of resuscitation have increased the number of near-death experiences (which are instigating more and more investigations by previously narrow-minded medical practitioners), the therapies of hypnotic regression, that at first looked for the origin of repressed traumas in the past of *this* life, are bringing to the surface an ever increasing number of pre-uterine memories.

The public in general thinks that this approach of inducing retrocognitions through hypnosis is extremely novel, when in fact it is nothing more than a recycling of old knowledge, observations and techniques.

MECHANISMS

The parapsychic phenomenon of retrocognition can be explained as being an evocation of retrothosenes or, in other words, as a reflux of mnemothosenes related to the past, prior to rebirth in this life. The retrocognition, seen in this light, and depending on the depth and amplitude of the area of the holomemory being accessed, can be considered, to a greater or lesser degree, as being a certain type of cosmoconsciousness or expansion of the consciousness, and for that reason, a process of recovery of cons.

It is logical to state that memories recovered during retrocognition are not encoded in the physical brain, since that organ did not exist concurrent to the facts being recollected. Rather, it is clear that they are stored in some other type of "file" or consciential database.

From the point of view of paraphysiology, retrocognition reflects the change of focus of attention of the consciousness from the physical memory to the extraphysical one - a movement of the consciousness from the brain to the parabrain. This idea reinforces the hypothesis presented by some researchers that retrocognition is the access to an *extracerebral memory.*

In most cases of retrocognition, the recovered memories have a strong affective-emotional content, that is to say, it is the accessing of mnemothosenes with the emphasis on the sen (as in sentiment). In practice and in retrocognitive reports it is generally observed that the moments remembered are those with strong emotional content, and not ones with greater intellectual substance.

It is common for a certain period to exist (sometimes spanning more than one life) that is inaccessible to the recollections of the intraphysical consciousness, although many lives prior or following the blocked period may be remembered. With a higher level of personal maturity the individual can overcome any blockage.

Normally, access to past experiences, contrary to what might be expected, does not occur in an inverted chronological sequence, meaning, firstly remembering the last physical life and then earlier lives, sequentially with lives remembered progressively getting older.

Studies of cases of retrocognitions demonstrate that most individuals access their past lives in a seemingly random order. The antiquity of a certain life does not necessarily determine a greater difficulty in its recollection. In other words, it is possible for someone to remember first an existence that happened six centuries ago, then later, another from 3,000 years ago and next a life that occurred just prior to the last. The current life can be the retaking or continuation of a certain previous life, which is not, chronologically speaking, necessarily the last one. Theoretically, that previous life would have been one of the easiest to remember.

The next opportunity to reencounter most of the people around us today might be a few lives from now, not necessarily the next in sequence. For this reason, the self-corruption of leaving certain disagreements to be solved in the next life should be avoided (groupkarmic procrastination). Centuries could pass before there is another opportunity for living together with those consciousnesses. This, without a doubt, constitutes an evolutionary delay.

It can be affirmed with certainty that it is easier to recall a past intraphysical existence of 30 centuries ago than to recall our last intermissive period. This is due to the limitations in cerebral analogies and the 3 differences among these different types of memories. However distant the past intraphysical existence under study may be, there exist many commonalities with current life, such as: breathing, eating, the use of spoken language, architecture, the use of clothing, family and human drama.

During the intermissive period, the style of existence was radically different: there was no breathing, feeding or other limitations characteristic of the soma; we could fly; there was no family in the sense that is understood on this planet because there was no reproduction; the organization of para-society was completely different; and several other points. This difficulty is similar to that which arises in conscious projections. It is easier to remember visits to the denser (crustal) extraphysical dimensions/communities than visits to the more transcendent and developed extraphysical communities which lack particular connections to physical humanity.

The following example might be viewed as analogous to the difficulty inherent in recollection and communication of our last intermissive period. Imagine sending a native aboriginal, with no previous contact with our technological civilization, on a space shuttle flight. On his return, how would he remember and communicate his experiences of the take-off, the orbital flight, and the vision of Earth? Inevitably, he would forget many details, some memories would become similar to dreams, many events would become symbolic and mystical, and he would have to use his life experiences in the forest as analogies, not only for his own understanding and association of ideas, but to describe it to others as well.

Thus, the larger and deeper the theoretical and experiential erudition of a person, the easier and more reliable that person's recollections of conscious projections or past experiences can be.

OTHER HYPOTHESES

Several authors who have a materialistic point of view, or who are blind followers of the physicalist paradigm, try to explain memories of past experiences through hypotheses that do not include the seriality of existences of the consciousness. None of them withstands a deeper analysis, as is discussed in the following paragraphs:

1. **Fantasy** - The memories obtained would simply be the result of fantasies, oneirisms (dreams), deliriums, or hallucinations. *Counter-arguments:* I. Many memories that were not part of the previous intellectual knowledge of the retrocognitor can be proven by historical research; II. Several individuals can have joint retrocognitions in which, even though physically separated, they have the same recollection of a common life.

2. **Genetic or genealogical memory** - The remembered existences would be the retrospective of a life of a direct ancestor within a continuous genealogical line. This cellular memory would be inherited through the genes. *Counter-argument:* In most cases, the memories recovered do not fit any genetic ancestor, on some occasions the retrocognition points to a life in a body of a different ethnic group from the current genetic line.

3. **Time travel** - In this hypothesis, the retrocognitor would have an experience of traveling back to the past in reality, through some temporal-spatial anomaly

or quantum singularity. *Counter-arguments:* I. During many retrocognitions it can be confirmed that the body does not leave the here-and-now; II. The very well-known problem of the paradox of time would occur in which, for example, a person could return to the past, as in the film *Back to the Future*, and prevent their parents from getting married, which would prevent his birth, and therefore his trip to the past.

4. **The consciousness and its puppets** - One old hypothesis that is still very common in current New Age metaphysical culture proposes that each human individual is actually a ramification, tentacle, or puppet of pivotal consciousnesses. Each one of these pivot consciousnesses is seen as several seemingly independent individuals in countries, cultures, or even distinct periods and composes several egos of the same consciousness. According to this line of reasoning, retrocognition would be a mere transfer of data or information within this network of egos. *Counter-arguments:* I. The experience of conscious projection does not corroborate this hypothesis nor does it supply a vague hint that could lead to its confirmation. II. This theory was originally used to explain cases of multiple personality (many times a result of interconsciential intrusions) and of supposed soul mates (which are nothing more than the manifestation of affinities built inside the same evolutionary group of consciousnesses throughout their history).

9

TYPES OF RETROCOGNITION

*Retrocognition can only be considered healthy
when it drives the consciousness forward.*

Classification (taxonomy) is a resource thoroughly used in science with the objective of facilitating research, teaching, and understanding. It identifies common patterns within the field of study, and represents extrapolations of the possibilities raised by the association of ideas. However, it is important to point out that efforts at classification can restrict or impoverish research. Rarely can the complexity of reality be easily inserted into narrow academic pigeonholes; this is especially the case when the topics being studied are consciential phenomena or qualities.

Therefore, I propose to classify and sub-classify retrocognitions according to the following criteria:

REGARDING THE OBJECT OF RETROCOGNITION

Keeping in mind the seriality of the consciousness, it is possible to recall three basic types of experiences, prior to the current physical life:

Seriate lives: referring to previous physical lives, that is, the consciousness in an intraphysical condition, including lives on other planets.

Intermissive periods: referring to the period in-between lives (intermission, that is, the consciousness in an extraphysical condition).

Conscious projections: rare, yet a valid type of retrocognition in which the consciousness remembers conscious projections that occurred in previous intraphysical existences, that is, while temporarily out of the soma it was using in a previous life.

REGARDING THE SUBJECT OF RETROCOGNITION

Self-retrocognition: The recollection of one's own experiences, accessing his or her own holomemory.

Hetero-retrocognition: An occurrence in which a retrocognitor perceives previous existences of others, accessing the holomemory of another consciousness.

Psychometrical: An experience in which a retrocognitor accesses memories recorded in the holothosenes of environments or objects. The so-called *accessing of akashic records* would be included in this category.

REGARDING GROUPALITY

Individual: The retrocognition happens only with one consciousness (the retrocognitor).

Group: An experience in which different people have similar retrocognitions, interrelated, referring to the same historical period, almost always from an existence they shared together. In this case, the retrocognitions of each of the elements of the group match and occur almost concurrently.

REGARDING THOSENITY

Affective: Retrocognition in which the memories are primarily guided by affective relationships, love, passion, abandonment and heartbreaks of the past.

Emotional-traumatic: Memories of moments of intense suffering, most often related to a prior death. The emotions most frequently featured are: fear, sadness, solitude, regret, and pain.

Intellectual: The least common of the three types. It entails the memories of past moments in which there were no particularly strong emotions or affections involved.

Actions, experiences, or lessons with higher mentalsomatic content are remembered.

REGARDING THE CAUSE

Spontaneous: Happening naturally, with no specific or known cause. Normally, one can observe associated factors which predispose this. Example: retrocognitive flashes during hypnagogy.

Provoked: Stimulated by some, generally external, driving factor. Example: hetero-hypnosis.

Self-induced: Generated intentionally by the individual - the self-retrocognitor - using different techniques or specific stimulating factors. Example: use of a *retrocognitarium*.

REGARDING THE LUCIDITY LEVEL

Semiconscious: Retrocognitions obtained during altered states of consciousness with lesser levels of lucidity, or those in which the memories do not completely flow back, manifesting as vague and imprecise memories, and on many occasions not being recognized as retrocognitions. Examples:

- Misunderstood emotions and phobias.

- Dreams or nightmares of a retrocognitive nature (recurrent in many cases).

- Rejections and affinities without any apparent reason.

- Vague feelings, sensation of familiarity, déjàism (the most common being *déjà-vu*).

- Certain intuitions that are, in fact, ancient personal knowledge being recovered.

Conscious: Memories of past experiences recalled during states of greater consciential lucidity, and are usually identified as retrocognitions. Examples:

- *Ephemeral:* Quick and fleeting remembrances, usually of images, scenes, or people, in the form of visual flashes.

- *Relived:* A true altered state of consciousness in which the individual feels as though they had returned to the past and were reliving it, feeling the same pains, pleasures, emotions, and human involvements again. The individual experiences the sense of being the observer and the observed with alternate points of view from within the scene as participant and from outside as observer, as in a very vivid and multi-sensory movie. Often it is possible to identify some personalities from the past and associate them with people from the present (recognition).

REGARDING THE ALIGNMENT OF THE VEHICLES

In alignment: In this case, retrocognition happens with the consciousness inside the soma. Example: when provoked by watching an historical film.

In semi-alignment: During the partial nonalignment of any of the vehicles, usually the psychosoma; meaning the consciousness is partially out of the soma. Example: a recurring dream with retrocognitive characteristics.

In non-alignment: During a projection of the consciousness, semi-lucid or lucid, through the psychosoma or mentalsoma. Example: recollection of a previous life provoked by the approach of an extraphysical consciousness during a projection.

REGARDING THE HOST-VEHICLE OF THE CONSCIOUSNESS

Somatic: With the consciousness hosted by the soma. Example: déjàism with a retrocognitive basis.

Psychosomatic: With the consciousness manifesting through the psychosoma, also called a retroprojection. Example: memory of the intermissive period during a projection to the consciousness's extraphysical origin.

Mentalsomatic: With the consciousness projected through the mentalsoma. Example: state of cosmoconsciousness.

REGARDING THE SANITY OF THE EXPERIENCE

Pathological: Retrocognition that generates a serious and lasting state of emotional, mental, and bioenergetic imbalance in the individual. In these cases, there is usually the involvement of extraphysical intruders, often related to the recalled period. On other occasions, individuals involve themselves too deeply in their recently recovered memories and alienate themselves, partially or totally, from the present physical life. In these cases, even in the long term, no growth or greater maturation of the personality is observed.

Healthy: Recollection that brings greater self-knowledge, sense of responsibility and maturity to the individual, even after a brief phase of instability and fragility. In these, the hand of the helpers is usually observed, and they will probably provoke new retrocognitions, in accordance with the utilization of information recovered by the consciousness being helped, and his or her possibilities and evolutionary needs. *Retro*cognition can only be considered healthy when it impels the consciousness *forward*.

Regarding the Binomial Animism - Parapsychism

Animic: or autonomous - occurring without energetic coupling or influence of other consciousnesses. In this case, individuals obtain the experience by themselves alone, through their own predisposition, or as the consequence of their intention.

Parapsychic: or co-promoted - provoked or assisted, intentionally or not, by another consciousness, generally extraphysical, through auric coupling and the resulting thosenic exchange or influence.

10
RELATED PHENOMENA

*Self-experimentation and the study of cases of
recollection of experiences previous to the present
intraphysical life show that retrocognition rarely
occurs in an isolated or pure fashion.*

Normally, retrocognition is associated with other paraperceptions or consciential phenomena (better known as parapsychic, paranormal or extrasensory phenomena) like the ones listed below:

CLAIRVOYANCE

In certain types of clairvoyance, particularly the facial variety, when the holochakral coupling is more intense a clairvoyant can access a previous existence of the other person. Many times, that coupling is more complex due to the participation of the helpers of the individuals involved. Generally, in this case, the helpers seem to sponsor and administer the experience.

DÉJÀISM

Déjàism is the perception of familiarity or pre-existing knowledge of a place, person, object, or event. It is most well known in the form of *déjà-vu*. It can, however, be reminiscences of past experiences with those same people, places, objects, and events. There are several reported episodes of déjàism that originate from projections and some others that can be the result of cerebral dysfunctions.

NEAR-DEATH EXPERIENCE (NDE)

NDEs - as well as electric shocks (many times due to lightning), and claimed legitimate abductions by UFOs - are among the most powerful stimulating factors precipitating paraperceptions, often of a persistent quality.

Due to several predisposing factors that coincide with a near-death experience, such as trauma, non-alignment, and the presence of a helper or an evolutionary advisor (evolutionologist), some individuals partially recover memories of a past life, and often of the previous intermissive period. This phenomenon is evidenced by cases in which the individual who has experienced an NDE reorientates their life towards tasks and behaviors that facilitate the execution of their existential program, planned during their last intermission.

INTUITION

If we can define intuition as the capacity to know, discover or understand something beyond the regular sequential process of the elaboration of thoughts, we can understand that inspirations, insights, hunches and 'eurekas' can also be due to the reflux of abilities or learned knowledge (mnemothosenes) acquired, developed and elaborated in periods prior to the current physical life.

PANGRAPHY

This complex and advanced form of paraperception, the result of the synergy of the best of animism and parapsychism (namely the expansion of the mentalsoma of the pangraphist and a close coupling with a helper), can provoke deep and healthy retrocognitions.

CONSCIOUS PROJECTION

Through the facility of the parabrain, the consciousness, when projected, has a greater predisposition towards having retrocognitions. The consciousness is thus free from the limits of the physical brain, where memories of previous existences are unlikely to reside. This predisposition can be considerably intensified during a projection by other factors such as: returning to the extraphysical origin; a re-encounter with a kindred extraphysical consciousness; the direct performance of a helper, including visual projections; thosenic intrusion from intruders; and energetic rapport with the former human milieu. In these cases, the extraphysical experience is called retroprojection.

PSYCHOMETRY

In this type of energetic or holothosenic reading of objects, places, or people, the rapport created can evoke mnemothosenes, in a process of *temporal tuning* of the memory, provoking retrocognitions. This mechanism is used in the technique of the retrocognitarium (see Chapter 18). The psychometrist can, sometimes, have a retrocognition of a prior existence of another person.

PANORAMIC VISION

Panoramic vision is the retrospection on life that some individuals experience soon after somatic deactivation, during an NDE, precipitated by a critical physical illness, or in situations of imminent death, among others. This intraprojection, or existential revision, can, in a certain sense, be considered a retrocognition, by virtue of its depth, extension, and meaning. In addition, it is technically the recovery of memories of a previous existence lived in another dimension (in the case of individuals finding themselves between the first somatic deactivation and recuperative sleep).

11
RELATED CONSCIENTIAL STATES

The consciousness is extremely
dynamic and has multiple characteristics.
It is impossible to separate consciential states
into watertight and mutually exclusive sets.
In fact, consciential states superimpose
themselves on different levels.

Along with the different consciential phenomena studied in the previous chapter, retrocognition is most often associated with different altered states of the consciousness, either as a cause or effect, as detailed in the following analysis:

HYPNAGOGY

Many retrocognitions occur in this everyday consciential state, while there is a predominance of alpha activity in the cerebral cortex. This state can be perceived as an intermediary level of lucidity between the ordinary physical waking state and light sleep.

In hypnagogy, the consciousness, still basically manifesting itself through the physical brain, presents a greater predisposition towards dreaming and concentration, offering less resistance to the blooming of old memories from this or other existences. In such a context, the borders between conscious, semiconscious, and unconscious memories become blurred. Most techniques used to obtain a retrocognition have helping the individual reach this state as an objective.

DREAMS

Dreaming acts as a mechanism of reorganization of the brain's synapses and, therefore, of memories as well as an escape valve for several forms of psychological pressures. This facilitates the reflux of certain older, often traumatic memories.

During the simulation of reality produced by dreams, recent or old memories are relocated and reprioritized. Throughout this process, certain information from the parabrain, due to its proximity to the soma, can become mixed in the physiological flow of mnemonic data, thus being able to interfere with or determine the basic plot of the dream.

The origin of many recurrent or repetitive dreams lies within blocks of mnemothosenes originating in past existences. Sometimes, when they are not reminiscences of conscious projections, extensive, vivid and plausible dreams - true films or epopees - can be caused by fragments of memories of previous existences.

NIGHTMARES

Taken as a form of unpleasant dream, nightmares have, basically, the same characteristics as dreams.

During the unfolding of a common dream, the consciousness has a tendency to integrate into it, through images or simulations of context that justify the captured perception, certain external or internal stimuli. For example: the sound of a door banging in the wind can be integrated into a dream as an explosion. In the same way, unpleasant sensations can distort the natural progression of the dream, transforming it into a nightmare, as can be the case with high environmental temperatures, digestive indisposition, fever, or atmospheres with insufficient oxygen. Psychological factors such as worries, various conflicts, and even extraphysical factors such as consciential intrusions, with the consequent pollution of the normal thosenes of the dreamer with xenothosenes from an intruder, can generate nightmares as well.

Following the same line of reasoning, we can understand that certain subliminal memories of traumas from
previous lives, no less important because they are unconscious, can cause nightmares, especially when associated
with energetic intrusions based on those same memories.

MEDITATION

Originally practiced as a means to elevate one's consciential level, seeking to obtain the state of cosmoconsciousness (discussed later), meditation is, today, understood
and applied by most people as a form of physical and mental relaxation, stress control and energetic recovery. By
taking most people to the hypnagogic state, meditation
predisposes its practitioners towards retrocognitions for
reasons already discussed.

However, this practice is not among the most effective
techniques for obtaining retrocognitions or conscious projections, because many meditators tend to fall asleep during their practice.

HYPNOTIC TRANCE

The hypnotic trance is a state in which the individual's
own will is reduced. It is very similar to hypnagogy, in that
it induces the alpha state and resembles the dream state.
In practice, this state is usually induced by another person
(hetero-hypnosis) who directs or guides the recovery of
specific memories. This form of retrocognition is the most
in use today in the form of so-called past life or past experience therapies (see Chapter 14).

PARAPSYCHIC TRANCE

When the consciousness is in this altered state, popularly
known as mediumistic trance, incorporation, or channel-

ing, the parapsychic can have retrocognitions provoked by close energetic contact with the communicating consciousness. This can occur either during psychophony (vocal communication), psychography (through writing), assistential energization through a coupling with an extraphysical consciousness, or by any other form of consciential symbiosis. The deep bi-directional transfusion of thosenes can work as an element of evocation of old memories, in many cases from lives common to both, that is, from lives in which they coexisted together.

CONSCIENTIAL INTRUSION

A consciential intrusion (obsession, greater or lesser possession, etc.), via the mechanisms discussed in the previous item, can induce a retrocognition, in this case virtually always pathological. An interesting fact is that in this mechanism the extraphysical consciousness frequently has the intention, as well as the means, to provoke a recollection in the person being intruded, with the intention of evoking specific memories that are negative and pathological. The purpose herein is to weaken its victim both emotionally and energetically, causing the victim to lose what energetic self-defense remains, as a result of guilt, shame, or a lack of motivation towards the present life and its challenges.

ANIMIC TRANCE

In certain circumstances, some individuals manifest trances that seem to be parapsychic. However, the perceptions of a veteran clairvoyant can reveal that this trance might not have the participation of any extraphysical consciousness. In these circumstances, the individual in trance changes his voice, intonation, physical posture, and even language. Yet many of these occurrences are, in fact, a retroactive dive into the person's own integral memory so that they reassume a personality from their past. This case is more than a recollection as the person is temporarily incorporating that past ego into the present.

A classic example studied at the end of the 19th century was of the French astronomer Camille Flammarion, who was supposedly channeling Galileo Galilei, until it was discovered, as claimed by the Kardecist spiritualists, that Flammarion had been Galilei in a previous life.

MULTIPLE PERSONALITY

This form of psychosis, within the limitations of the materialistic paradigm, has resisted all attempts at explanation and dissection of its mechanisms and causes. Considering multidimensionality and the seriality of the consciousness, it is understood with certain obviousness that, beyond the great majority of cases that are caused by consciential intrusions, many can be the result of personalities or prior egos of the same consciousness, that appear again without the organizing element of lucidity, as previously discussed in the most benign case of the animic trance.

COSMOCONSCIOUSNESS

Also known as cosmic consciousness, samadhi, nirvana, satori, illumination, oceanic consciousness, universal integration, among many other expressions, this is one of the rarer consciential states, yet one of the most advanced and positive ones. It is the result of healthy exacerbation of mentalsomatic activity, which manifests itself beyond the limitations of the psychosoma, facilitating experiences that transcend space, time, shapes, and emotions.

The expansion of the consciousness and several of its attributes precipitates, in certain cases, a superior form of retrocognition, that does not present itself as indistinct flashes, or as a sequential recollection of events, but as an in-block recovery of vast areas of the holomemory, some-times of several lives at the same time.

12
BLOCKING FACTORS

*The trauma of rebirth is generally greater
than that of somatic deactivation. The interruption
in continuity suffered because of somatic rebirth
represents the main factor blocking
our memories of the past.*

In using theorice to study retrocognitions it is very important to study the causes of why we forget experiences we have had in the past, and the difficulties in recovering those memories.

The mechanisms of mnemonic blocks are many, and the relative influence of each one of them depends on the individual.

The following is a discussion of several important blocking factors:

PARAPATHOLOGY OF THE MENTALSOMA

The lack of development of the mentalsoma, understood here as a form of parapathology, is perhaps the most important blocking factor of retrocognitions. Actually, this is a lack of evolution of the consciousness and of the development of its attributes. Being at an evolutionary level in which we still lose one third of our lives with the natural evolutionary coma of physiological sleep, there is no reason to be surprised by the difficulty in remembering past lives or intermissions.

LOW LEVEL OF MULTIDIMENSIONAL SELF-AWARENESS

The average intraphysical consciousness may display a reasonable level of lucidity in its day-to-day existence, identifiable through trivial intraphysical manifestations, such as the capacity to rationalize, decide, perceive, and create. However, in practice what is observed is that the great majority of people are practically unable to manifest this same mediocre level of lucidity when outside the soma, in other dimensions; that is to say, the human consciousness lacks holosomatic adaptability and flexibility.

Multidimensional self-awareness (MS) is the capacity of the consciousness to be lucid with regards to several different dimensions, perceiving clearly its respective realities and acting in a conscious and coherent way.

MS can be measured according to, at least, the following three determining factors:

1. Average level of hyperacuity (measured in cons) that can be reached in each dimension.
2. Number of different dimensions in which the consciousness can lucidly manifest itself.
3. Ability and speed in changing dimensions while maintaining the maximum of consciential continuity.

Based on the aforementioned ideas, it can be concluded that one cause for the difficulty in recovering retrocognitive memories is the inability of the intraphysical consciousness to access its parabrain while out of the body, close to the physical dimension, or in other dimensions that have a weaker connection with the planet. For this reason, among others, the exercise of lucid projection is one of the main procedures in the development of retrocognitions.

SHOCK OF SOMATIC REBIRTH

Contrary to what most people think, the trauma of rebirth is generally greater than that of somatic deactivation. During somatic rebirth the consciousness passes through a condition of intense restriction that reduces its lucidity and robs the consciousness of its extraphysical freedom and its perceptual acuity. It is further restricted by the limitations of the physical body (gravity, breathing, fatigue, pain, and illnesses among others). On the other hand, in the process of somatic deactivation the consciousness returns to a condition of greater subtlety and capacity.

If undergoing somatic rebirth implies an inevitable and chronic state of limitation in the consciousness, it is easy to infer that the condition of repression that the consciousness suffers when starting a new physical life, in an immature and unprepared soma, is even greater, due to the undeveloped condition of the central nervous system.

Taking into consideration the total amount of time of the intermissive period plus that of the current life, somatic rebirth imposes a very sudden change in dimension to: the host body of the consciousness, the thosenating vehicle (body that generates and manifests thosenes), and consciential energies. The shock of this abrupt change causes a rupture in the continuity of lucidity; in other words, a fissure in the continuity of manifestation.

In the same way that a night's sleep makes us forget some details of the previous day; or a small lapse can cause a *pseudo-déjà-vu*; or an abrupt change in the focus of attention makes many people forget what they were saying or intending to do, so too the sudden and dramatic change accompanying somatic rebirth may deeply block our memories of other existences. This mechanism is similar to the projective blackout at the moment of reinteriorization into the body, which blocks the recollection of that extraphysical experience.

LACK OF CONSCIENTIAL MATURITY

For the great majority of consciousnesses, physical life is mediocre and monotonous. It creates stresses, conflicts and suffering which lead many to pseudo-escapes, like drugs or suicide. What then would happen if a good part of the population were to remember previous experiences resulting in an indigestible overload of conflicts and problems? How would a normal individual react to knowing that his son was his wife's lover in a past life? What would be the quality of education and energy a mother could give her son after discovering that he was one of her worst intruders up to the beginning of her pregnancy? What would we do if we had an affective retrocognition that reawakened an old passion for a person that today is off limits to our feelings and energy?

These and many other examples extracted from daily reality indicate that we do not have retrocognitions because of our lack of consciential maturity. Here consciential maturity is understood as emotional stability, psychological balance, thosenic self-control, experiential structure, and cosmoethical impeccability.

ENERGY BLOCKS

The study of the holosoma and the observations made by conscious projectors indicate that the consciousness commands the physical body through the consciential energies of the holochakra. That is to say, the chakras, together, act as an interface between the psychosoma and the soma.

Energetic blocks in the cranium, specifically in the frontalchakra and predominantly in the coronochakra, limit the intensity and affect the quality of the flow of information between the parabrain and the physical brain.

Because the parabrain is the most accessible source of memories that transcend the current life, it is understood that these blocks hinder lucid retrocognitions and even recollections of conscious projections.

It is this same mechanism that makes it easier to recover information of other existences while the individual is projected or partially disconnected, as in the cases of the hypnagogic state or hypnosis.

RETRO-PSYCHIC SCARS

As injuries to the physical body can leave scars, many traumas, energetic decompensations and intrusions in the past leave "scars" in our subtler bodies, mainly in the psychosoma or emotional body. Such scars are not necessarily marks visible to extraphysical sight. They are, in the majority of cases, thosenic records enmeshed in the psychosoma's structure.

An example of such a mechanism is the real case of a person who regularly suffered severe asthma attacks. Following regressive hypnotic therapy in which the patient remembered his death by smoke suffocation during a fire in his previous life, the illness was overcome.

The suffering and despair associated with such a death imprinted mnemothosenes - with a great emphasis on the sen - in the psychosomatic structure of that consciousness. Upon rebirth in a new soma, the psychosoma - the matrix for the formation and maintenance of the soma - marked the new body with characteristics from that moment in the past.

Upon remembering and contemplating that event in a more lucid and rational way, the individual dissipated a good amount of the emotional-energetic load from the experience, reducing or completely ceasing the physical manifestations of asthma (catharsis). However, those memories will never be forgotten because they are part of the holomemory of that person.

The last thosenes of a life - omegathosenes - generated with uncommon intensity immediately before and during the process of the first somatic deactivation, heavily influence or determine several characteristics of the following life.

What will probably be the quality and intensity of your omegathosene?

REPRESSIONS

Studying common ego-defense mechanisms, and particularly memory repression, is a starting point for understanding that the consciousness unconsciously blocks certain traumatic memories of the past, whether *from this life or others*, in order to avoid further suffering.

In the same way that harmful experiences of this physical life, painful at first, in time begin to lose their intensity until intellect and rationality trump emotionality, so too do the traumas of the past need to be brought 'to the surface' of the consciousness for them to be emptied of their repressed emotional content

BLOCKS PROGRAMMED IN THE INTERMISSION

As part of the planning and preparation for the next physical life, and to avoid either ectopic deviations in the existential program or improper consciential evocations, the consciousness may receive a thosenic intervention from the helpers or evolutionary orientor, so as to block certain memories or specific periods of its parahistory or multiexistential biography. This also explains the greater difficulty in recovering the memories of certain lives.

HELPERS

Through mechanisms similar to the one discussed in the previous item, and for the same reasons, helpers often act in a way as to maintain the thosenic blocks enacted during the intermissive period, through the physical life. Often, to protect the homeostasis of the intraphysical consciousness, they, unlike some intruders, are forced by circumstances to discourage retrocognitions rather than stimulate them.

LACK OF INTEREST AND MENTAL LAZINESS

Awareness of the existence of previous lives is a great step towards recycling thosenes and overcoming blocks and conditioning. However, most of the time more than just this is needed.

To obtain the evolutionary triumph of healthy and regular self-retrocognitions, dedication and work are necessary. Many people never have recollections of their past prior to being reborn simply because they have never tried to make an effort to have them.

One can experience retrocognitions by using appropriate techniques (see Chapters 17 and 18).

PHYSICAL HYPOMNESIA

Deficiencies in physical memory imply difficulties in recollecting past experiences in a regular and autonomous way. If we do not remember simple, physical, accessible memories, how can we remember data which is more complex and more difficult to access?

For the intraphysical consciousness, the holomemory is rooted in the physical memory. To reach the first, it is usually necessary to conquer and to dominate the second (see Chapters 3 and 17).

Do you remember what you had for lunch yesterday?

13
WARNINGS AND PRECAUTIONS

Caution and energetic asepsis are necessary
when exhuming our own or anyone else's past,
the same way physical asepsis is necessary
when exhuming a corpse.

With the objective of enhancing the evolutionary benefits of a healthy retrocognition, avoiding pathological retrocognitions and minimizing the possible subsequent negative effects, it is important to be aware of the following factors. Possessing knowledge of the following points before embarking allows the consciential self-explorer to prepare himself objectively and subjectively for what may come.

CERTAINTY

The human consciousness is very complex, dynamic, and variable. The great majority of retrocognitions, particularly spontaneous ones, occur during consciential states that are experienced with lower than normal levels of lucidity, like hypnagogy, dreams, and hypnotic trances. Due to this fact, it is important to always maintain a balanced level of self-criticism, so as to avoid mistakes.

Certain experiences, which appear to be retrocognitions, can actually be the result of some form of oneirism (semiconscious fantasy); spontaneous images that naturally arise during hypnagogy; a reflux of memories from this current life; or even thosenes received from other physical or extraphysical consciousnesseses (intruders, blind guides or helpers).

Countless cases exist where people have had a brief singular flash of an image - of Ancient Egypt for example - and subsequently assume with certainty that they actually lived there during that period.

To avoid such a mistake, the following formula should be applied: *10 healthy retrocognitions = 1 certainty*. In other words, in order to confirm the possibility of having had a particular life in the past, we should wait for the accumulation of several similar, complementary, and coherent experiences that are mutually confirmed and present more points in common than differentiating factors.

The individual, with the accumulation of corroborated and complementary retrocognitions assembles, piece by piece, the puzzle of his multiexistential autobiography and, with time, will better understand the panorama of his past.

Fixed Idea

Some individuals, upon recalling experiences from the past, accurate or not, begin to invest most of their consciential resources (time, space, and energy) in that specific existence, which has supposedly been recalled. In this case, the person develops a fixed idea with regards to the past. This mainly occurs when remembering facts that have great impact, as with a great lost love, intense suffering, or a life in which the person enjoyed social or economic status.

That fixed idea, when it becomes more intense and lasting, can lead to a state of obsession or self-intrusion. It is important to stress that the only real time is 'Now!', because we can act only now. We should remember the past in order to get to know ourselves better, so as to avoid making the same mistakes, and to direct our path in the future with greater accuracy.

PSEUDO-INTRUSION

Someone who has had a significant retrocognition can, to a greater or lesser degree or in a temporary or more permanent way, manifest changes in his behavior, ideas, or preferences. When accessing vaster areas of its holomemory, the intra or extraphysical consciousness partially incorporates that prior personality.

That change can be understood by the retrocognitor himself, or by his acquaintances, as being an intrusion arising from some extraphysical consciousness. In certain cases, that process may be manifested as a case of double or multiple personalities. In many situations, both types of intrusion occur in parallel - self-intrusion and hetero-intrusion, one intensifying the other.

CONSCIOUS SELF-MIMICRY

It is not rare for some people, having experienced some form of retrocognition, to consciously decide to give continuity to the way or pattern of life recalled, sometimes deeply altering their course in the present life. Retrocognitors might feel attracted or seduced by that old holothosene, and try to escape or alienate themselves from the present.

In the absolute majority of these cases, the result of this "return to the past" will simply be ectopic and lead to existential incompletism.

EVOCATIONS OF INTRUDERS FROM THE PAST

Somatic rebirth can be, for many people, the consciential or holokarmic equivalent of the American government's *Witness Protection Program.* Due to the fact that the intraphysical consciousness forgets the past and undergoes a somatic rebirth with the inherent effects of a new body, culture, family, energies and, even up to a certain extent, holothosene, it becomes inaccessible to its old intruders, who are now incapable of energetically tracing and locating this consciousness.

The moment the individual has a retrocognition, the memories (retrothosenes) can evoke or attract those same intruders from the past, subsequently creating a typical scenario of inter-consciential intrusion.

For that reason it is very important that the individual who plans to begin a program of self-retrocognitions studies, practices and controls, as much as is possible, all of the different types of bioenergies and bioenergetic techniques that he or she can, placing particular emphasis on the VS or vibrational state, which is the basic procedure for energetic self-defense.

Another simple yet effective approach to avoiding these evocations and continuation of intrusion is the application of techniques for mental hygiene. These techniques help the practitioner temporarily to discard his or her fixed ideas and, therefore, help change his or her thosenes.

For individuals who induce hetero-retrocognitions, the need for energetic self-defense is also necessary. Many times it is even more pertinent for them, because during the exhumation of their patients' past, they risk becoming thosenically involved with these *pasts* and the respective personalities, whether they are presently intraphysical or extraphysical consciousnesses.

GROUPKARMIC RELATIONSHIPS

Many retrocognitions can reveal information regarding the roles played in the past by several consciousnesses who are in our evolutionary group and who currently have a degree of interaction with us. Many were our relatives, friends, lovers or even our enemies or torturers. Sometimes it is not easy to co-exist with certain people and the memories associated with them, after we become aware of certain historical facts.

This warning is especially valid in cases of people with whom we shared profound love in the past, and who are now forbidden or 'off limits' to our affection or sexuality. Experience shows that, many times, consciousnesses that today are in the role of a father and daughter, or mother and son, were lovers in the past. How many families would have maturity enough to be aware of this fact through affective retrocognitions?

Consciential maturity and cosmoethical understanding are essential in forgiving and in being forgiven. Ideally, retrocognitions should, over the medium and long term and after the necessary recomposition period, improve, not worsen our groupkarmic balance.

EMOTIONAL DECOMPENSATIONS

Using techniques and approaches made available by conscientiology and projectiology, we should avoid, and when necessary heal, common emotional imbalances stemming from memories of past existences, such as: sorrow, resentment, melancholy, longing, shame, guilt, lack of motivation, foreigner syndrome, affective frailty, and others of a similar nature.

ENERGETIC DECOMPENSATIONS

The control of bioenergies in all its forms of manifestation, beyond everything previously discussed regarding self-defense against intrusions from the past, is noticeably important as a resource for keeping the holosomatic balance of the retrocognitor. Retrothosene refluxes can provoke states of energetic, physiological, or emotional imbalance. The lucid consciousness that possesses control over its own energies can clean up or attenuate the effects, mainly of the affective variety, common to retrocognitions.

SOMATIZATIONS

Retrocognitions can provoke more objective physiological processes besides just emotional and energetic decompensations. These processes can be felt and seen as health problems or diseases. The best way of contending with those deviations in homeostasis is by utilizing the vibrational state, and also by absorbing and exteriorizing energies when necessary.

There are cases, like those reported by the English author Arthur Guirdham, in which certain pseudo-illnesses precede, by some days, the recollection of memories of the past that provoked those illnesses. This characterizes a sort of incubation phase for the retrocognition.

14
DISCUSSING HYPNOSIS

Hypnosis can be a powerful and valid tool
for assistance and research when well employed.
It is, however, an energetic intrusion – a close
relative to brainwashing – and must be
avoided whenever possible.

When studying reservations and precautions associated with retrocognitions, it is impossible not to touch upon the subject of hypnosis, which here receives an individual chapter due to its importance and complexity.

Techniques that are today called hypnosis have existed for a long time, in one form or another (mesmerization, magnetization, among others), as have conscious projections, near-death experiences and retrocognitions.

Franz Anton Mesmer (1734-1815) is considered the pioneer of what was called magnetization, and first applied these techniques in a therapeutic and popular way. Mesmer stated that a force, which he called animal magnetism or magnetic fluid (bioenergy), was exchanged between the therapist and patient, causing the effects that were observed. From Mesmer's day to the present, hypnosis has been a source of much polemic, fear, ignorance, and misapplication.

The classical view is one in which the hypnotist uses a monotonous and soft tone of voice, sometimes using an object with a repetitive movement, to capture the usually disorganized and anxious attention of the subject.

Current consensus is that approximately 10% of the population does not yield to hypnotic trance, another 10% enters into a deep hypnotic trance, and the remaining 80% can be induced into a superficial level of hypnotic suggestion. It has also been observed that, in general, more creative and intelligent people (at least using the conventional concept of intelligence) are more predisposed to being hypnotized, while it is almost impossible to place schizophrenics in a hypnotic trance.

In the last decades, hypnosis has been used with countless objectives in mind, for instance: anesthesia (mainly odontological); obtaining more precise and complete testimonies; recovery of memories in cases of abductions by UFOs; public shows and demonstrations; and regressions of memory seeking to overcome repressed traumas from this or other lives. Yet the great majority of people are not aware of important factors that become essential, from a multidimensional, bioenergetic, and cosmoethical point of view, as well as from other approaches explained by conscientiology.

There are many types of hypnosis, some more subtle and others more forceful. It is impossible to live without applying or receiving a certain level of hypnotic imposition or suggestion. We all influence others, and are to a greater or lesser degree open to being influenced by others, all at the same time. Some hypnotic suggestions exist in most of our relationships, as the following examples of daily experiences show: during a class; in the course of a discussion; while meeting with friends; when purchasing or selling something; while watching television or a movie; and during a project presentation for the management of the company.

Contrary to what is affirmed and defended by many professionals of hypnosis, its practice decreases the level of lucidity of the hypnotized, rather than increasing it. That assertion is a cause for concern, because it demonstrates the lack of knowledge on the part of many professionals regarding the mechanisms and characteristics of altered states of consciousness.

The person being hypnotized enters a consciential state in which certain attributes of the consciousness, such as attention and memory, become exacerbated. Yet, this practice is the complete opposite of the highly desirable phenomenon of cosmoconsciousness. During hypnosis, the will, which is the main force of the consciousness, is subdued by an external will.

We may find parallels in the consideration of the *idiot savant* (wise idiot), an autistic person who displays extraordinary capacities within one domain despite cognitive deficiencies in all others. We would hardly consider these attributes sufficient to equate being in a state of super-consciousness. In the *idiot savant's* case, perhaps those consciential attributes are amplified at the expense of a drastic reduction in several others, exactly like that which occurs in the case of the hypnotic trance.

There are cases of individuals proclaiming to remember, at each retrocognitive session, a different life with a plot totally different from the others. Over the course of several sessions, analyzing the totality reveals that the stories do not match, do not mutually corroborate each other, and that the individual does not seem to change or improve their general characteristics - exactly the opposite of what generally happens with those who have authentic retrocognitions. Such behavior should be analyzed and clarified by the individuals doing the hetero-retrocognitions, because it may be a simple manifestation of a very fertile imagination.

Hypnosis can be a powerful and valid tool for assistance and research. However, it can be compared to surgery, being in this case an intervention into the intimacy of the consciousness, into its subtle bodies, thosenes, memories, and energies. In the same way that a surgical procedure should be the last medical resource, hypnosis is acceptable when all other known techniques have already been tried and discarded after careful analysis. Just as some medical practitioners appeal for surgery in a simplistic and hasty way, some therapists use hypnosis as exploratory surgery, and this can produce more negative consequences than benefits.

Clearly, there are conscious and capable hypnotherapists, yet in my experience over the years I have observed that most know nothing of bioenergies and consciential intrusion. They do not understand that hypnosis, an energetic intrusion, is *closely related to brainwashing.* Hypnosis has profound similarities with interconsciential intrusion, and establishes an energetic ascendancy, sometimes permanent, of the therapist over the patient. It should be avoided whenever possible.

Extreme proficiency in hypnosis, to the extent of being able to induce a trance without need of speaking, employing just a glance or a physical touch, a snap of the fingers, or the placing of a hand on the forehead of the subject, might indicate the possibility of the practitioner having recently been a veteran extraphysical intruder. Helpers never act in such a manner. Not the smallest of their actions has any similarity with hypnosis. On the other hand, many approaches tried by intruders utilize traits related to hypnosis.

Someone knowing they are easily influenced should consider exercises to reinforce their energies, self-defense, and willpower. They should regularly install vibrational states seeking, among other objectives, to verify the presence of extraphysical consciousnesses in their psychosphere.

For therapists using hypnotic regression techniques, the following additional points should be taken into account.

First, it is important to avoid regression sessions performed in group, whereby the hypnotherapist, simultaneously and in the same location, leads several people into past existences. It is very common for many people, due to auric couplings and sympathetic assimilations, to access memories of other individuals present, whether they are intraphysical or extraphysical consciousnesses. In many instances, it is easier to have a retrocognition of another person than of ourselves, due to the personal blockages previously discussed. The didactic comparison with surgery is important even here: it is necessary to maintain asepsis, therefore avoiding thosenic contamination among different patients.

Caution and energetic asepsis are necessary when exhuming our own or anyone else's past, in the same way that physical asepsis is necessary when exhuming corpses.

Many therapists who work with regression therapies contend that they do not use hypnosis. However, they place the patient in a comfortable position, ask them to close their eyes - sometimes there is soft music playing - and then begin to lead the subject, vocally instructing them to relax, disconnect from the moment and place, render attention to certain ideas and images that come to mind, follow them, and so forth. Many therapists do not recognize this procedure as a form of hypnosis, in this case, perhaps a little less intrusive.

Another serious point is that many therapists are not aware of the role, presence, and work of extraphysical consciousnesses - intruders, blind guides, or helpers - in their sessions. In cases where hypnosis is appropriately used for obtaining regressions, the hypnotherapist acts as a catalyst or facilitator, while the primary control of the whole process is in the hands of the helpers.

It is also important to note the need for support and follow-up on the part of the therapist after the retrocognitions have been induced. Often these processes open a Pandora's Box and it is indispensable to dedicate time and energy until the crisis has been overcome.

I have seen cases of unprepared people take a weekend course in hypnosis, and begin to assist individuals seeking therapy through past life regression. They are subsequently unable or unwilling to render the necessary support (equivalent to the postoperative, UTI). If you, the reader, should decide to obtain retrocognitions induced by a hypnotherapist, even after trying to produce recollections of prior existences on your own, verify with all your lucidity if:

1. The therapist is experienced and performs the necessary preparation.
2. The therapist only performs individual sessions.
3. The therapist is outside of your circle of friends or acquaintances.
4. The therapist is lucid regarding the reality of bioenergies and extraphysical consciousnesses.
5. The therapist is positive and holosomatically balanced.
6. The work environment has a positive and assistential holothosene.
7. The environment is free of intruders
8. You notice your own and the therapist's helpers, before, during and after the session.

Beyond these precautions spend the whole week prior to the scheduled retrocognitive session installing vibrational states several times a day.

Based on consciential and evolutionary facts, there is no hetero-healing, but only self-healing. The physician, psychologist, teacher of conscientiology and projectiology, this author, or any one else, can, at best, be triggering or facilitating elements in the process of self-development.

Only the consciousness itself has the conditions, elements and opportunities to heal the real causes of illnesses. That is why *hypnotic intervention,* as well as energetic cures, will always only be some form of consolation, since the work is in the therapist's hands, and they may establish emotional and energetic dependencies. In these cases, clarification as a way of enabling the individual to solve their own problems will not occur.

15
BENEFITS

Nowadays, the therapeutic effects of retrocognition, sometimes sought in a superficial and immediate way, are valued more highly than the permanent and profound evolutionary results obtainable through auto-retrocognitions.

Retrocognition, when not pathological, even in many cases when achieved through hetero-hypnosis, presents undeniable benefits. To better understand the ample universe of positive effects of retrocognitions, the following classification is presented:

THERAPEUTIC BENEFITS

Remission or relief from physical illnesses - Many traumas as well as physical, emotional, and mental illnesses from the past leave marks in our paragenetics. Those retrothosenes, previously discussed under the name of retro-psychic scars, can affect the constitution of the present soma. If they are not overcome now, they can interfere with the structure of your future body. Our current body is the result of the combination of genetics, inherited from our parents, and our paragenetics, inherited from ourselves. The psychosoma, through the energies of the holochakra, acts as a mold or matrix for the formation of the physical body (a hypothesis also known as the biological organizational model or the morphogenetic field). In this way, certain health problems can be manifested from birth or they can start to appear little by little throughout the years, as a result of flaws or imperfections in that mold or matrix. Several studies conducted by researchers in this area, among them Ian Stevenson, have shown cases where fatal wounds (omegathosenes) suffered in the immediate previous life had a repercussion in the new body in the form of a birthmark. As an example, a child who died by a shot to the top of one of his ears was reborn with the corresponding ear deformed. Also there is the case of a boy who died from a cut to his throat, and was reborn with a scar in the same place. On many occasions, the lucid and balanced recollection of certain memories removes (catharsis) the excessive energetic load of mnemothosenes acting in an anti-biological form, thus allowing the cure or attenuation of some health problems.

Overcoming traumas and phobias - In the same manner as in the previous item referring primarily to physiological problems, retrocognition can, using the same mechanisms, result in the relief of emotional disorders or decompensations. In practice, among psychological or behavioral disorders, the area most intensively explored is that of overcoming phobias. Upon remembering a past trauma, the consciousness can reprocess traumatic memories (traumatothosenes) with greater lucidity and balance, and integrate them smoothly into his or her consciousness. What is not valued or often misunderstood is the de-intruding effect of certain retrocognitions. In these cases, psychological-emotional relief is mainly a result of the removal or distancing of extraphysical consciousnesses, previously present and active, who had based their energetic coupling on those semiconscious memories.

Improvement of interpersonal relationships – All people with whom we live (family, friends, and work colleagues) are part of our evolutionary or karmic group. From this perspective, and based on logic and practical observation, we can see that these human relationships were initiated in the past, and that each of them brings an energetic inheritance or specific holothosene. Passions, admirations and hatreds did not begin today. The consciousness, while becoming aware of the past, and if in possession of a minimum level of maturity, can change the tendency of the mechanical repetition of past mistakes (self-mimicry). The consciousness is capable of establishing strategies and plans to heal certain relationships, even with consciousnesses that are now in an extraphysical condition. The basic tools required, without *adolescent romanticism* or *religious demagogy*, are altruism, discernment, understanding, and forgiveness. *There is no other way out.*

EVOLUTIONARY BENEFITS

Multiexistential self-knowledge – In time, accumulating and matching the pieces of our millenary puzzle, we start to discover our parahistory, and we become more able to write our multiexistential and multidimensional autobiography; recognizing that we are today the expression of our millenary curriculum or the living summary of our past. It is essential to recognize our conditionings, fixed ideas, brainwashing, belief systems, intrusive stigmas, deviations of ethics and patterns of repression that have been established and cultivated since time immemorial. Thus it can be considered impossible to have a higher level of self-knowledge without retrocognitions. According to conscientiology, retrocognition is inevitable in the evolutionary process of the consciousness.

Intraconsciential recycling - In practice, most cases of intraconsciential recycling are caused by crises (NDE, death of loved one, etc.). However, intraconsciential recycling may also be the result of a planned process of self-study that inevitably includes retrocognitions. This greater self-knowledge drives the consciousness to eradicate some of the fossilized weak traits in its holosomatic structure. If a near-death experience (considered by the researcher of conscientiology to be an elementary occurrence in the majority of cases) can result in observed changes in nature, character, behavior, values and life principles, how much would we change with a series of healthy and profound retrocognitions? Lucid individuals know that they will not be able to completely change in one life alone, and for that reason they begin to sketch the first draft of their plan for the next life.

Conscientiotherapy - It is quick and easy to recognize physical, emotional, and human relationship problems. It is subtler and less common to recognize the deviations and faults in the structure of our holosoma and in the origin of our thosenes, within our intimacy as a consciousness. The recovery of certain specific memories can have, in the long term, deeper effects on the structure of the mentalsoma itself (body of discernment) producing consciential cures and predisposing one to a condition of holosomatic homeostasis.

Healing groupkarma - The consciousness, upon understanding not only its own multiexistential history, but also that of its evolutionary group, conquers the essential elements required to clean up its groupkarmic account, opened long ago in the *"Holokarmic Bank."* These memories can help one to overcome the initial phases of the consciential polykarmic process, particularly those of victimization and recomposition (reconciliation).

Connection with the better part of the evolutionary group - Broadening the understanding we have of our entire evolutionary group and its particular elements allows us to create a stronger coupling with more cosmoethical and positive consciousnesses, while overcoming dependencies, intrusions and fixations with less healthy individuals of the group.

Aid for the recovery of the existential program - By remembering our last intermissive period through retrocognitions, we can recover the awareness, even if only partially, of what we should be doing here and now (existential program). Upon recalling our past intraphysical lives, we become conscious of what we should not be doing in this dimension (ectopy).

Understanding our present physical life - With the wider vision acquired in time through the recollections of past existences, and particularly of the last intermissive period, it is possible to profoundly and serenely understand the rhythm of our current life: its reasons, the how, the where, the when and the with whom.

Expansion of Universalism - Universalism is the antithesis of bigotry, egocentrism, sectarianism, machismo, feminism, nationalism, patriotism, regionalism, provincialism, racism, parochialism, dogmatism, selfishness, corporativism, fanaticism, discrimination, segregation, and many other similar concepts, which indicate the separation of consciousnesses into isolated or privileged groups. Universalism comes to be an inevitable acquisition of a more lucid consciousness. In this context, we can clearly understand that many individuals increase their level of universalism by remembering past lives. For example: the case of the racist who remembers having been an element of the oppressed minority of a specific culture and time; or the macho man who remembers having been an oppressed and abused woman, with several children, working 18 hours a day to maintain the family.

Consciential maturing - We could say that we grow, develop, and mature through the sum of our experiences, which become increasingly complex, broad, and deep as time passes. If we increase the quantity, quality, and originality of our experiences, by use of conscious projection, for example, we can develop more quickly. The same happens when we recover, reselect, reanalyze, and relive the memories of the past stored in the holomemory, with the higher level of discernment and acuity we have today, taking better advantage of our past experiences.

16
INDUCING FACTORS

The most powerful trigger for any psychic phenomenon is a decided and constant Will.

From case studies and understanding of the mechanisms of physical memory, holomemory, consciential energy, thosenes, holothosenes, auric coupling, rapport, and the structure and paraphysiology of each of the vehicles of the holosoma, we can enumerate several factors which induce or facilitate retrocognitions. These factors, whether natural or artificial, are outlined below:

Age

Children have a natural predisposition to remember experiences of past lives. The younger the children, taking into account the limits of their capacity for mental elaboration and communication, the easier the recollection. Most observed cases occur in children less than 5 years of age.

This predisposition seems greater in the case of consanguineous somatic rebirths. This is when the individual returns to the same family or genealogical tree (e.g. being one's own great-grandchild).

One researcher who spent a great deal of time studying this form of infantile retrocognition, as illustrated in the French film *Manika*, was Ian Stevenson. Stevenson published several books on the subject.

This predisposition of children is basically due to the following factors:

1. The memories of a previous life (or even intermission) are more recent;

2. Less conditioning exists, as the physical brain and current memory are still quite virgin;

3. In the condition of a newly reborn consciousness, the individual has less rigid connections with the soma, presenting a larger predisposition to several parapsychic phenomena.

4. During the phase of the consciential basement, when there is a high rate of cons recovery (number of cons recovered over a period of time - e.g. cons per month), many mnemothosenes flow back to the physical memory.

EMOTIONS

Certain traumas, crises, or intense emotional states experienced now can evoke memories of certain past events, where a similar emotion was present. Example: if someone were to suffer from cynophobia (fear of dogs), they might remember the event that generated the phobia when feeling threatened by the presence of a dog today.

MUSIC

Due to its affective-emotional appeal, some music evokes old memories, particularly songs that are evocative of historical periods or have folkloric characteristics. Because of thosenic tuning, it can also attract extraphysical consciousnesses.

It is important to stress that some erudite compositions and many popular pieces are frankly negative and can produce pathological evocations.

HISTORICAL FILMS

Through their emotional and bi-sensorial stimulation (images and sounds - including music) that simultaneously act directly and evoke several types of memories, some historical films, or documentaries of certain periods, past cultures or outstanding historical events (the French Revolution, for example) can generate refluxes of mnemothosenes, and therefore retrocognitions.

SCENTS

When studying the physical memory, it is a well-known fact that smells, scents and perfumes are among the most powerful elements that exist for evoking recollections in this life, as they act more directly on the limbic system or *reptilian brain.*

The perception of a certain scent can, in this way, assist in the evocation of resonant mnemothosenes, consequently triggering a retrocognition in a predisposed individual.

NDEs

During near-death experiences, recollections of past existences may occur due to the sum of predisposing factors, such as: temporary liberation from the limitations of the soma; occurrences of panoramic vision; assistance by an extraphysical helper or even an evolutionary orientor; existential recycling; physiological trauma; or evocation of the omegathosene of some past life due to the similarity of circumstances.

HYPNAGOGY

During hypnagogy (alpha state), the intraphysical consciousness is more deeply predisposed to retrocognitions as a result of the following factors: physical and mental relaxation; disconnection with the here-and-now; focus of attention; liberation of memories; and partial non-alignment of the psychosoma, with the consequent increase in participation of the parabrain and paramemory.

HYPNOSIS

In addition to the factors common to hypnagogy, hypnosis, when exercised by another person upon a subject (hetero-hypnosis), includes the catalytic and directing action of the therapist and his or her consciential energies, as well as (sometimes) the performance of specialized technical helpers. (See Chapter 14)

HOLOCHAKRAL HOMEOSTASIS

The installation of regular high quality VSs creates a condition of greater flexibility and non-alignment of the individual's consciential energies, called looseness of the holochakra. This condition can be occasional, temporary, or permanent. It increases the paraperceptions of an intraphysical consciousness, along with the likelihood of retrocognitions. In this case, the occurrence of the phenomenon is facilitated because holochakral stimulation increases the exchange of information (mnemothosenes) between the parabrain and its physical counterpart.

ENERGETIC RAPPORT

Energetic rapport is when an intense energetic connection with elements external to the consciousness occurs; also known as auric coupling. This connection allows the reading, reception, scanning, sweeping, psychometry, or analysis of external thosenes and holothosenes. If the perceived thosenes and holothosenes resonate with mnemothosenes (evocation of intraconsciential retrothosenes), that is to say, with memories of events already lived, then events, images or people connected to those memories can be recalled.

In greater detail, the following coupling targets can be enumerated:

- Objects (physical and extraphysical)
- Places (physical and extraphysical)
- Intraphysical consciousnesses (or groups of intraphysical consciousnesses)
- Extraphysical consciousnesses (or groups of extraphysical consciousnesses):
  - Intruders
  - Blind guides
  - Helpers
  - Evolutionologist (evolutionary orientor)

PENTA

Penta (personal energetic task), since it is a daily energetic donation seeking to do as much polykarmic assistance as possible, is a catalyzing agent for retrocognitions, with the same benefits discussed regarding the VS being relevant. Other factors that predispose the Penta practitioner to retrocognitions include closer energetic coupling with the helpers, or even with intruders being assisted (many of them old acquaintances).

It is to be expected that in most cases helpers will wait for the conclusion of penta's critical period (initial phase of approximately six months) to liberate such memories.

TRAVEL

The consciousness, upon leaving its little daily world, arid in terms of new experiences, increases the amount and diversity of the stimuli received or the inputs perceived. In the case of traveling, this stimulation is multisensorial, holosomatic and multidimensional. In addition are the effects of sensorial evocations and energetic rapports that have already been discussed.

If an intraphysical consciousness returns to a place where it has lived before, it will re-encounter familiar holothosenes and consciousnesses who have been friends for many centuries, even if everything is not entirely clear or easy to remember at first. Such re-encounters can trigger old memories related to those existences.

Such a condition becomes even richer and deeper in the case of trips to teach conscientiology courses (clarification task), due to the synergy of the following factors of the assistance rendered: couplings with students, closer monitoring of helpers, and intensification of parapsychism and conscious projections.

SELF-ANALYSIS

While the previous items referred more to external approaches (extra-consciential), in this approach the decision of the consciousness to deeply explore its inner-self is emphasized.

Upon accomplishing a more serious, systematized, mature, multidimensional, and millenary study of oneself, the individual will unavoidably uncover information regarding his past through a form of *intraconsciential rapport*. This holothosene can also trigger synchronicities favorable to retrocognitive research.

Upon deciding to undertake such a task, the intraphysical consciousness increases its merit. By the consciousness's demonstrating that it has matured and awoken to the importance of self-evolution, the helpers are then motivated to sponsor retrocognitions.

Within the spectrum of this author's experiences, the best example of this specific type of approach is the course 'Extension in Conscientiology 1' (EC1), offered regularly by the IAC in several countries around the world.

17
OPTIMIZATIONS

*To obtain retrocognitions, it is ideal,
more efficient, and effective to use a set
of several techniques and predisposing
factors in parallel, working on different
fronts at the same time.*

The reader interested in advancing his self-knowledge can, using the ideas presented earlier, establish a plan for the short, medium and long term, with the objective of obtaining healthy self-retrocognitions without losing the overall perspective of the reasons for this effort and of the role of these memories in one's evolutionary moment.

The points discussed below increase the individual's predisposition to refluxes of memories that can generate retrocognitive episodes, acting as true retrocognitive techniques. Ideally, the most efficient and effective approach is to use these techniques and predisposing factors together in parallel, working on different fronts at the same time.

Seeking to be didactic in the presentation of practical instructions, a more imperative language is used here, although the objective is not to impose or to subliminally condition or hypnotize.

For its optimum execution, it is important to use pen, paper, library, videotape, computer, and an Internet connection, as well as other artifacts of knowledge.

PHYSICAL MEMORY

The golden rule with memory is: *conquer and dominate the intraphysical memory, so as to then work with the holomemory.*

For that, it is worthwhile to invest in the following points:

1. Take care of your physical memory and enlarge it through regular use.

2. Study and practice techniques for improvement of memory (mnemonics), and then go beyond them.

3. Avoid stress, lack of sleep, sleeping excessively, emotional outbursts, intoxicating food, illegal drugs, medication (when possible), cholesterol and saturated fats, shallow breathing and a sedentary life.

4. Fight against *experiential monotony*.

5. Avoid the pattern of an unbalanced life without rhythm or discipline.

6. With discernment, much care, and competent technical supervision, use nutritional supplements that can improve your brain's performance.

VS AND ENERGETIC BALANCE

Learn everything you can about bioenergy and its manifestations. Understand that we live immersed in an ocean of energy that has several degrees of density, and that this vital energy is the foundation for life in this universe. To be able to perceive and control it is to be more capable of living and acting in this dimension, as well as in the more subtle ones (see Chapter 5).

Verify and maintain your energetic self-defense, installing vibrational states (VSs) 20 times a day for example. Always act with cosmoethical and assistential thosenes.

It should be emphasized that the most important consciential lever to execute these techniques is the *will*. Forget imagination, visualizations, rituals, amulets, and other similar resources when wanting to work with your energies. As an example, notice that for you to close your hand (action of the consciousness on the soma), nothing else is necessary but will. Therefore, face your training with energies in an equally natural way, since you, as a consciousness, will simply be acting on another of your bodies - the holochakra.

In the beginning, when you do not have much experience, a certain level of physical and mental relaxation is needed, a calm place that allows a certain privacy, and a certain amount of time. As you develop, your *control and sensitivity* regarding bioenergies will become second nature to you. It is possible to work with your energies while walking, moving, or talking; under the sun or in the water; and in any mood or state of health. It becomes possible to execute the techniques in a way that is efficient, fast, and imperceptible to others.

To define the sensation of energy is almost impossible. It is like trying to explain, in words, a color, a scent, or a flavor; typically analogies with other sensory perceptions already experienced are used. So using this approach, we can say that the most common sensations experienced when working with energy are: chills, increase or decrease in temperature, shivers, electric current, static electricity, numbness, tingling, lightness, pressure in certain points of the body (chakras), pulsation, dizziness, vibrations, and many others. Therefore, when developing control over your energies, try to be aware and attentive to these occurrences, memorizing them permanently, registering and analyzing them to discover their patterns, causes and effects, until you are able to recognize your *energetic signals.*

In quantitative terms all applications, manipulations, and mobilizations of energy can be reduced to three basic operations or techniques: 1. Absorption, 2. Exteriorization, and 3. Closed Circulation.

In the context of this book and its methods, we are mainly interested in the last one. The objective of this technique, the most difficult of the three, is the installation of the *vibrational state* (VS).

The technique is developed in the following way:

1. Preferably with the body in a linear position (lying down or standing) - always feeling your energies - try to move your energies, using your determined will, from your feet to your head, creating a wave of intense energies that moves along your body.

2. As soon as the wave, under the strong and permanent command of your will, arrives at the head, immediately invert the flow, steadily moving it down, until reaching your feet - always attentively following the entire trajectory. When the wave arrives at your feet invert the direction of the flow again.

3. Maintain this cyclic and repetitive movement, with the wave repeatedly ascending and descending, without missing, jumping, or excluding areas.

4. While the wave of energy moves, try to trace its course, detecting blockages that are almost always felt as energetically "dead" areas or areas resistant to the flow.

5. Avoid imagination or visualization, and try to reach a tempo that is stable and clear; try, little by little, to accelerate the speed of this movement. When attempting to accelerate, it is common to lose the rhythm or tempo. If this occurs, just restart the whole process, as many times as is necessary.

6. When you are able to accelerate the wave and increase the volume of energy, you will start to feel surges of vibrations in the body, very ephemeral at the beginning, but they will progressively arrive and install themselves in a more permanent, broad and intense way. At this point, you will feel as if your body were a vibrating and humming generator, with electric currents of thousands of volts, as if all cells, molecules, and atoms in your body were in a vitalizing frenzy.

It is necessary to point out that it usually takes some time until full and intense vibrational states can be reached, regardless of the time, place, and independent of any factor (internal or external) other than your determined will. Remember, before all else, that this is an exercise - as well as a test - of your will, self-development, motivation, and discipline (words that are rarely used in this period of the politically correct and still largely infantile society).

MAINTENANCE OF EMOTIONAL BALANCE

Emotional serenity increases the action of the mentalsoma and the holomemory, facilitating the recovery or evocation of memories. It is useful to remember that high concentrations of adrenaline for long periods cause hypomnesia.

Determine if you are addicted to emotions and stop stimulating them. Be determined to keep your emotional balance (the largest challenge in our evolutionary phase).

The following are indispensable instruments in this field:

1. Discernment
2. Discipline
3. Energetic control
4. Healthy and active affectivity and sexuality

Another example of a practical resource that supplies a reference or more visible goal would be a progression chart. The same way that large companies and industries maintain a chart controlling the number of days passed without work-related accidents (generally maintained by ICPAs - Internal Commission for Prevention of Accidents, or the Health and Safety Authority in the UK and OSHA, Occupational Safety & Health Administration in the USA), you can maintain a small chart, slate, or erasable board in which you can follow and visually represent the counting of the number of consecutive days you have lived without any great emotional outbursts or surges (positive or negative), remaining fraternal, understanding, affectionate and generous, and maintaining your level of affinity with the intraphysical consciousnesses with whom you coexist. Update this chart daily and restart the counting after each surge of emotion. Make an effort to *beat your record.*

DETAILED STUDY OF THE EVOLUTIONARY GROUP

First, study your family (nuclear), extended family, and your current and previous circle of friends, social contacts, and work groups. List names of key-people in this physical life and establish the common, basic characteristics (holothosene) of your evolutionary group.

Without limiting yourself to only the points suggested below, analyze the general characteristics, common denominators, or holothosene of your evolutionary group:

1. Assistential or closed with mafia-like intentions.
2. Conscious of multidimensionality or materialistic.
3. Knowledgeable or intellectually mediocre.
4. Consisting of paranormals (psychics) or energetically locked individuals.
5. Expanding or withering.
6. More universalistic or limited to a region, culture or religion.
7. Numerous or small.
8. Progressive or old-fashioned.
9. Linked to science, industry, trade, art, religion, or militarism.

Study the basic characteristics of the two branches of your genealogical tree (father and mother). Which one prevails genetically (nature) and mesologically (nurture, or environmental influences or upbringing) in you? *Are you a mutant in your genealogical tree?*
Conclude this entire study by establishing the respective relations and associations with the extraphysical consciousnesses (helpers, blind guides and intruders) that you usually encounter while out of the body, during the physical waking state or when communicating during parapsychic sessions, now or in the past.

STRONG AND WEAK TRAITS CHART

We must always keep in mind that we are basically the result of our past. Strong traits (qualities, talents, intelligences, capacities, brilliance) and weak traits (defects, limitations, inabilities, blind points) were established, cultivated, or reinforced over millennia.

The technical analysis, logic and clarity utilized in a chart that details strong and weak traits can give us very plausible tracks or themes of our parahistory and therefore of our current existential program. Our existential program is planned so that we can use our strong traits to fulfill it, and to help us overcome our weaker traits.

1. Do your own self-analysis and work to compile a list of your strong and weak traits.
2. Enrich it with the opinion of relatives, friends, enemies, and work and evolutionary colleagues. Make an intensive study of cross-referenced similarities and singularities on these lists so as to accurately compile the rightful inclusions or exclusions.
3. After filtering the information received, include in this study all of the technical assessments already done on you, such as IQ and competency tests, psychological analyses and vocational tests.

4. Consult dictionaries and thesauruses (dictionaries of analogies, synonyms, and similar ideas) in order to always use the best expression for each strong and weak trait.

5. Use your memory, discernment, honesty, and depth of self-observation to do successive versions and revisions of this strong and weak traits chart.

6. Identify your mega-strong trait and your mega-weak trait.

Consciential Biography

It is not necessary to wait until old age to begin writing our memoirs or autobiography, especially when it assists our self-awareness.

Based on the unfortunate fact that there is a strong tendency for the consciousness to repeat its past, the study of the present physical life will supply clues to stimulate refluxes of retrothosenes, as well as aid in studying similar personalities (see Chapter 18).

1. Begin to register, by listing in chronological order, the most relevant facts and episodes of your current life. For now do not worry about the literary composition. Use topics or very short sentences. This will give you the chronological line or backbone of your autobiography.

2. Continue to accumulate your biographical data, emphasizing the *whens, hows, whys* and *with whoms*, correctly inserting them in the chronological line.

3. Gradually add more detail to the existing information, paying attention to the events that are being recalled as part of the natural association of memories.

4. List everything that your life gave or offered in terms of opportunities, synchronicities and evolutionary conveniences, mainly if these were uncommon in

your community at that time, or for your evolutionary group. The analysis of this list will give you more data for the discovery of your existential program.

5. Take advantage and mark which decisions, choices, and actions were productive for your evolution and for the evolution of others, and that could inspire similar results in your next life. Would some of them be repetitions of previous existences?

6. Also indicate which ones were unproductive or negative, and hindered your, your evolutionary group's, or humanity's evolution, and that you would like not to repeat again in the next life. Could they be repetitions of mistakes committed in the past, as part of undesirable self-mimicry? Read and review this list several times, saturating yourself with it in order to indelibly record the topics in your holomemory, without negative obsessions. This helps you to remember these facts in your next physical life, and in this way you have already begun the technique of preparing for your next life.

SELF-DESCRIPTION

Besides mature and immature points there is a series of other characteristics that sometimes transcend the dichotomy of good or bad. These characteristics cannot be classified as strong or weak traits, yet they are important indications of our past, and therefore, must be recognized and registered. Analyze yourself and list, among others, your:

1. Accidents.
2. Genetic characteristics.
3. Diseases, health problems and their causes.
4. Favorite sports.
5. Personal style.
6. Phobias.
7. Preferences.

8. Hobbies.

9. Languages spoken or appreciated.

10. 'Shock organs' (*locus minoris resistenciae*; Achilles heel - organs, areas, or systems of your soma more fragile or susceptible to illnesses or problems, specific to each person).

11. Paragenetic patterns.

12. Patterns of energy blocks.

13. Predisposition to making a rapport with certain people or situations.

14. Personal principles.

15. Intolerances.

16. Recurring dreams or nightmares.

17. Tendencies.

18. Physical type.

19. Types of friendships.

20. Traumas.

21. Life values.

MATURITY

For the reasons previously discussed (see Chapter 12), invest in the development of your level of consciential maturity and in the enhancement of your universalism, utilizing all the cosmoethical resources that are within your reach. With this purpose in mind, conscientiology proposes several theorices beyond those discussed in this book (see the book *700 Experiments of Conscientiology*, by Waldo Vieira).

18
TECHNICAL PROCEDURES

Retrocognition is not a universal panacea.
The only possible panacea is evolution, and
this can be obtained only step by step, and
accelerated only through much work.

Regarding the conscientiological approach to consciential autonomy, the objective is learning, acquiring, and developing new evolutionary capacities, overcoming the need to depend on others for obtaining advances that, ultimately, are our own responsibility.

In this sense, after some general premises, the following techniques for obtaining self-retrocognitions are presented.

Premises:

1. Such techniques should not be applied without understanding the topics already discussed.
2. To increase the effectiveness of your self-research, it is suggested that you apply more than one technique (or all of them) at the same time, in parallel.
3. As with any technique of development or research of the consciousness, do not get anxious if you do not obtain results the first time you try. The best way to obtain retrocognitions, as well as conscious projections, is to continue trying.
4. Instead of lamenting what we fail to obtain, thoroughly value and explore the results that are achieved. Value the results and progress you get.
5. Maintain updated and complete records of everything that you notice, remember, or understand (retrocognitive diary).
6. Always be alert to your personal energetic signals, so as to be conscious of any and all changes in your psychosphere, be they for the better or worse.

7. Precede your period of retrocognitive explorations with, at least, a month of daily vibrational states (20 times a day).

If you are seeking to produce a conscious projection with the psychosoma, or projections with the mentalsoma, you can find more information on technical procedures involved in the books *Projectiology* and *700 Experiments of Conscientiology* by Waldo Vieira (see Bibliography).

STUDY OF SIMILAR PERSONALITIES

Perhaps you, the reader, may have appeared in an historical record in one or more of your previous lives. Even more likely is the possibility that some members of your karmic group, who have characteristics and a holothosene similar to yours, have been thus registered.

During the development of your research, synchronicities and retrocognitions may occur due to the stimulation of your holomemory or because of holothosenic resonance with the personality under study.

1. Utilizing the tips obtained from the analyses proposed in chapters 16 and 17, look for historical profiles in encyclopedias, in your family history and from other sources of historical personalities that have some similarity with you, your characteristics, and life profile. Do not limit yourself to famous personalities.

2. Take into account any special interest or admiration you have experienced since your childhood for some individual(s) or historical personalities that have already passed through somatic deactivation.

3. From this small list of names, start by selecting the personality that seems to be the most similar to you.

4. Begin extensive historical research, making use of all the biographical sources with regards to that person-

ality (books, magazines, newspapers, museums, the Internet, interviews, and other means).

5. List the strong and weak traits of that personality and, paying attention to details, write down the main events of that life.
6. Compare yourself with this person; look for and list affinities, similarities, coincidences and synchronicities.
7. In a similar way, construct a list of radically different or excluding factors with regards to your personality and theirs.
8. Compare similarities and differences and, according to the result, deduce the probability that you may have been this historical personality or someone close to him or her.
9. Perform the same analysis with the other names on your list.
10. Beyond the result of the comparison, use all the pictures, books, letters, testimonies, and information obtained during this research to establish a rapport with such a personality, and use them to serve as valuable hints for the following procedures, including the construction of your *retrocognitarium.*

It is essential to be aware of the fact that certainty of a specific life in the past can only be concluded through authentic healthy retrocognitions (10 healthy retrocognitions = 1 certainty), even if the result of the similar personality analysis proposed here is very compelling.

RETROCOGNITIVE SELF-HYPNOSIS

The following technique can be used even if you have no clues about your past. However, it will be more effective when you have some place to start.

1. Prepare your routine in advance so that you will not be worried about time or commitments.

2. Make sure you are well rested to avoid being sleepy during the experiment.

3. Isolate yourself in an environment where you can be comfortable and not worried about possible interruptions.

4. Work with your energies and install the vibrational state. Evaluate your thosenes and holosomatic condition. Proceed only if everything is fine. If you find yourself indisposed, depressed or irritated, even after installing the VS, leave the experiment for another day.

5. Exteriorize the maximum amount of energy you can and tune in to your helpers, *without being passive.*

6. Assume a comfortable position, lying, or sitting in a reclining chair. Close your eyes and apply a relaxation technique.

7. Forget your present life and disconnect yourself from your plans for the future. Let the hypnagogic state settle in.

8. Imagine a staircase starting at ground level - from an expansive lawn, for example - and going underground (down towards a basement, for instance). Picture yourself walking towards the staircase and going down each one of its steps.

9. Associate a decreasing counter (30 to zero, for instance) with each step you descend: a number for each stride or step. At each step/count, induce and suggest to yourself the idea that you are entering into the archives of your past. Tell yourself that you are approaching your past and that you can feel it closer with each step. Reinforce the idea that your retrocognition will be positive and recalled later. Think about your helpers assisting you. Count slowly, giving time for the induction to take effect, and reinforce it by

using different words and approaches, always with the same theme and objective.

10. When arriving at the bottommost step, envision a very long corridor with several doors on each side. Suggest to yourself that each one takes you to a specific past existence, physical or extraphysical. Observe the corridor for some time and reflect upon this.

11. Imagine yourself walking through the corridor and try to use your intuition to choose a specific door that seems to lead to your most productive past life. Walk up to it and open it slowly, entering the associated past/room, without fear or preconceptions.

12. Allow yourself to be taken by the plot and scenes (or seemingly disconnected flashes) that appear. Be an observer that does not interfere or judge.

13. During the whole time, pay attention to the images and intuitions that may appear. Follow them, allowing them to occur without your direct intervention. Do not analyze, compare or criticize what reaches you, or else you might block the process. You will analyze and take notes later, but at this moment simply watch what happens.

14. Continue until you feel that you should stop and return to the physical base in the here and now. If you fall asleep, you might have a retrocognitive dream. In this case, do not worry, you will awake naturally.

15. Upon feeling your body again, breathe deeply and review everything that was perceived.

16. Smoothly recover control of your physical body, get up and register on paper or in your computer everything that you saw, felt or perceived, even if during the first attempts it does not seem to be clear, coherent or worthy of note. Always record everything.

17. Repeat the same procedure with a certain frequency, changing doors, until you obtain results.

18. If you want to enrich the technique, use a tape recorder to register and afterwards playback messages or relative inductions towards the retrocognition that you wish to obtain. If you already have a starting point (culture, specific period or previous retrocognition), use it to make the inductions more precise. Take care so that the mechanism that automatically stops the recorder does not abruptly wake you.

RETROCOGNITARIUM

Preparation:

1. Choose a room of your house that can be totally modified.

2. Completely empty that environment, removing all pieces of furniture, pictures, and other objects, until nothing remains inside that evokes the current epoch.

3. Based on some clue, hint or hypothesis of some past life in a certain time or culture, decorate the environment with objects representative of that culture or time. Preferably use authentic objects belonging to that period. If possible, gather furniture, pictures, decorative objects, books and anything else that you might find. If it is impossible to obtain real antiques, use reproductions. The objective is to create an environment that simulates, as closely and accurately as possible (including energetically), the conditions in which you might have lived.

4. Ensure with all your ability, using your paraperceptions, the positive energies of the objects you collect to include in your *retrocognitarium*. Most old objects bring negative holothosenic patterns, often provoking auric couplings and evocations with less positive extraphysical consciousnesses. For example: never place weapons of any type, old or new, in your *retrocognitarium*.

5. Regularly, even before having completed the construction of your *retrocognitarium*, perform self-retrocognition sessions and studies in the room.

Execution:

1. Always begin by installing a prophylactic vibrational state.
2. Read something or watch a movie set in or related to that specific period of time.
3. Look at, study, and play with the objects that represent this past, taking a psychometric reading.
4. Exteriorize energy to the entire environment, establishing an auric coupling with those objects and their respective holothosenes, allowing yourself to become saturated by the retrocognitarium and its atmosphere.
5. Listen to music of that period for some time. Turn it off before continuing with the following steps.
6. Lie down, close your eyes and relax. Without fear, expectation, or anxiety, allow the energy of the environment to penetrate you.
7. Pay attention to the images that little by little come through the hypnagogy. Simply follow them without criticism or rationalization. Be a spectator and let them grow in intensity and precision. Watch any story that may unfold.
8. In case of falling asleep during the exercise, try later to remember dreams or even projections that may have occurred, always taking notice of all your perceptions and experiences.
9. If possible, try projective techniques with the objective of obtaining retroprojections.
10. Repeat this exercise regularly, since the results improve with practice and with a greater immersion in the holothosene of that specific period and culture - based on your *retrocognitarium*.

CONSCIOUS PROJECTIONS

1. Study everything you can about the conscious projection, its mechanisms, optimizations, techniques, phases, sensations, benefits, and cautions.

2. Choose the technique that might be the most productive in your personal case.

3. Apply the technique daily, if possible at the same place and time. The ideal would be to perform this exercise inside the *retrocognitarium*.

4. In conjunction with the execution of the chosen technique, use the technique of mental saturation daily; in other words, saturate your thoughts and memory with the idea of recalling a certain previous life. If you possess some clues or suppositions relative to a specific time and culture, saturate yourself with information regarding them.

5. Prioritize, in this case, having retrocognitions of your last intermissive period. Think deeply about your intermissive course and existential program. Try to awake in yourself the sensation of being in your extraphysical origin. Evoke the best thosenes you can regarding multidimensionality, detaching yourself from the conditionings of physical life.

6. Along with mental saturation, establish some projective target to direct your experience out of the body. Some examples of objectives are:

   - **Helpers and Evolutionologist:** plan encounters and interviews with the more evolved consciousnesses of your karmic group who can give you certain information that contributes to your self-research.

   - **Extraphysical Origin:** establish the goal of leaving the body and going to your extraphysical hometown, or place of origin, that is, the extraphysical community where you spent the better part of your last intermissive period. Target revisiting the extraphysical places where you attended intermissive courses, so as to remember, while being there, what you studied and for what you were preparing yourself.

PROJECTION OF THE MENTALSOMA

After acquiring experience and skill controlling bioenergies and generating conscious projections through the psychosoma, invest your time in obtaining projections through the mentalsoma to achieve the profound temporary state of cosmoconsciousness (see Chapter 11).

SECTION III:
TIME AND EVOLUTION

19
SIMULCOGNITION

The only real time is the present,
because it is when you can use your
free will, decide, and act.

BASIS

To continue with the objectives of this book, namely seeking the acceleration of an individual's maturing and evolution, and after analyzing the past and the ways in which we can perceive, it is necessary, to complete the general picture, to continue with a discussion of the relationship between consciousness and time, specifically the individual's perception of the present (simulcognition) and the future (precognition).

Simulcognition is usually defined as any form of parapsychic or paranormal sensing that allows the consciousness to capture or become aware of facts or situations that are happening at the moment the perception occurs (simultaneously), although the events are out of the scope of their conventional intraphysical perceptions, either due to distance or difference in dimension. In this sense, the best known type of simulcognition is traveling clairvoyance or remote viewing, in which the individual can see or perceive facts that are happening in some distant place, well outside of their normal reach.

However, using conscientiological criteria we are able to define simulcognitions in a more general and complete way: as the capacity of the consciousness to be integrally lucid regarding the present multidimensional moment. This encompasses simultaneously perceiving extraphysical or distant physical events in full, while remaining fully aware of the present physical moment (the here-and-now).

Even full awareness of the present physical moment eludes most people.

The ideal simulcognition is the continuity of hyper-acuity to the highest degree.

HYPERACUITY

For the expanded consciousness, the past and the future are illusions. The past exists only as an effect of our personal and group memory, or by the observation of the consequences left by naturally occurring events (memory of nature - fossils, geological formations and many others). The future is a set of probabilities that is changeable, and those probabilities increase or decrease depending on each present event.

The only real time is the present, because it is the moment when you can apply your free will, decision and action. Therefore, the highest possible level of lucidity in the present moment (simulcognition) is a higher priority than lucidity regarding the past (retrocognition) or the future (precognition).

This high level of lucidity - broad, deep, profound, intense, penetrating, precise, multidimensional, continuous, and stable - is more technically called multidimensional hyperacuity. To develop this multidimensional self-awareness it is necessary to invest in the greatest possible level of stable and continuous lucidity regarding the intraphysical here-and-now.

Most human beings live with myopic lucidity, acting like sleepwalkers or zombies, distracted, mentally disorganized, and completely disconnected from the reality of multidimensionality. During daily tasks they oscillate between the internal perception of themselves and external reality, generally without reaching the necessary depth in either of them. Many actions become automatic, conditioned, or mechanical; this occurs to such a degree that it is very common, for example, for someone to forget if they locked the door or turned off the iron after leaving the house. Many people forget what they were talking about in mid-sentence, or look for something in a room and realize they have completely forgotten what they were looking for.

To understand how our multidimensional hyperacuity is generally limited, let us propose a small test or check-up for your immediate answer (to be performed in this same instant, while you read this book).

At this exact moment, can you:

1. Feel your own energy?
2. Discriminate the energy of your environment?
3. See the energetic dimension?
4. Perceive or see the extraphysical dimensions that coexist with your environment or your surroundings? How many can you perceive?
5. Notice if there are helpers in the area, how many there are, who they are, and what they are doing?
6. Verify, in a similar way, if there are intruders in your environment?
7. Know what your existential program is?
8. Remember the essential parts of your last physical life?
9. Recover the information learned in your intermissive course?
10. Have a general idea of what has already been drafted for your next life?

The ideal goal to be reached, in terms of hyperacuity, corresponds to sustaining a high level of lucidity in all of these 10 points. To reach this, there are several mutually complementary procedures proposed by conscientiology and projectiology. Yet, before anything else, it is indispensable for the individual to want to reach this objective.

The following list has been enumerated to summarize in a practical way what procedures can be used to improve your hyperacuity (some have already been mentioned in this book):

1. Control of your bioenergies.
2. Preventive and corrective energetic self-defense to avoid intrusion and blockages.
3. Sufficient care of the body, especially the central nervous system.
4. Good habits, organization, and a stable life (affective, sexual and economic).
5. Increase your level of multidisciplinary knowledge and theorice.
6. Effort to maintain emotional balance.
7. Training of paraperceptions.
8. Practice of lucid projectability (projections).
9. Development of the mentalsoma and its capacities.
10. Strengthening the connection with helpers through maximum self-incorruptibility, and through the exercise of assistance with a predominance of the clarification task.

CONTINUITY

Everyone can have certain moments of high hyperacuity, but these are usually spontaneous and fleeting. In many cases, these *outbursts* of higher awareness can be caused by different factors, such as: presence of a helper, life crisis, physical trauma, imminent death, or even drugs.

The greatest challenge of all is to consistently maintain a high level of balanced hyperacuity, without abrupt changes or disruption of continuity. The goal is the production of an uninterrupted flow of thosenes in coherent succession, a continuous chain, a logical and stable sequence, with flexible yet resistant connectivity.

In practice, however, what is observed is exactly the opposite. The linearity or constancy of our lucidity suffers frequent breaks and flaws. We lose the continuity of our hyperacuity while sleeping, by becoming too emotional, when changing dimensions, when deactivating or reactivating the soma (rebirth), and transmigrating.

Continuously exercising our hyperacuity in a certain dimension, even the intraphysical one, will facilitate the manifestation of this level of lucidity in any other dimension. With time, we will start having projections of continuous consciousness (out-of-body experiences without blackouts or gaps of awareness), and then nights of continuous consciousness, until one day, we will arrive at the state of continuous consciousness.

20

CURRENT LIFE vs. PREVIOUS LIVES

Life on this planet is better now than it has ever been.

Individuals currently enjoying a higher level of lucidity, on both a personal and collective scale, are more able to recall certain memories of past lives, and can begin to compare their current life with past ones.

Knowledge of the main points of this comparison demystifies several esoteric, political and social *pseudo-truths*; this gives the retrocognitor a deep sense of safety and optimism regarding his evolution and that of others. This exercise supports the continuity mentioned earlier, since it makes a link between the past and the present in a critical, productive, and mentalsomatic way.

COMPARISON

Among the countless points that can be compared, the following stand out due to their evolutionary effects:

Larger population – This planet, which today has approximately 6.4 billion people, has never before provided for so many intraphysical consciousnesses. This increase in population has implications in most of the following areas.

Longer life expectancy – Contrary to what many people think, most individuals now live a longer and healthier life. This longer life expectancy is still not a reality in all nations of the world, yet it has clearly surfaced in several developed nations. This indicates that soon we will be living up to 130 years, the age believed to be the maximum duration of our nominal life as programmed in our genes. The extension in life, made possible by progress in medicine, allows for a larger accumulation of experiences and facilitates a greater number of accomplishments in one lifetime. It is worth remembering that during the Middle Ages in Europe the average life expectancy was approximately 35 years, an age that, today, corresponds to the conclusion of the preparatory period of the existential program.

Greater number of human contacts – In this present life, we can have contact with approximately the same number of people in one week that we would have encountered during an entire life in the Middle Ages. This fact shows that a person's current groupkarma is, unavoidably, closer to polykarma than during previous lives. The multiplication of personal and group contacts, including those due to the presence of recently transmigrated consciousnesses, accelerates the maturation of the consciousness through an amplification and diversification of experiences.

Greater access to knowledge – Today, most intraphysical consciousnesses on this planet have more access to information and knowledge than in their previous lives, primarily due to television, computers, the Internet and the popularization and diminishing prices of printed media - books, magazines and newspapers (today many can be obtained free). In spite of the current world crisis in teaching, more people attend schools, and knowledge is becoming ever more accessible.

Greater transportation speed – Today, we are not obliged to spend a lifetime in a small fortified feudal village, nor are we limited to an area of some hundreds of square kilometers. Contemporary means of transportation surpass all previous methods in speed and convenience. This facilitates fast and relatively cheap access to practically any part of the planet. As a result, people can save a great deal of time and experience a greater theoretical and practical universalism, through interaction with other cultures and people, consequently multiplying their life experiences.

More free time – Within the first world, due to the increase in wealth, it is possible today to work fewer hours. In the distant past most people were forced, by necessity, to ceaselessly work to survive. Even before the invention of money, the need for shelter, heat, safety, water, and food consumed all of an intraphysical consciousness's available time - we lived only for the body. Only kings, leaders, and some priests had what we call today free time. At the time of the Industrial Revolution, in England, for example, adults and children worked at looms in shifts of up to 18 hours, without resting on Saturday or Sunday. At the end of the 20th century, most people in developed - and many in developing - countries can afford the luxury of working only 40 hours a week. This gives them several hours a week for leisure, study, and interpersonal contact.

More comfort – Technological progress and the reduction of prices resulting from economies of scale have made inventions that simplify intraphysical life available to many. Electricity, supermarkets, microwave ovens, telephones and many others have turned physical life into less of a slavish existence. We no longer need to spend hours preparing a meal, or days weaving a piece of cloth.

Greater freedom of expression – In many countries there is already a reasonable degree of freedom of speech (of the press and expression). This encourages a consciousness to be less inhibited, to be more creative, and to participate more fully in social and political processes and in its historical moment.

More democracy – Beyond freedom of speech, democracy has also expanded into other areas. In several countries, it is possible for the population to choose their leaders, allowing them to transcend the foolishness of monarchies and empires, where power was limited to only one group or family for generations. Another effect promoted by the expansion of democracy is a relative improvement in justice. Authoritarian decisions, corruption, discrimination, and other unethical practices will become progressively more difficult to perpetrate.

More consciential energy – A greater number of people and the accumulation of centuries of human civilization has been building an ever stronger field of consciential energy on this planet. Through the constant natural exteriorization of CEs, and the permanent natural recycling of matter, molecules and atoms - which come from nature to construct human bodies and later, in the process of death, are returned and reused in the construction of new bodies - we observe that the dense matter of this planet is becoming increasingly energized and *thosenized*. One cannot yet foresee all the effects of this process, however it can be inferred that physical matter will become more compliant and malleable to consciousness, and that the expression of multidimensionality on this planet will become more trivial.

It is important to clarify that the presentation of the previous points is not intended to excuse the current model of society with hypocritical pride. We are still suffering serious problems. The current social-economic paradigm continues to be radically unjust. Beyond that, among many other problems, it is causing the destruction of the planet, a fact that will change only when consumerism is abandoned and self-sustainable models are created. Wars, hunger, authoritarianism, fanaticism, intolerance, lack of lucidity and an absence of cosmoethics, unfortunately, continue and will continue to exist for a long time.

In any case, many individuals who have already had a good number of healthy retrocognitions arrive at the same conclusion, namely that, in global terms and considering seriality, *most consciousnesses have never had it so good.*

21
PRECOGNITION

*To what extent are you passive in your
perceptions of the future, and to what
level are you an active author of the
events supposedly foreseen?*

Precognition is the consciential capacity or ability of perceiving, seeing, capturing or intuiting future events. Regarding chronological time it is the third paraperception of the consciousness, retrocognition (perception of the past) and simulcognition (lucidity of the present) being the other two. It is popularly known as premonition, the *sixth* sense or prophecy.

In spite of being one of the more difficult consciential phenomena to explain, it is one of the most common and popular ones. There are few people who have never had some kind of confirmed precognition.

Precognition, nowadays, has already overcome the category of supposition or farce, having been repeatedly tested and verified in laboratory experiments, usually by utilizing statistical observations of deviations in random events. The use of Zener cards (five kinds of card: a star, three vertical wavy lines, a plus sign, a circle and a square) is an example of such an experiment. Like other types of paraperception, it can occur in several different ways and may be combined with other parapsychic abilities, and associated with distinct altered states of consciousness.

The most common form of precognition occurs during dreams, a state in which the reduction of the *influence* of rationality, the predominance of the alpha state, and the partial non-alignment of the vehicles of manifestation of the consciousness predispose its occurrence.

It also manifests during the ordinary physical waking state, through non-visual intuitions, or as visions or flashes of scenes.

Extraphysical precognition, perceived by projected individuals or extraphysical consciousnesses, is the clearest and most precise. In this condition, the consciousness is less limited by the objective or subjective influence of time, or more accurately, the space-time continuum.

The strongest type of projective precognition - if we can refer to it in this way - is the entire perception of time, in-block, obtainable through some projections of the mentalsoma, a state in which the borders between past, present, and future disappear.

Most often, the precognition occurs seconds, hours or several days before the foreseen event; yet, in a few cases, it may occur many years or centuries earlier.

For some as yet not understood reason, most parapsychic forecasts foresee accidents, disasters, catastrophes, or traumatic events, occurrences that might be categorized as negative. As with retrocognitions, perceptions with a stronger emotional impact prevail. Perhaps, owing to the higher emotional susceptibility of the human being, whose holothosene still has greater emphasis on the *sen*, this type of information impresses the memory more, allowing it to be *brought* to intraphysical awareness through a process of affinity or thosenic resonance. Another fact that should be taken into account is that hetero-intrusions or self-intrusions predispose the individual to negative recurring precognitions.

A common discussion concerning precognition is its implication of a predetermined destiny. So many premonitions of a personal or public character have been confirmed that many people, including some scientists, have hypothesized that free will plays no part in our decisions. According to this theory, no matter what our individual decision, it would simply be the one already predetermined in the course of our destiny. This idea is also reflected in certain Hindu philosophies.

Another contributing factor to this theory is the occurrence of events that could not be avoided, even with extreme effort and foreknowledge. In some of these cases, all of the impelling factors for its occurrence had been dominated or controlled; nonetheless, the event had such determinism that it infiltrated through the *holothosenic breaches* and occurred, in spite of all efforts to the contrary. On the other hand, certain experiences, which at first were assumed to be precognitions, "lapsed" and were never confirmed.

One of the most logical explanations for this 'destiny-freewill' paradox is that the future is changeable and is permanently open. Events closer in the future can be foreseen (even in a rational or conventional way) with larger precision, while those more distant are more uncertain.

All future events have associated probabilities; that is to say, anything is possible. Some events have probabilities closer to zero and are considered unlikely, while others are close to 100% and are seen as nearly certain.

If it is possible to record the largest possible number of factors and variables of a certain system throughout an extensive period of time in order to calculate its laws or tendencies, its future behavior can be deduced with a certain probability. This was the original pretense of the mechanistic (materialistic) paradigm, which had the goal to discover all the laws of the universe by measuring the variables at the present and using them to calculate the future in an unequivocal way. This train of thought was derailed by the discovery of Heisenberg's uncertainty principle, which added an indeterminate variable to the *equation for the future.*

An analogy can aid in elucidating the mechanism of precognition. Imagine flying over a great city in a helicopter or balloon, observing and analyzing the flow of urban traffic below. It is impossible to foresee the trajectory of a single car in particular, or its driver's actions. However, it would be quite easy and precise to observe and foresee the behavior of the traffic as a whole. After some time, the patterns would emerge and the more congested times, days, and routes could be foreseen.

This materialistic approach is very easily understood and applied in a conventional non-parapsychical way, in areas like weather forecasting; investments, stock markets; political forecasting; sporting predictions; and in anticipation of certain mass social and cultural trends. Many forecasts and predictions come true, yet there are always many surprises and mistakes. As in the case of traffic, it is almost impossible to foresee individual behavior, although it is usually possible to forecast larger trends.

According to the consciential paradigm, it is understood that other variables interfere with the future. Some of them are: other dimensions; *Homo sapiens serenissimus*, helpers, intruders; energies or thosenes; and the holothosenes of the past. The sum or convergence of the *holothosenic forces* and synchronicities of today tend to create larger probabilities for certain future events. The closer the clearer; the more distant the more diffuse and changeable.

Perhaps the most important factor of all is the timeless (atemporal) characteristic of the consciousness. While restricted in the soma, it suffers the maximum degree of objective and subjective influence from the time factor. When manifesting through the psychosoma, a more subtle body, that influence is largely reduced; and when liberated through the mentalsoma, it seems to completely transcend these influences or restrictions. Using this line of reasoning, a precognition could be a quick and semiconscious expansion of the mentalsoma and its capacities.

Following this line of thought, conscious projections of the psychosoma or mentalsoma allow a wider and more complete perception of reality, and its past, present and future events, as in the previously discussed analogy of the balloon and the traffic.

Of course, our helpers and their evolutionologists can also have their own precognitions, by means of their more subtle extraphysical condition, and their previous knowledge of our individuality, group, collective, global and (depending on their degree of lucidity) universal existential program. Nothing obstructs some of the perceptions we call precognitions from being second hand perceptions, captured and transmitted to us by these extraphysical consciousnesses.

This raises a pertinent question: can intruders instill *pseudo-precognitions* into more susceptible minds, so that false forecasts become reality due to suggestions to the intrudee and the actions that result from their own thosenes? Experience shows that this actually happens.

Even in a healthier and cosmoethical form, this possibility can be real. To what extent are we passive in our perceptions of the future, and to what level are we active authors of events supposedly foreseen?

Most of the previously discussed ideas regarding retrocognitions are also valid for precognitions. Techniques for obtaining retrocognitions, like the example of the *retrocognitarium*, often produce precognitions (*precognitarium*).

The type of precognition that is most important at this time is that relating to our next physical life. It is possible to capture the basic plan traced out for our evolutionary group and, consequently, for each individual.

More than a simple passive inspiration, the individual should wake up to the logical and feasible theorice of preparing for his next intraphysical life.

22
THEORIES CONCERNING THE END OF THE WORLD

Only pathological, entropic, and dull consciousnesses,
intruders or the intruded, can create and divulge
ideas concerning the end of the world.

Humanity has always lived with apocalyptic prophecies. Towards the end of centuries or millennia these prophecies tend to proliferate. On these occasions several theories - visions, supposed messages and premonitions regarding the end of the world, the final Day of Judgment, or the end of our time - multiply beyond our capacity to keep track.

In this book we are studying the interrelation of the evolution of the consciousness with time. It is essential to discuss the subject of apocalypse, so as to demystify it and, hopefully, calm some of the more suggestible individuals. Through a higher level of lucidity regarding the evolution of the consciousness and humanity, mainly obtained by the experience of lucid projectability, and healthy retrocognitions, it is understood that there is no logical argument to support these apocalyptic theories.

Many arguments can be used against these kinds of theories:

1.   At the end of the 10th century and of the 1st millennium, around the year 999, several cataclysmic forecasts proliferated, just as occurred at the end of the 2nd millennium.

2.   The idea of the end of the century or the beginning of the 3rd millennium is based on the Gregorian calendar that, in spite of being used by most people of this planet, is nothing more than a non universal reference or convention. The Chinese and Jewish communities count time in a different way, and they are already beyond the year 5,000.

3.   A deep change in the rhythm of life on Earth would affect other planets and civilizations due to interplanetary transmigrations. The evolution of the cosmos does not follow a calendar that bears the name of one human being, who represents a specific religion (all religions are anti-universalistic) among many others on a small planet in the periphery of one of the countless galaxies of the visible universe.

4.   The majority of these theories are based on a materialistic vision of existence, geocentric models, or religious approaches that defend the idea that the nature of the consciousness is physical and not extraphysical. This can be observed, for example, when it is affirmed that after the Day of Judgment we will live eternally on Earth again, in an intraphysical form.

5.   The concept of the Age of Aquarius comes from the presuppositions of Astrology, which in its basis still uses the paradigm of Earth being the center of the universe. Several of the constellations used in astrology are not true constellations, in the technical sense of stars kept together by gravitational forces or born from the same genesis. They seem to be a stellar group only because they are aligned visually in the same portion of the sky, but among its stars, some are closer to Earth and others are light-years away. The constellations, true or virtual, are where they have always been in respect to the timescale of human civilization. It is the relative position of the Earth, with its countless types of movement (mainly rotation, translocation and precession) that gives, for inhabitants on its surface, the illusion of movement of the sky. In comparison to the scale of relative astronomical distances between the constellations and Earth, those movements, including the one of orbiting around the Sun, are minute. That is to say, on an astronomical scale, in the last few thousand years, the Earth has hardly moved.

6.   The knowledge of the existence and action of the *Homo sapiens serenissimus* shows that evolution on this

planet does not run unattended, and that everything is under the supervision of consciousnesses more developed than we are.

7.   Humanity has already experienced deep crises, or even catastrophes, and still survived. For example: we have already had several plagues and epidemics that decimated millions of people (black plague in the Middle Ages and the Spanish influenza at the beginning of the 20th century). In addition, *Homo sapiens* experienced the last great glacial era on this planet.

8.   Everything indicates that the rhythm of transmigrations have increased in the last three or four centuries. Such a fact would be illogical if we were about to face some great crisis of cosmic magnitude.

More developed consciousnesses, justifiably optimistic and good humored, do not promote such apocalyptic theories. More pathological, entropic, and somber intraphysical or extraphysical consciousnesses create and proclaim them.

It would be a mistake to think that the history of humanity from here onwards will be an ascending straight line, without highs and lows. We will probably still endure several crises, like: overpopulation, pollution, lack of potable water, lack of food, agricultural plagues, global epidemics, increasing crime rate indexes, and perhaps large scale wars. However, just as before, the rhythm of evolution will continue.

23
CONSCIENTIOLOGICAL SOCIETY OF THE FUTURE

*Despite almost always resulting in non-confirmed
predictions, futurology essays are good practice
for our lucid perception of the continuity of the
past, present and future.*

FUTUROLOGY

Futurology: the branch of knowledge that speculates about
the future of society and its political and economic institutions, in order to forecast humanity's possible futures, con-
centrating on topics such as: humanity's demographic
explosion, probable genetic mutations, and revolutions in
biology, medicine, and technology.

PREMISES

To conclude this book's ideas about the evolution of the
consciousness, memory, time and the perceptions of the
consciousness relative to time, following is an exercise in
futurology. This exercise is based on the consciential paradigm, on the leading-edge relative truths of conscientiology, and on the extrapolation, as logically as possible, of the
current scientific, technological, and social trends.

It is important to point out that the majority of exercises in futurology do not reach a significant percentage of
success or confirmation - sometimes erring completely -
due to the constant change in the direction of history, and
human inability to appreciate the trends of the present
moment. It is usually only possible to have a more accurate and profound vision of historical cultures and facts at
least 50 years after their occurrence.

Examples of uses of Futurology are found in science fiction works (books or films). Some of these forecasts have been confirmed, such as the orbiting telecommunications satellite foreseen by Arthur C. Clark; or the submarine and the trips to the Moon anticipated by Jules Verne. On the other hand, several conceptions regarding the future have not been confirmed, at least not yet, as in the case of *Metropolis* (Fritz Lang), *1984* (George Orwell) and *A Brave New World* (Aldous Huxley).

Another obvious limitation of Futurology, which attempts to quantify historical variables and to simulate possible futures through computer modeling, is its imprisonment in the materialistic, Newtonian, Cartesian, physicalist or reductionist paradigm.

The objective of this chapter is to exercise the reader's mentalsoma, provoke debate, unsettle conditionings, associate different ideas, and expand horizons, so as to stimulate your precognitions, mainly regarding your next intraphysical life, inviting you to do a critical analysis of this draft of conscientiological futurology described in the following pages.

So that one can understand the proposed panorama, it is important to understand that a conscientiological intraphysical society, a less pathological intraphysical society, is based on the following concepts or principles:

- Advanced Groupkarmality

- Assistentiality

- Clarification task

- Conscientiological Companies

- Conscientiotherapy

- Cosmoethics

- Holochakrality

- Mentalsomatics

- Multidimensionality

• Polykarmality

• Universalism

Many of the changes pointed out in the following draft are already underway, and others will be able to be accomplished in the medium term. Some of them, however, will only be realities on this planet some millennia in the future.

ESSAY

Knowledge / Science / Technology

• Worldwide network of information and telecommunications;

• Versatile domestic terminals (Computer + telephones + televisions + radio + video game + CD + interactivity);

• Proliferation of portable, light and inexpensive personal computers with telecommunications capacities, and voice and writing recognition;

• Decrease in the use of printed paper (tele-informatics);

• Human knowledge being doubled in increasingly smaller periods of time (every 1.5 months by 2004);

• Virtual reality education and training;

• Robotics in the home;

• Vulgarization of genetic manipulations (genetic engineering, Genome Project, genetic treatments);

• Use of cloned tissues and organs, bionics and cyborgs in medicine;

• Use of artificial reproduction or generation;

• Consciential Paradigm invigorating science;

- Practical application of bioenergetic technology;
- Use of projectability in general and in scientific research.

Ecology

- Drastic decrease in the number of subhuman species;
- Water, air, energy and physical space increasingly more expensive;
- Older population (less children);
- Super-valuation of nature;
- Shortage of potable water;
- Extreme care for the environment (pollution, urbanization, domes and dikes);
- Shortage of food;
- End of consumerism and the disposable society;
- Inevitable mutations and biological adaptations.

Behavior / Psychology

- Problems with an increase in free time (risk of excess in entertainment, virtual infantilism, drugs, video games) and the necessity to use this time better;
- Increase in the need for escapism (idiosyncrasies, eccentric life and behavior, adrenal sports, etc.);
- Critical polynomial: education - transportation - feeding - survival;
- Greater freedom of expression and manifestation, including sexually-affective, although with more discernment and responsibility;
- Greater sense of groupality and respect for individuality and privacy;
- Greater authenticity in inter-consciential relations;

• Larger availability for multidimensionality, due to the reduction of the working day and a larger presence of computers and robots;

• Greatest human sport: conscious projection;

• Coexisting inside the largest possible Universalism;

• Cosmoethics as common sense.

Sociology / Politics / Legislation

• Coalition of ever larger companies, with the consequent formation of economic conglomerates (some of them more powerful than some nations);

• Information becomes the most important and expensive commodity;

• Personal identification by DNA;

• Reduction in the use of paper money (electronic money);

• Confrontation of overpopulation and its implications;

• Obligatory donation of organs upon somatic deactivation;

• Appearance of ecological religious sects;

• Multiplication of conscientiological companies;

• Unification of countries;

• Greater individual and group freedom;

• Greater number of existential invertors;

• Organization and formalization of evolutionary groups;

• Application of techniques of conscientiometry, like the Conscientiogram, for the formation of evolutionary couples, recruiting of employees, electing of politicians, etc.;

- A stable population in terms of number and profile (at this time the UN forecasts that it should reach 8.9 billion people by 2050);
- Popularization of volunteer work and the consciential link;
- Changes in the structure of family;
- World government;
- Human colonies outside of Earth and the sociological implications of that;
- Increasing regularity of waves. According to Alvin Toffler: 1st wave = Agricultural Revolution; 2nd wave = Industrial Revolution; 3rd wave = Information Revolution. According to Conscientiology, the 4th wave = Multidimensionality;
- Longer intraphysical life (approximately 130 years, according to some lines of research);
- Universal language (natural coalition, in different percentages, of the current most important languages);
- Contact with extraterrestrial civilizations;
- End of wars.

Multidimensionality

- Intensification of interplanetary transmigrations (interplanetary immigration and interplanetary emigration);
- An increase in the number of consciential epicenters;
- Expansion of conscientiotherapy;
- Larger number of consciousnesses with high level intermissive courses;
- More energetic springtimes experienced;

- Life's comforts will lead people to a clearer perception of the energetic dimension or of the *energetic haze*;

- Larger difficulty for somatic rebirth (competition for the few spaces available, necessity of prerequisites to merit somatic rebirth);

- Larger number of well-known serenissimus;

- General tendency towards the mentalsoma (care of the soma prioritizing the mentalsoma, avoiding the current *Athens-Sparta dichotomy*);

- Larger use and value of parapsychism, projectability, and bioenergy;

- Consciential leaders that have been negative for many centuries gradually becoming positive and cosmoethical;

- End of extraphysical reurbanizations - only maintenance continues;

- Increase in the average evolutionary level of the population;

- Larger exchange of lucidity: intraphysicality - extraphysicality;

- Physical matter more energized and amenable to consciousness(es);

- Knowledge of multidimensionality as a public domain (taught from childhood);

- Decrease in the percentage of inter-consciential intrusion, increase in the percentage of permanent-totally intrusion-free consciousnesses;

- Physical lives without the necessity of such ostensible assistance on the part of helpers, as it is today;

- Intraphysical society will move closer to the healthy extraphysical societies;

- Public discovery of the *Homo sapiens serenissimus* (historical equivalent to the discovery of fire, agriculture and the wheel);

- Consciential era;

- Exhaustion of the vital charge of Earth's bioenergy and the necessity for total transmigration;

- Reaching the state of continuous consciousness;

- 3rd somatic deactivation and the state of free consciousness (FC).

Conclusion

Within the larger context of lucidity regarding consciousness, time and evolution, it would be interesting if you, the reader, thought about the following subjects:

- *In practical terms, what are you doing regarding all of this?*

- *Do you help the serenissimus in their evolutionary role or do you become associated with mega-intruders, creating even more entropy?*

- *Are you lucid of your self-evolution and trying to catalyze it, or are you simply taken in by the relentless river of general evolution?*

- *Do you have proactive precognitions, and when they are positive go into battle to transform them into reality, or do you have passive precognitions, and wait to see if they come true?*

SECTION IV:
APPENDICES

GLOSSARY

The following are definitions of conscientiological and projectiological terms, compound words, and expressions. Not all are used in this book.

Abdominal brain – The umbilicochakra (center of consciential energy located above the navel), when unconsciously selected by the intraphysical consciousness, who is still fairly unevolved, as the basis of his/her manifestations. The belly-brain, gut brain, abdominal brain, abdominal *pseudo*-brain, or abdominal sub-brain, is the *gray eminence* of the natural, encephalic brain (coronochakra and frontochakra); an indefensible obstacle to conscious self-evolution.

Admiration-disagreement binomial – The posture of an intraphysical consciousness who is mature in regard to consciential evolution, knows how to live in peaceful coexistence with another intraphysical consciousness who he/she loves and admires, but with whose points of view, opinions and positions he/she is not always in 100% agreement.

Advanced existential program – The existential program of the intraphysical consciousness who is an evolutionary leader, within a specific libertarian groupkarmic task that is more universalistic and polykarmic in nature. This individual acts as a lucid, *mini*cog within a *maxi*mechanism of the multidimensional team.

Altered state of consciousness – See xenophrenia.

Alternant intraphysical pre*serenissimus* – The intraphysical consciousness who is capable, from time to time, of simultaneously living consciously in the ordinary, physical waking state, as well as projected in extraphysical dimensions.

Androsoma (*andro* + *soma*) – The masculine human body, or the soma specific to a man.

Androthosene (compound word: *andro* + *tho* + *sen* + *e*) – The thosene specific to the primitive male intraphysical consciousness or the *macho man*.

Animism (Latin: *animus*, soul) – The set of intracorporeal and extracorporeal phenomena produced by the intraphysical consciousness without external interference. For example, the phenomenon of lucid projection induced by one's own will.

Antithosene (*anti* + *tho* + *sen* + *e*) – The antagonistic thosene, common in refutations, omniquestioning and productive debates.

Artifacts of knowledge – Intellectual tools; resources used by the consciousness to store, retrieve or process information, such as books, computers and the internet.

Assisted lucid projection – The projection wherein the intraphysical consciousness finds him/herself to be directly assisted, during the experiment, by a helper which is almost always an expert in lucid projectability (LPB).

Assistential – Related to or denoting assistance. An assistential task is universalistic, cosmoethical, fraternal and should ideally be clarifying (clarification task) instead of consoling (consolation task).

Auric coupling – Interfusion of the holochakral energies between 2 or more consciousnesses.

Belly-brain – See abdominal brain.

Biothosene (*bio* + *tho* + *sen* + *e*) – The thosene specific to the human or intraphysical consciousness.

Bithanatosis – The deactivation and discarding of the holochakra after the first desoma, including removal of the remaining energetic connections of the holochakra in the psychosoma; *second death*; second desoma.

Blind guide – The amoral or inexperienced consciousness which helps another consciousness – in an anticosmoethical manner, according to its momentary egotistic interests – to the detriment of others.

Bradythosene (*brady* + *tho* + *sen* + *e*) – The thosene having a sluggish flow, pertaining to the bradypsychic human consciousness.

Cardiochakra (*cardio* + *chakra*) – The fourth basic chakra, the influential agent in the emotionality of the intraphysical consciousness which vitalizes the heart and lungs. Also known as the heart chakra.

Chakra – A nucleus or defined field of consciential energy, the totality of which basically constitutes the *holochakra* or energetic parabody inside the body. The holochakra forms a junction between the soma and the psychosoma, acting as a point of connection through which consciential energy (CE) flows from one consciential vehicle to the other. The word *chakra* is one of our *critical* *neologistic limits.* The author has not encountered another single international word that is more adequate, or apt, to put in its place and eliminate the *philosophical preconception* that exists with respect to this term (as well as its derivations and cognates). What is above all important, in this context, is *conceptual content* and not *linguistic form.* We live in *deficiencyland,* but consciential evolution proceeds with holo*chakro*logy.

Chirosoma (*chiro + soma*) – The soma considered specifically in terms of the use of the hands or manual labor.

Clarification task – The advanced assistential task of elucidation or clarification which can be performed individually or in group. Plural: clarification tasks.

Coincidence – The state of alignment of the vehicles (holosoma) of manifestation of the consciousness.

Communicology – The area or subdiscipline of conscientiology that studies all natures and forms of communicability of the consciousness, including interconsciential communication between consciential dimensions, considering lucid consciential projectability and the "entire" consciousness (holosoma, holobiography, holomemory).

Con – The hypothetical unit of measurement of the level of lucidity of the intraphysical or extraphysical consciousness.

Confor (*con + for*) – The interaction of content (idea, essence) with form (presentation, language) in the processes of interconsciential communication (communicology).

Conscientese – The telepathic, non-symbolic idiom that is the native language in the consciential dimensions of very evolved extraphysical societies.

Consciential amentia – The condition of the consciousness which is incapable of thinking with reasonable mental balance.

Consciential basement – The phase of infantile and adolescent manifestation of the intraphysical consciousness up to adulthood, characterized by a predominance of more primitive strong traits of the multivehicular, multiexistential and multimillenary consciousness.

Consciential bond – The cosmoethical, self-lucid, voluntary and polykarmic link between a volunteer and an institution. The consciential bond goes beyond the employment bond.

Consciential co-epicenter – The helper that works with an intraphysical consciousness who is a veteran consciential epicenter in his/her personal energetic task (penta). This helper can work as a colleague in the daily practices of penta as well as in the assistance continuously provided to extraphysical consciousnesses which are brought to the epicenter's extraphysical clinic.

Consciential concentration – The direct, unwavering, focusing of the consciousness' senses, consciential attributes, will and intention upon a singular object.

Consciential continuism – The condition of wholeness – without gaps – in the continuity of consciential life, through opportune foresight and evolutionary self-relay. In other words, the incessant linking of the experience of the present moment to immediately prior and subsequent experiences, in a cohesive and unified whole, with neither interruption in continuity nor staunched consciential experiences.

Consciential ectopia – Unsatisfactory execution of one's existential program in an eccentric, dislocated manner, outside the programming chosen for one's own intraphysical life.

Consciential energy (CE) – The immanent energy that the consciousness employs in its general manifestations; the *ene* of thosene.

Consciential epicenter – The key intraphysical consciousness of operational epicentrism who becomes a fulcrum of interdimensional lucidity, assistentiality and constructiveness through the extraphysical clinic. Directly related to *penta* or the personal energetic task.

Consciential era – That era in which average intraphysical consciousnesses find themselves sufficiently evolved, through the impacts, redefinitions and revolutions created through their experiences of lucid projectability (LPB), implanting *self-conscientiality first and foremost.*

Consciential eunuch – The intraphysical consciousness who is conscientially castrated and manipulated by sectarians, domesticators of *satisfied robots*, the modern slaves pertaining to the unthinking masses.

Consciential gestation – Useful evolutionary productivity, on the part of the human consciousness, within the framework of the personal works of his/her existential program.

Consciential hyperspaces – Extraphysical consciential dimensions.

Consciential micro-universe – The consciousness when considered as a whole, including all of its attributes, thosenes and manifestations during its evolution. The microcosm of the consciousness in relation to the macrocosm of the universe.

Consciential monoendowment – Intraphysical life under the pressure of constant intrusion by ill beings. This is experienced by mediocre intraphysical consciousnesses having few talents and no versatility.

Consciential paracoma – The state of extraphysical coma of a projected intraphysical consciousness who invariably remains unconscious, therefore having no recall of extraphysical events.

Consciential paradigm – Leading-theory of conscientiology, based upon the consciousness itself.

Consciential restriction – Restriction of the consciousness due to the process of manifestation in the physical state, in which one's natural level of awareness is reduced.

Consciential retailing – The rudimentary system of individual behavior characterized by lesser, isolated consciential actions having a minimum of productive results or great evolutionary effects.

Consciential scaffolding – Dispensable psychological or physiological *crutches* used by the consciousness.

Consciential self-bilocation (Latin: *bis,* two; and *locus,* place) – The act whereby an intraphysical projector encounters and contemplates his/her own human body (soma) face-to-face, when the consciousness is outside the soma, headquartered in another vehicle of consciential manifestation.

Consciential self-relay – The advanced condition in which the consciousness evolves by consecutively interweaving one intraphysical existence with another (*connected existential programs*), in the manner of the links of a chain (existential seriality), within one's multiexistential cycle (*holobiography*).

Consciential tri-endowment – Quality of the 3 conjugated talents most useful to a conscientiologist: intellectuality, parapsychism and communicability.

Consciential wholesaling – The behavior of an individual characterized by a tendency to approach consciential acts in a comprehensive or wholesale manner, not leaving negative evolutionary loose ends or gaps behind.

Conscientiocentric institution – The institution that centralizes its objectives on the consciousness and its evolution, as is the case with the International Academy of Consciousness (IAC); a consciential cooperative within conscientiological intraphysical society, based on employment and consciential bonds.

Conscientiocentrism – The social philosophy that concentrates its objectives on the consciousness itself and its evolution. Conscientiocentrism is a subject covered by *conscientiocentrology*, the subdiscipline of conscientiology that studies the creation and maintenance of the conscientiocentric institution based on consciential and employment bonds – like a consciential cooperative – in conscientiological intraphysical society.

Conscientiogram – The technical plan for measuring the evolutionary level of the consciousness; the consciential megatest having *Homo sapiens serenissimus* as a model – *serenissimus* being responsible for a positive egokarmic account. The conscientiogram is the basic instrument employed in conscientiometric tests.

Conscientiologist – The intraphysical consciousness who is engaged in the continued study and objective experimentation in the field of conscientiological research. The conscientiologist operates as an agent of evolutionary renovation (*retrocognitive agent*), in the libertarian work of consciousnesses in general.

Conscientiology – The science that studies the consciousness in an integral, holosomatic, multidimensional, multimillenary, multiexistential manner and, above all, according to its reactions in regard to immanent energy (IE), consciential energy (CE) and its multiple states.

Conscientiometry – The discipline or area that studies conscientiological (of the consciousness) measurements, using the resources and methods offered by conscientiology, that are capable of establishing the possible bases for the *mathematicization of the consciousness*. Main instrument: the conscientiogram.

Conscientiotherapy – The subdiscipline that studies the treatment, relief or remission of disturbances of the consciousness, executed through the resources and techniques derived from conscientiology.

Consciousness, the – The individual essence or intelligent principle in constant evolution. In conscientiology the word consciousness (as in "the consciousness") is considered to be synonymous with mind, ego, intelligent principle, and others, and is not being used to refer to a state of consciousness. Outworn synonyms: soul, spirit.

Consolation task – Elementary, personal or group, assistential task of consolation.

Contrathosene (*contra + tho + sen + e*) – The *intra*consciential thosene of the intraphysical consciousness; mute mental refutation; *mental word*; mute thosene; a type of *intrathosene*.

Co-projector – The helper who works with the intraphysical consciousness in the development of his/her lucid, assisted consciential projections.

Coronochakra (*corono + chakra*) – The chakra in the area of the sinciput, *crowning* the holochakra; crown chakra.

Cosmoconsciousness – The consciousness' inner perception of the cosmos, of life and the order of the universe, in an indescribable intellectual and cosmoethical exaltation. In this condition, the consciousness senses the living presence of the universe and becomes one with it, in an indivisible unit. Interconsciential communication occurs in this singular condition.

Cosmoethical mimicry – The productive social impulse of imitating the evolved forebears of the intraphysical consciousness.

Cosmoethicality – The cosmoethical quality of the consciousness.

Cosmoethics (*cosmo + ethics*) – The ethics or reflection upon cosmic, multidimensional morality, or the cosmic moral code, which defines holomaturity. Cosmoethics surpasses social, intraphysical morals or those morals presented within any human classification. It is a subdiscipline of conscientiology.

Cosmothosene (*cosmo + tho + sen + e*) – The thosene specific to conscientese or the state of cosmoconsciousness; the form of communication of conscientese.

Counterbody – The same as the holochakra, the specific vehicle of the intraphysical consciousness' consciential energy (CE).

Daydream – The fanciful story created by the imagination during the ordinary, physical waking state of the human consciousness.

Dermatologies of the consciousness – The compound expression attributed to the conventional, physicalist sciences that are subordinated to the Newtonian-Cartesian, mechanistic paradigm and focus their research only upon the soma, because they do not avail themselves of the instrumentation necessary for direct, technical investigation of the consciousness itself; dermatologies of the intraphysical consciousness; periconsciential sciences.

Desoma (*de + soma*) – Somatic deactivation, impending and inevitable for all intraphysical consciousnesses; final projection; *first death;* biological death; monothanatosis. *First* desoma, or simply desoma, is the deactivation of the human body or soma. *Second* desoma is the deactivation of the holochakra. *Third* desoma is the deactivation of the psychosoma.

Desomatics – The study of the physical context of desoma and of the psychological, social and medicolegal contexts related to deactivation of the soma. It is a subdiscipline of conscientiology.

Destructive macro-PK – Harmful PK (psychokinesis) capable of causing injuries to the intraphysical consciousness. Destructive macro-PK can even prove fatal to the soma.

Discoincidence – The state of non-alignment of the vehicles (holosoma) of manifestation of the consciousness.

Domiciliary holothosene – The holothosene specific to the intraphysical consciousness' physical base, energetically shielded bedroom and extraphysical clinic.

Dream – The natural consciential state which is intermediary between the ordinary, physical waking state and natural sleep. Dreams are characterized by a set of ideas and images that present themselves to the consciousness. The afflictive dream that has the effect of agitation, anguish and oppression is termed: *nightmare; night terror; nightmarish hallucination.*

Egokarma (*ego + karma*) – The principle of cause and effect active in the evolution of the consciousness, when centered exclusively on the ego itself. The state wherein free will is restricted by infantile egocentrism. The word *karma* is another of our *critical neologistic* *limits.* The author has not encountered another single, international, word that is more adequate, or appropriate, to put in its place and combat the *philosophical preconception* that exists with respect to this term (as well as its derivations and cognates). What is above all important, in this context, is *conceptual content* and not *linguistic form.* We live in *deficiencyland*, but consciential evolution proceeds with holo*karm*ology.

Egothosene (*ego + tho + sen + e*) – The same as self-thosene; the *unit of measurement* of consciential egotism according to conscientiology or, more precisely, according to conscientiometry.

Energetic dimension – The energetic dimension of consciousnesses; the holochakral dimension; the *three-and-a-half* dimension. The natural dimension of the holochakra.

Energetic maxispringtime – The condition of a maximized or prolonged energetic springtime.

Energetic minispringtime – The condition of a minimal or ephemeral energetic springtime.

Energetic springtime – The more-or-less long-lasting personal condition wherein one's consciential energies (CEs) exhibit an optimal, healthy, constructive profile.

Energetic springtime by two – The energetic springtime of the evolutionary duo, the partners of which truly love each other and control the application of healthy consciential energy with complete lucidity, building their existential programs through consciential gestations.

Energivorous – Energy consuming, energy draining; in reference to intruder(s).

Enumerology – The didactic technique of processing texts based on informative self-critiquing.

Evolutient – The consciousness that is in the process of evolution and utilizing the services of a conscientiotherapist to further this process; outworn synonym: patient.

Evolutiologist – The consciousness which assists in the intelligent coordination of the existential program, or the consciential evolution of one or more consciousnesses of the same karmic group. The evolutionary condition between the petifree consciousness and *serenissimus.* A more adequate expression than *evolutionary orienter.*

Evolutiology – The subdiscipline of conscientiology that studies the evolution of the consciousness, which is addressed in a high-quality, integral manner. This subject is specifically related to the evolutiologist or evolutionary orienter.

Evolutionary duo – Two consciousnesses that interact positively in joint evolution; the existential condition of *cooperative evolutivity* by two.

Evolutionary orienter – See *evolutiologist.*

Existential completism – The condition wherein the existential program of the human consciousness is complete.

Existential incompletism – The condition wherein the existential program of the human consciousness is incomplete.

Existential inversion – An advanced evolutionary technique consisting of inverting sociocultural values and projects in human life, according to the principles of projectiology and conscientiology. It is based upon the prioritization of and the fulltime dedication to the execution of the existential program, beginning at a young age.

Existential inverter – The intraphysical consciousness who is inclined to execute existential inversion in intraphysical life.

Existential maximoratorium – The condition of the greater existential moratorium which is given to an existential *completist*. It is an addition to his/her completed existential program. It is therefore the execution of a *healthy extension* to an existential mandate that has been concluded.

Existential maxiprogram – The maximal existential program having a *wholesale approach*, or targeting the execution of tasks of applied universalism and maxifraternity with polykarmic bases.

Existential minimoratorium – The condition of the lesser existential moratorium or one which happens to the *incompletist* intraphysical consciousness in order for him/her to compensate for a *holokarmic deficit* (deficit-based) or to achieve the condition of existential completism regarding his/her existential program. It is therefore the finishing of a still incomplete existential mandate.

Existential miniprogram – The minimum, *retail-oriented*, existential program targeting the execution of a minimal, groupkarmic task.

Existential moratorium – An extension of (a complement to) intraphysical life which is provided to select intraphysical consciousnesses according to their holokarmic merit. The existential moratorium can be either deficit-based (lesser), an existential minimoratorium; or can be profit-based (greater), an existential maximoratorium, with regard to the results of the individual's existential program.

Existential multicompletism – Existential completism obtained through the execution of various existential programs in diverse consecutive intraphysical lives (existential seriality).

Existential program – The specific program of each intraphysical consciousness, in his/her intraphysical existence.

Existential recyclability – The quality of the intraphysical execution of existential recycling.

Existential recycler – The intraphysical consciousness who is inclined to execute existential recycling.

Existential recycling – The evolutionary technique in which the intraphysical consciousness adopts a new set of values and priorities in his/her life, enabling the execution of the existential program.

Existential robotization – The condition of a tropospheric intraphysical consciousness who is excessively enslaved by intraphysicality or four-dimensionality.

Existential self-mimicry – Imitation on the part of the intraphysical consciousness of his/her own experiences or past experiences, whether they pertain to his/her current intraphysical life or previous intraphysical lives.

Existential seriality – 1. Evolutionary existential sequencing of the consciousness; successive existences; intraphysical rebirths in series. 2. Human or intraphysical life. Synonym outworn and exhausted by excessive use: *reincarnation;* this archaic word no longer serves those more serious individuals dedicated to leading-edge consciousness research.

Extraphysical – Relative to that which is outside, or beyond, the *intra*physical or human state; the consciential state *less* physical than the soma.

Extraphysical agenda – A written list of high-priority extraphysical, consciential targets – beings, places or ideas – that the projected projector seeks to gradually reach, in a chronological manner, establishing intelligent plans for its own development.

Extraphysical approach – The contacting of one consciousness by another consciousness in the extraphysical dimensions.

Extraphysical catatonia – The fixed condition wherein a projected intraphysical consciousness performs repeated stereotypical acts that are generally useless or dispensable in terms of its evolution.

Extraphysical clinic – The extraphysical treatment center of the intraphysical epicenter (penta practitioner). The resources and extraphysical *installations* of the extraphysical clinic are numerous and remarkable. The extraphysical clinic is a domiciliary holothosene.

Extraphysical community – A group of extraphysical consciousnesses living together in an extraphysical dimension.

Extraphysical consciousness – The paracitizen of an extraphysical society; a consciousness which no longer has a soma. Outworn synonym: *discarnate.*

Extraphysical euphoria – The condition of euphoria experienced after somatic deactivation, generated due to the reasonably satisfactory completion of the existential program; *post-mortem* euphoria; para-euphoria; postsomatic euphoria.

Extraphysical gang raid – The action of a group of energivorous extraphysical consciousnesses, including extraphysical blindguides, in the paratropospheric dimensions, with the objective of vampirizing the intraphysical consciousnesses in the environments of intraphysical celebrations or events which gather persons who are predisposed to the condition of collective victimization through consciential energies.

Extraphysical melancholy – The condition of extraphysical, postsomatic or *post-mortem* melancholy due to the unsatisfactory execution of the existential program; paramelancholy.

Extraphysical monitoring – The condition wherein assistance is provided by healthy extraphysical consciousnesses to a balanced intraphysical consciousness, while that intraphysical consciousness is performing balanced tasks of consolation or clarification.

Extraphysical precognition (Latin: *pre*, before; *cognoscere*, to know) – The perceptive faculty through which the consciousness, while fully projected outside the human body, becomes aware of unknown upcoming facts, as well as objects, scenes and distant forms in the future.

Extraphysical romance – The set of acts whereby an intraphysical consciousness dates or maintains a healthy or positive romantic relationship while projected outside the body.

Extraphysical society – Society of extraphysical consciousnesses.

Free consciousness (Latin: *con* + *scientia, with knowledge*) (FC) – The consciousness – or, more precisely: the extraphysical consciousness – which has definitively freed itself (deactivation) from the psychosoma or emotional parabody and the series of lifetimes. The free consciousness is situated in the *evolutionary hierarchy* above *Homo sapiens serenissimus.*

Geoenergy (*geo* + *energy*) – Immanent energy (IE) deriving from the soil or earth and absorbed by the intraphysical consciousness through the *pre-kundalini.* Archaic expression: *telluric energy.*

Golden cord – The alleged energetic element – similar to a remote control – that maintains the mentalsoma connected to the parabrain of the psychosoma.

Graphothosene (*grapho* + *tho* + *sen* + *e*) – The *thosenic signature* of the human or intraphysical consciousness.

Groupality – The quality of the evolutionary group of the consciousness; the condition of evolutivity in group.

Groupkarma (*group* + *karma*) – The principle of cause and effect active in the evolution of the consciousness, when centered in the evolutionary group. The state of individual free will, when connected to the evolutionary group.

Groupkarmic course – The set of the consciousness' levels within the evolutionary consciential group.

Groupkarmic interprison – The condition of groupkarmic inseparability of the evolutionary consciential principle or the consciousness.

Groupthosene (*group* + *tho* + *sen* + *e*) – The sectarian, corporatist and antipolykarmic thosene; however, the groupthosene can also be constructive.

Gynosoma (*gyno* + *soma*) – The female human body, or that which is specific to a woman, specialized in the animal reproduction of the intraphysical life of the intraphysical consciousness; the aphrodisiac body.

Gynothosene (*gyno* + *tho* + *sen* + *e*) –The thosene specific to feminine language and communicability.

Hallucination (Latin: *hallucinari,* to err) – The apparent perception of an external object that is not present at the moment; mental error in the perception of the senses, which is baseless in an objective reality.

Helper – The extraphysical consciousness which is auxiliary to one or more intraphysical consciousnesses; extraphysical benefactor. Archaic equivalent expressions that have been outworn through continued use: *guardian angel; angel of light; guide; mentor; spirit guide.*

Heterothosene (*hetero* + *tho* + *sen* + *e*) – The thosene of another in relation to ourselves.

Holobiography – The multidimensional, multiexistential personal history of the consciousness.

Holochakra (*holo* + *chakra*) – The energetic parabody of the human consciousness.

Holochakral existence – Intraphysical life or the lifetime of the human consciousness.

Holochakral seduction – The energetic action of one consciousness upon another (or others) with a more or less conscious intention of domination.

Holochakrality – The quality of the manifestations of the intraphysical consciousness deriving from the holochakra or energetic body.

Holokarma (*holo* + *karma*) – The grouping of the 3 types of consciential actions and reactions – egokarma, groupkarma and polykarma – within the principles of cause and effect, that are active in the evolution of the consciousness.

Holomaturity (*holo* + *maturity*) – The condition of integrated maturity – biological, psychological, holosomatic and multidimensional – of the human consciousness.

Holomemory (*holo* + *memory*) – The causal, compound, multimillenary, multiexistential, implacable, uninterrupted, personal memory that retains all facts relative to the consciousness; multimemory; polymemory.

Holo-orgasm (*holo* + *orgasm*) – Holosomatic orgasm; maximum ecstasy generated by the energies of the entire holosoma.

Holosoma (*holo* + *soma*) – The set of vehicles of manifestation of the intraphysical consciousness: soma, holochakra, psychosoma and mentalsoma; and of the extraphysical consciousness: psychosoma and mentalsoma.

Holosomatic homeostasis – The integrated, healthy state of the holosoma's harmony.

Holosomatic interfusion – The state of maximal sympathetic assimilation between two consciousnesses.

Holosomatics – The specific study of the holosoma. It is a subdiscipline of conscientiology.

Holotheca – Compilation of information from artifacts of knowledge.

Holothosene (*holo* + *tho* + *sen* + *e*) – Aggregated or consolidated thosenes.

Homo sapiens serenissimus – The consciousness which is integrally experiencing the condition of lucid serenism. Popular synonym: *serenissimus*.

Homothosene (*homo* + *tho* + *sen* + *e*) – The thosene of telepathic transmission and reception; the *unit of measurement* in telepathy, according to conscientiometry.

Hyperacuity – The quality of maximum lucidity of the intraphysical consciousness, achieved through the recuperation – to the maximum degree possible – of cons.

Hyperthosene (*hyper* + *tho* + *sen* + *e*) – Heuristic thosene; original idea of a discovery; neophilic thosene; *unit of measurement* of invention, according to conscientiometry.

Hypnagogy (Greek: *hipnos*, sleep; and *agogos*, leader, bringer) – The transitional twilight condition of the consciousness between the ordinary, physical waking state and the state of natural sleep. It is an altered state of consciousness.

Hypnopompy (Greek: *hipnos*, sleep; and *pompikós*, procession) – The transitional condition of natural sleep, introductory to physical awakening, during the semi-sleep state that precedes the act of awakening. This state is characterized by oneiric images with auditory effects and hallucinatory visions that continue after awakening. It is an altered state of consciousness.

Hypothosene (*hypo* + *tho* + *sen* + *e*) – The same as protothosene or phytothosene.

Immanent energy (IE) – Energy that is primary, vibratory, essential, multiform, impersonal, diffuse and dispersed in all objects or *realities* of the universe, in an omnipotent fashion. Immanent energy has still not been tamed by the human consciousness. It is too subtle to be discovered and detected by existing technological equipment.

Incomplete couple – The couple composed of a man and a woman who do *not* form an intimate couple (a couple that practices the complete sex act), but who, nevertheless, maintain strong affectionate ties.

Integrated maturity – The state of a more evolved consciential maturity, beyond biological (physical) or mental (psychological) maturity; holomaturity.

Inter-vivos apparition – Appearance of the consciousness of the projected human projector to intraphysical consciousnesses.

Interconsciential climate – The condition of multi-understanding in an interconsciential encounter, established through similar thosenes, especially those *with an emphasis* on consciential energies (CEs). There are interconsciential climates, *mini-climates* and *maxi-climates*.

Interdimensionality – Interaction, interrelation or interconsciential communication between intraphysical and extraphysical dimensions.

Intermissibility – The quality of the period of intermission between two intraphysical lives of a consciousness.

Intermission – The extraphysical period of the consciousness between two of its physical lives; intermissive period.

Intermissive course – The set of disciplines and theoretical and practical experiences administered to an extraphysical consciousness during the period of consciential intermission. This course occurs when one has achieved a certain evolutionary level within one's cycle of personal existences. The intermissive course objectifies consciential completism (existential completism) of the upcoming intraphysical life.

Intraconsciential compensation – The conscientiometric technique based upon the greater use of a consciential attribute that is more developed (strong trait) over another, or other less developed consciential attributes (weak traits) in the micro-universe of the intraphysical consciousness.

Intraconsciential recycling – Intraphysical, existential, *intra*consciential recycling or the cerebral renovation of the intraphysical consciousness through the creation of new synapses or interneuronal connections. The newly created synapses are capable of allowing the adjustment of the existential program, execution of existential recycling, existential inversion, the acquisition of new ideas, neothosenes, hyperthosenes and other neophilic conquests of the self-motivated human consciousness.

Intraconscientiality – The quality of the manifestations specific to the intimacy of the consciousness.

Intraphysical assistant – The intraphysical guardian of the projector's inactive human body that is emptied of the consciousness during lucid projection.

Intraphysical consciousness – Human personality; citizen of intraphysical society. Outworn synonym: *incarnate*.

Intraphysical euphoria – The condition of euphoria experienced before somatic deactivation that is generated by the reasonably satisfactory completion of the existential program; *pre-mortem* euphoria. The ideal condition predisposing one to have a positive existential moratorium.

Intraphysical melancholy – The condition of intraphysical or *premortem* melancholy generated by incompletion of the existential program.

Intraphysical society – The society of intraphysical consciousnesses; human society.

Intraphysicality – The condition of human, intraphysical life, or of the existence of the human consciousness.

Intrathosene (*intra* + *tho* + *sen* + *e*) – The *intra*consciential thosene of the human consciousness.

Intruder – The perturbed, ill, needy, anticosmoethical consciousness; especially an extraphysical consciousness when performing a thosenic intrusion upon an intraphysical consciousness.

Intrusion – Invasion of a consciousness by another; this can be through consciential energies (CEs) or the holochakra, psychosoma, holosoma, or thosenes. It can also be interconsciential or intraconsciential.

Intrusive stigma – An evolutionary failure or derailing that is always dramatic and generally pathological, generally stemming from consciential self-obcaecation. This process generates either intraphysical or extraphysical melancholy and often results in parapsychic accidents.

Intrusiveness – Ill, interconsciential thosenic intrusion. Archaic equivalent expression: *obsession*; many intraphysical consciousnesses are defensive regarding this word.

Joint projection – An experience outside the human body in which two or more projected intraphysical consciousnesses participate.

Locked existence – Human experience or lifetime without the production of lucid projections (LPs); tropospheric human life with only unconscious, vegetative projections that are characteristic of the state of evolutionary paracoma; locked lifetime.

Looseness of the holochakra – The condition of relative freedom of action of the energetic parabody of the intraphysical consciousness, relative to the psychosoma and soma.

Lucid projectability (LPB) – The lucid, projective paraphysiological quality of the consciousness that is capable of provoking its discoincidence or taking its vehicles of manifestation out from the alignment of its holosoma, even through the impulsion of its willpower.

Lucid projection (LP) – Projection of the intraphysical consciousness beyond the soma; extracorporeal experience; out-of-body experience (OBE).

Lucidity-recall binomial – The set of the two conditions that are indispensable to the intraphysical consciousness for his/her achievement of a fully satisfactory lucid projection (outside the soma).

Macrosoma (*macro + soma*) – The soma that is *supercustomized* for the execution of a specific existential program.

Materthosene (*mater + tho + sen + e*) – The mother-idea or matrix for the complete development of a thesis, theory or analysis, the *leitmotif*, major pillar or predominant thosene in a holothosene.

Maxifraternity – The most evolved, universalistic, interconsciential condition that is based on pure fraternity on the part of a self-unforgiving and heteroforgiving consciousness. Maxifraternity is an inevitable goal in the evolution of all consciousnesses. Synonym: megafraternity.

Maxithosene (*maxi + tho + sen + e*) – The thosene specific to FCs or free consciousnesses.

Megagoal – The consciousness' greater self-evolutionary objective.

Megapower – The evolved condition of great, cosmoethical lucidity of the consciousness.

Mega-strong-trait – The maximal strong trait of the consciousness.

Megathosene (*mega + tho + sen + e*) – The same as orthothosene.

Mega-weak-trait – The maximal weak trait of the consciousness.

Mentalsoma (*mental + soma*) – Mental body; *parabody* of discernment of the consciousness.

Paraphysiology – Physiology of the vehicles of manifestation of the consciousness, excluding the human body or soma. It is a subdiscipline of conscientiology.

Parapsychic – That which is paranormal or multidimensional in nature.

Parapsychic accident – Physical or psychological disturbance generated by sick energetic, intersciential influences, generally of an extraphysical or multidimensional origin.

Parapsychic signage – The existence, identification and self-aware use of the energetic, animic, parapsychic and extremely personal signs (indicators) that every intraphysical consciousness possesses.

Parapsychism – Parapsychic capacities of the consciousness.

Parapsychophysical repercussions – Reactions between 2 vehicles of consciential manifestation, when they come into contact with each other. This can occur between different vehicles of one consciousness or between similar vehicles of two or more consciousnesses. These repercussions can be intraphysical and extraphysical.

Parasanitary encapsulation – Assistential isolation and the temporary, energetic annulment of thosenic manifestations – notably energetic or intrusive ones – from one or more ill intraphysical and/or extraphysical consciousness, in the manner of sanitary isolation (quarantine) wards in hospitals for infectious and contagious illnesses with patients who present a high potential for disease, radioactive or toxic contamination.

Parathosene (*para* + *tho* + *sen* + *e*) – The thosene specific to the extraphysical consciousness.

Parawoman – The extraphysical consciousness having the appearance of a woman or a projected female intraphysical consciousness. Synonymous expression outworn through use: *female spiritual entity.*

Pathothosene (*patho* + *tho* + *sen* + *e*) – The pathological thosene or the thosene of consciential dementia; *mental peccadillo*; pathological will; sick intention; *cerebral rumination.*

Penile aura – The sexochakral energy around the penis, notably when in erection, perceivable by any motivated individual, especially by the sexually excited man.

Penta (*p* + *ene* + *ta*) – The multidimensional, daily, personal energetic task that receives continuous assistance from the helpers on a long-term basis or for the rest of one's life. Outworn expression: *passes-to-the-void.*

Personal experience (PE) – Practical, personal, direct, non-transferable experimentation of the intraphysical consciousness on his/her evolutionary way.

Personal principles – The set of guiding values and initiatives of consciential life which are chosen by the consciousness based upon holomaturity, multidimensionality and applied cosmoethics.

Petifree – The intraphysical consciousness who is permanently and totally free of intrusion, and is completely self-aware of being in this condition.

Phenomenon concomitant with LP – That which occurs either inside or outside of the time-space *continuum*, but does so simultaneously with the experience of the lucid projection, in a spontaneous and unexpected manner.

Physical base – The safe location, chosen by the intraphysical consciousness for leaving the soma stationary or resting while lucidly projecting to other, external, consciential dimensions; *duodrome*. A domiciliary projectiogenic holothosene. It is directly related to: the energetically shielded chamber; penta; consciential epicenter; extraphysical clinic; *projectarium; precognitarium;* and *retrocognitarium.*

Phytothosene (*phyto* + *tho* + *sen* + *e*) – The rudimentary thosene of a plant; the *lexical unit* of a plant, according to conscientiology.

Podosoma (*podo* + *soma*) – The soma, when considered specifically in regard to the application of the feet or work performed with the feet, as in the case of a soccer player.

Polykarma (*poly* + *karma*) – The principle of cause and effect, active in the evolution of the consciousness, when centered in the sense of and the experience of cosmic maxifraternity, beyond egokarma and groupkarma.

Polykarmality – The quality of the polykarmic manifestations of the consciousness.

Postsomatic intermission – The extraphysical period of the consciousness immediately following somatic deactivation.

Precognitarium – The physical base which is technically prepared for the production of precognitive LPs (lucid projections).

Pre-couple – The preliminary, initial or flirting stage of human sexuality, a practice within intraphysical society.

Pre-intraphysical mandate – The existential program for human life, planned before the intraphysical rebirth of the consciousness; existential program.

Prekundalini – The secondary plantar (sole of the foot) chakra. There are 2 plantochakras in the holosoma of the intraphysical consciousness. This is an expression pertaining to conscientiology.

Pre-serenissimus – The intraphysical or extraphysical consciousness that does not yet live a life of lucid serenism.

Presomatic intermission – The extraphysical period of the consciousness immediately preceding its intraphysical rebirth.

Primothosene (*primo* + *tho* + *sen* + *e*) – The same as the *primary cause of the universe*; the first compound thought. This term has no plural form.

Projectarium – The physical base which is technically prepared for the production of projections of the consciousness (PCs).

Projectiocritique – Critiquing performed with a projectiological perspective. It is a subdiscipline of conscientiology.

Projectiography – The technical study of projectiological registers. It is a subdiscipline of conscientiology.

Projectiology (Latin: *projectio,* projection; Greek: *logos,* treatise) – The science that studies projections of the consciousness and their effects, including projections of consciential energies (CEs) outward from the holosoma. It is a subdiscipline of conscientiology.

Projectiotherapy – The science of the prophylaxes and therapies derived from the research and techniques of projectiology.

Projective mental target – The predetermined goal that an intraphysical consciousness plans to reach using the will, intention, mental focus and decision, upon finding itself lucid outside the body.

Projective phenomenon – The specific parapsychic occurrence within the scope of projectiology research.

Projective recess – The existential phase of the intraphysical consciousness characterized by the spontaneous cessation – almost always temporary – of lucid projective experiences, within a sequence of intensive experiences.

Protothosene (*proto + tho + sen + e*) – The more rudimentary thosene; the same as phytothosene or hypothosene.

Psychosoma (Greek: *psyche,* soul; *soma,* body) – The emotional parabody of the consciousness; the *objective body* of the intraphysical consciousness. Outworn expression: astral body.

Rethosene (*re + tho + sen + e*) – The repeated thosene. The same as *mono*thosene, fixed idea, or monoideism.

Retrocognitarium – The physical base which is technically prepared for the production of retrocognitive lucid projections (LPs).

Retrocognition (Latin: *retro,* back; *cognoscere,* to know) – The perceptive faculty through which the intraphysical consciousness becomes aware of facts, scenes, forms, objects, successes and experiences that pertain to a time in the distant past. These issues are commonly related to one's holomemory.

Retrothosene (*retro + tho + sen + e*) – The thosene specific to self-retrocognitions; the same as the *engram* of mnemotechnics; the *unit of measurement* of retrocognitions, according to conscientiometry.

Self-conscientiality – The quality of the level of self-knowledge on the part of the consciousness; megaknowledge.

Self-mimeticity – The consciential quality of existential self-mimicry.

Self-projection – Departure of the intraphysical consciousness to another consciential dimension in the mentalsoma or the psychosoma, when intentional or provoked by the will.

Self-thosene (*self* + *tho* + *sen* + *e*) – The thosene of the consciousness itself.

Self-unforgiver – The intraphysical consciousness who, in the individual's self-discipline, does not pardon his/her own errors or omissions, in order to eliminate conscious self-corruption. This healthy condition is contrary to the likewise healthy condition of *hetero*forgiver, a sincere *universal forgiver* of all beings, forever – *a basic principle of maxifraternity.*

Semilucid projection (SLP) – The oneiric experience in which the projected intraphysical consciousness finds itself to be partially lucid, in a disordered manner. It is not an ideal consciential projection; lucid dream.

Sene (*sen* + *e*) – Sentiment and consciential energy.

Serenissimus – Popular name for *Homo sapiens serenissimus.*

Seriality – The quality of the consciousness subjected to existential seriality (rebirth cycle).

Sexochakra (*sex* + *o* + *chakra*) – The root or basic sexual chakra of the human consciousness. An ancient expression related to the consciential energy (CE) of this chakra: *kundalini* (*the serpentine fire*).

Sexosoma (*sex* + *o* + *soma*) – The soma when considered specifically in relation to its sex.

Sexosomatics – The specific study of the soma in regard to its sex, or sexosoma, and its relations with the intraphysical consciousness, whether male or female. It is a subdiscipline of conscientiology.

Sexothosene (*sex* + *o* + *tho* + *sen* + *e*) – The sexual fantasy; the *unit of measurement* of mental adultery, according to conscientiometry.

Shielded chamber – The energetically defended and extraphysically "aseptic" private room in a house or apartment, especially a bedroom; intrusion-proof bedroom.

Silver cord – The energetic connection between the soma and the psychosoma which is present in a projection of the consciousness, resulting from the holochakral energies.

Sleep – The natural state of rest in humans and superior animals that is especially characterized by the normal and periodic suppression of perceptive activity, voluntary motor activity and daily interpersonal exchanges, through the relaxation of the senses and muscles, a reduction in the heart and respiratory rates, as well as by oneiric activity, during which the organism recuperates from fatigue.

Soma – Human body; physical body. The body of the individual of the *Animal* kingdom, *Chordata* phylum, *Mammiferous* class, *Primate* order, *Hominidae* family, *Homo* genus, and *Homo sapiens* species, being the most elevated level of animal on this planet; nonetheless, this is the most rudimentary vehicle of the holosoma of the human consciousness.

State of suspended animation – That state in which the essential vital functions of the cellular body of the intraphysical consciousness are temporarily suspended, whereupon its normal physiological conditions later return. In certain cases, this occurs without any damage being done to one's personal health, the cells surviving in a metabolism of human hibernation.

Strong trait – The strong trait of the personality of the intraphysical consciousness; the positive component of the structure of the consciential micro-universe that impels the evolution of the consciousness.

Subthosene (*sub + tho + sen + e*) – The thosene having an emphasis on consciential energy restricted to the abdominal brain, notably energy of the umbilicochakra; the *unit of measurement* of the abdominal brain, according to conscientiometry.

Sympathetic assimilation – The willful assimilation of consciential energies (CEs). This condition is often accompanied by the decoding of a set of the thosenes of one or more consciousness.

Sympathetic de-assimilation – Cessation of sympathetic assimilation of consciential energies (CEs) performed through the impulsion of one's will, normally by installing the vibrational state (VS).

Tachythosene (*tachy + tho + sen + e*) – The rapid flowing thosene, pertaining to the tachypsychic (quick-thinking) intraphysical consciousness.

Telethosene (*tele + tho + sen + e*) – The same as homothosene.

Theorice (*theor + ice*) – The experience of combined theory and practice, on the part of the intraphysical or extraphysical consciousness.

Thosen (*tho + sen*) – Thought and sentiment.

Thosene (*tho + sen + e*) – The practical unit of manifestation of the consciousness, according to conscientiology, that considers thought or idea (concept), sentiment or emotion, and CE (consciential energy), as being 3 inseparable elements.

Thosener – The instrument through which the consciousness manifests its thoughts and acts. In the specific case of the intraphysical consciousness, the fundamental thosener is the soma.

Thosenity – The quality of one's thosenic awareness.

Thosenization – The process whereby the consciousness generates thosenes.

Trithanatosis – The deactivation and discarding of the psychosoma with the subsequent entrance of the consciousness of the *Homo sapiens serenissimus* into the condition of free consciousness (FC); *third desoma*.

Umbilicochakra (*umbilic + o + chakra*) – The umbilical chakra (located above the navel) or that chakra related to the (abdominal) physiology and paraphysiology of the human consciousness.

Universalism – The set of ideas derived from the universality of the basic laws of nature and the universe which, through the natural evolution of the consciousness, inevitably becomes its dominant philosophy; cosmism.

Vehicle of the consciousness – The instrument or body through which the consciousness manifests in intraphysicality (intraphysical consciousness) and in the extraphysical dimensions (projected intraphysical consciousness and extraphysical consciousness).

Verbaction (*verb + action*) – The practical interaction of what is said and done in the coherent behavior of the consciousness; a result of one's word being ratified by example through the testimonies experienced by the intraphysical consciousness.

Vibrational state (VS) – The technical condition of the maximal dynamization of the energies of the holochakra, through the impulsion of the will.

Virus of intraphysical society – Any social weak trait in the intraphysical life of the human consciousness.

Volitional intrusion – Invasion of the will of one consciousness upon another by way of heterosuggestion or heterohypnosis.

Waking discoincidence – The parapsychic condition of the intraphysical consciousness projector in which one perceives that the psychosoma is outside the state of coincidence, while in the full ordinary, physical waking state, without feeling completely integrated in the soma. This generates the intensification of paraperceptions and energetic and parapsychic phenomena.

Weak trait – The weak trait of the personality of the intraphysical consciousness; the negative component of the structure of the consciential micro-universe that the consciousness has still not been able to discard or rid itself of.

Xenophrenia (Greek: *xenos,* strange; *phrem,* mind) – The state of the human consciousness outside the normal pattern of the ordinary, physical waking state, induced by physical, physiological, psychological, pharmacological or parapsychic agents; altered state of consciousness.

Xenothosene (*xeno + tho + sen + e*) – The intrusive thosene of the intruder in the occurrences of thosenic intrusion or intrusiveness; *mental wedge; unit of measurement* of interconsciential intrusion, according to conscientiometry.

Zoothosene (*zoo + tho + sen + e*) – The thosene of the sub-human animal lacking self-conscientiality; *unit of measurement* of the consciential principle of the sub-human animal, according to conscientiometry.

FILMOGRAPHY

The movies that follow (compiled in 1998) are listed here as a source of additional information regarding the subjects approached in this book, and also - why not - as a possibility for entertainment.

Movies can be used as an illustration for certain contexts and also to inspire certain ideas or approaches. Nevertheless, the majority lack truthfulness to the multidimensionality.

Obviously, the artistic sense, the fantasy, the sensationalism, ignorance and pressure for a big box-office hit cause many distortions in regards to extraphysical reality. Always maintain your critical sense, discernment and, inclusive, in some of them, energetic self-defense.

It is important to emphasize here the universality of the subjects of seriality, retrocognition, survival of physical death, and other correlated topics, as represented by the following statistic in regards to the list of movies indicated.

- *Number of films*: 92
- *Countries of production*: 16 - Germany, Argentina, Austria, Canada, Denmark, EUA, France, Hong Kong, India, England, Italy, Yugoslavia, Japan, Mexico, Portugal, Sweden.
- *Languages*: 11 - German, Cantonese, Spanish, French, Dutch, English, Italian Japanese, Portuguese, Serbian and Swedish.
- *Genre*: 10 - action, adventure, comedy, crime, drama, fiction, scientific, romance, satira and horror.
- *Media*: 5 - sounded-color-movie, silent-black-and-white-movie, sounded-black-and-white-movie, color-TV, black-and-white-TV.
- *Largest number of re-makes*: 9 - *She*
- *Year of oldest movie*: 1908 - *She*

1. Adding Machine, The (1969)
USA 1969 Color
Produced by: Regional
Language: English
Genre/keyword: Drama / fantasy / murder / employment / after-life / electric-chair / based-on-play
Directed by Jerome Epstein
Written by Jerome Epstein & Elmer Rice (play)

2. Almost an Angel (1990)

USA 1990 ColorProduced by: Ironbark Films
Language: English
Genre/keyword: Comedy / angel
Runtime: USA:96
Directed by John Cornell
Cast: Paul Hogan: Terry Dean; Elias Koteas: Steve; Linda
Kozlowski: Rose Garner; Doreen Lang: Mrs. Garner
Written by Paul Hogan
Produced by John Cornell & Paul Hogan (executive), Mark
Turnbull (associate), Kelly Van Horn (line)

3. Always the Woman (1922)

USA 1922 Black and White
Produced by: Betty Compson Productions
Genre/keyword: Romance / Drama / reincarnation
Directed by Arthur Rosson
Cast (in credits order): Betty Compson: Celia Thaxter; Emory
Johnson: Herbert Boone; Arthur Delmore: Gregory Gallup
Written by Arthur Rosson & Perley Poore Sheehan (story)

4. Always (1989)

USA 1989 Color (DeLuxe)
Produced by: Universal Pictures US / Amblin Entertainment
Language: English
Genre/keyword: Drama / Romance / guardian-angel / reincarna-
tion / aviation / fantasy / firefighting / grief / true-love / pilot
Runtime: USA:106 / UK:103 / Netherlands:121
Directed by Steven Spielberg
Cast (in credits order): Richard Dreyfuss: Pete Sandich; Holly
Hunter: Dorinda Durston; John Goodman: Al Yackey; Audrey
Hepburn: Hap
Written by Chandler Sprague and David Boehm (story: A Guy
Named Joe), Frederick Hazlitt Brennan (adaptation A Guy
Named Joe), Dalton Trumbo (screenplay A Guy Named Joe),
Jerry Belson
Produced by Kathleen Kennedy, Frank Marshall (I), Steven
Spielberg
Remake of Guy Named Joe, A (1943)

5. Amy and the Angel (1981) (TV)

USA 1981 Color
Genre/keyword: Adventure / Comedy / afterlife
Runtime: USA:45
Directed by Ralph Rosenblum (I)
Cast (in alphabetical order): Jennifer Ashe: Sara; James Earl Jones:
The Angel Gabriel; Matthew Modine: Ralph; Rochelle Oliver:
Mrs. York; Meg Ryan: Denise
Written by Bruce Harmon
Executive Producer: Frank Doelger

6. Attack of the Mayan Mummy (1964)

USA 1964 Black and White
Language: English
Genre/keyword: Horror / mummy
Runtime: USA:70
Directed by Rafael Portillo & Jerry Warren
Cast (in credits order): Nina Knight; Richard Webb; John Burton
Written by Guillermo Calderón & Alfredo Salazar (also story),
Jerry Warren
Produced by Guillermo Calderón (original version), Jerry Warren
(final American version)

7. Audrey Rose (1977)

USA 1977 Color (DeLuxe)
Produced by: United Artists US
Language: English
Genre/keyword: Horror / reincarnation
Runtime: USA:113
Directed by Robert Wise
Cast (in credits order): Marsha Mason: Janice Templeton;
Anthony Hopkins: Elliot Hoover; John Beck (II): Bill Templeton
Written by Frank De Felitta (also novel)
Produced by Frank De Felitta & Joe Wizan

8. Beetlejuice (1988)

USA 1988 Color (Technicolor)
Produced by: Warner Bros. US / Geffen Pictures
Language: English
Genre/keyword: Comedy / fantasy / ghost / haunted-house /
music / screwball / surreal / afterlife
Runtime: USA:92

Directed by Tim Burton
Cast: Alec Baldwin: Adam; Geena Davis: Barbara; Annie
McEnroe: Jane Butterfield; Michael Keaton: Betelgeuse
Written by Michael McDowell (also story), Warren Skaaren, Larry
Wilson (I) (story)
Produced by Eric Angelson (I) (associate), Michael Bender,
Richard Hashimoto, Larry Wilson (I)

9. Belle histoire, La (1992)
Also Known As: Beautiful Story, The (1992)
France 1992 Color
Produced by: Les Films 13 FR / TF1 Films Productions FR
Language: French
Directed by Claude Lelouch
Written by Claude Lelouch

10. Between Two Worlds (1944)
USA 1944 Black and White
Produced by: Warner Bros. US
Language: English
Genre/keyword: Drama / fantasy / afterlife
Runtime: USA:112
Directed by Edward A. Blatt
Cast: John Garfield: Tom Prior; Paul Henreid: Henry; Sydney
Greenstreet: Thompson
Written by Daniel Fuchs, Sutton Vane (play Outward Bound)
Produced by Mark Hellinger

11. Beyond Tomorrow (1940)
USA 1940 Black and White
Produced by: RKO Radio Pictures
Language: English
Genre/keyword: Romance / christmas / fantasy / afterlife / senti-
mental
Runtime: USA:84
Directed by A. Edward Sutherland
Cast: Harry Carey Sr.: George Melton; C. Aubrey Smith: Alan
'Chad' Chadwick; Charles Winninger: Michael O'Brien
Written by Mildred Cram (story) and Adele Commandini (story)
Produced by Adele Commandini (associate), Lee Garmes

12. Bill & Ted's Bogus Journey (1991)

Also Known As: Bill and Ted Go to Hell (1991) (working title)
USA 1991 Color
Produced by: Interscope Communications
Language: English
Genre/keyword: Adventure / Comedy / historical / supernatural /
time-travel / afterlife / albert-einstein / android / fantasy / heaven /
hell / devil / game / robot / rock'n'roll / possession / séance /
death / god
Runtime: USA:98
Directed by Peter Hewitt (I)
Cast: Keanu Reeves: Ted "Theodore" Logan; Alex Winter: Bill S.
Preston/Granny; William Sadler: Grim Reaper
Written by Chris Matheson, Ed Solomon (I)
Produced by Paul Aaron (co-producer), Robert W. Cort (executive), Stephen Deutsch (II) (co-executive), Ted Field (executive),
Rick Finkelstein (executive), Scott Kroopf, Neil A. Machlis (supervising), Chris Matheson (co-producer), Ed Solomon (I) (co-producer), Barry Spikings (executive), Erwin Stoff (co-producer), Connie
Tavel (co-executive)

13. Bride and the Beast, The (1958)

Also Known As: Queen of the Gorillas (1958)
USA 1958 Black and White
Produced by: Allied Artists Pictures Corporation US
Language: English
Genre/keyword: Horror / gorilla / reincarnation
Runtime: USA:78
Directed by Adrian Weiss
Cast: Charlotte Austin: Laura; Lance Fuller: Dan Fuller; Johnny
Roth: Taro
Written by Adrian Weiss (story), Edward D. Wood Jr.
Produced by Adrian Weiss, Louis Weiss (I)

14. Bröderna Lejonhjärta (1977)

Also Known As: Brothers Lionheart, The (1977)
Sweden 1977 Color (Eastmancolor)
Produced by: Artfilm / Svensk Filmindustri (SF)
Language: Swedish
Genre/keyword: Adventure / Children's / afterlife / legend /
based-on-novel
Runtime: Sweden:102

Directed by Olle Hellbom
Cast: Staffan Götestam: Jonatan; Lars Söderdahl: Skorpan; Allan
Edwall: Mattias
Written by Astrid Lindgren (I) (also novel)
Produced by Olle Hellbom, Olle Nordemar

15. Bunker Bean (1936)
USA 1936 Black and White
Produced by: RKO Radio Pictures
Language: English
Genre/keyword: based-on-novel
Runtime: USA:67
Also Known As: His Majesty Bunker Bean (1936)
Directed by William Hamilton (I); Edward Killy
Cast: Owen Davis Jr.: Bunker Bean; Louise Latimer: Mary Kent;
Robert McWade: J.C. Kent
Written by Lee Wilson Dodd (play), James Gow, Edmund H.
North, Harry Leon Wilson (novel), Dorothy Yost
Produced by William Sistrom
Remake of His Majesty, Bunker Bean (1918)

16. Buried Treasure (1921)
USA 1921 Black and White
Produced by: Cosmopolitan Pictures
Language: English
Genre/keyword: Adventure / fantasy
Directed by George D. Baker
Cast: Marion Davies: Pauline Vandermuellen; Norman Kerry: Dr.
John Grant; Anders Randolf: William Vandermuellen
Edith Shayne: Mrs. Vandermuellen
Written by George D. Baker

17. Casper (1995)
USA 1995 Color (DeLuxe)
Produced by: Universal Pictures US / Amblin Entertainment /
The Harvey Entertainment Company
Language: English
Genre/keyword: Adventure / fantasy / ghost / part-animated /
based-on-comic
Runtime: USA:101 / UK:100 / Germany:100
Directed by Brad Silberling
Cast: Christina Ricci: Kat; Bill Pullman: Dr. Harvey

Written by (in credits order) Joseph Oriolo (book Casper, the
Friendly Ghost), Seymour Reit (book Casper, the Friendly Ghost)
Sherri Stoner, Deanna Oliver
Produced by Paul Deason (associate), Jeff Franklin (co-producer),
Gerald R. Molen (executive), Jeffrey A. Montgomery (executive),
Steven Spielberg (executive), Steve Waterman (co-producer),
Colin Wilson (II)
Version of Casper the Friendly Ghost (1945)

18. Chances Are (1989)
USA 1989 Color (Technicolor)
Produced by: TriStar Pictures
Language: English
Genre/keyword: Comedy / Romance / reincarnation / title-based-
on-song
Runtime: USA:108
Directed by Emile Ardolino
Cast: Cybill Shepherd: Corinne Jeffries; Robert Downey Jr.: Alex
Finch; Ryan O'Neal: Philip Train
Written by Perry Howze & Randy Howze
Produced by Leslie Benziger (associate), Andrew Bergman (execu-
tive), Mike Lobell, Neil A. Machlis (executive)

19. Cleo/Leo (1989)
USA 1989 Color
Produced by: DB Media / Platinum Pictures
Language: English
Genre/keyword: Comedy / sex-change / transsexual / reincarna-
tion
Directed, written and produced by by Chuck Vincent
Remade as Switch (1991)

20. Creature of Destruction (1967)
USA 1967 Color
Produced by: Azalea Pictures
Language: English
Genre/keyword: Horror / Sci-Fi / monster / hypnotism / murder /
reincarnation
Runtime: USA:80
Directed by Larry Buchanan
Cast: Les Tremayne: Dr. John Basso; Aron Kincaid: Captain
Theodore Dell; Pat Delaney: Doreena

Written by Enrique Touceda
Produced by Larry Buchanan
Remake of She Creature, The (1957)

21. Crowhaven Farm (1970) (TV)

USA 1970 Color
Produced by: Aaron Spelling Productions, Inc. US
Language: English
Genre/keyword: Drama / reincarnation
Runtime: USA:74
Directed by Walter Grauman
Cast: Hope Lange: Maggie Porter; Paul Burke: Ben Porter; Lloyd
Bochner: Kevin Pierce; John Carradine: Nate Cheever
Written by John McGreevey
Produced by Walter Grauman, John McGreevey (associate),
Aaron Spelling (executive)

22. Cyberella: Forbidden Passions (1996)

USA 1996 Color
Produced by: A Section 8 Production / Twilight Entertainment,
Inc. / Section 8 Production
Language: English
Genre/keyword: Sci-Fi / Romance / virtuosity / erotica / virtual-
reality / afterlife
Runtime: USA:87
Also Known As: Forbidden Passions (1996)
Directed by Jackie Garth
Cast: Debra K. Beatty: Mara; Marshall Hilliard: Bob; Rebecca
Taylor (III): Amy
Written by Randy Fontana
Produced by Alan B. Bursteen (executive) Suzi Mealing

23. Daibyonin (1993)

Japan 1993 Color
Language: Japanese
Genre/keyword: afterlife / cancer / tragicomedy
Runtime: Japan:116 / Germany:115
Also Known As: Last Dance, The (1993/II)
Directed by Juzo Itami
Produced by Yasushi Tamaoki

24. Dead Again (1991)

USA 1991 Black and White (Technicolor) / Color (Technicolor)
Produced by: Mirage / Paramount Pictures US
Language: English
Genre/keyword: Drama / Mystery / Romance / Thriller / murder
/ psychoanalysis / 1940s / reporter / scandal / wedding / composer
/ flashback / hypnotism / multiple-time-frames / passion / reincarnation / supernatural / amnesia
Runtime: USA:107
Directed by Kenneth Branagh
Cast: Kenneth Branagh: Mike Church/Roman Strauss; Andy
Garcia: Gray Baker; Emma Thompson: Amanda "Grace"
Sharp/Margaret Strauss
Lois Hall: Sister Constance
Written by Scott Frank
Produced by Lindsay Doran, Dennis Feldman (co-producer),
Charles H. Maguire, Sydney Pollack (executive)

25. Deadly Messages (1985) (TV)

USA 1985 Color (Metrocolor)
Produced by: Columbia Pictures Television US
Language: English
Genre/keyword: Thriller / ouija
Directed by Jack Bender
Cast: Kathleen Beller: Laura Daniels; Michael Brandon (I):
Michael Krasnick; Dennis Franz: Detective Max Lucas
Written by William Bleich
Produced by Paul Pompian

26. Defending Your Life (1991)

USA 1991 Color (Technicolor)
Produced by: Warner Bros. US
Language: English
Genre/keyword: Comedy / Romance / afterlife / fantasy
Runtime: USA:112
Directed by Albert Brooks
Cast: Albert Brooks: Daniel Miller; Michael Durrell: Agency
Head; James Eckhouse: Jeep Owner
Written by Albert Brooks
Produced by Robert Grand (co-producer) Michael Grillo - Herb
Nanas (executive)

27. Demonsoul (1994)
UK / USA 1994 Color
Produced by: Vista Street Entertainment / Gothic Films UK
Genre/keyword: Horror / lesbian-scene / lesbian / vampire
Runtime: UK:81
Directed by Elisar Cabrera (as Elisar C. Kennedy)
Cast (in alphabetical order) complete, awaiting verification
Michael Alexander (V): Mike
Suzanne Ballantyne: The Psychiatrist
Gavin Barnard: Disciple 2
R.J. Bell: Erica's Father
Katherine Blick: Vampire Woman 2
Nikita Blum: Vampire Woman 3; Mark Braby: The Brute; Allen
Bryce: Asylum Doctor; Mayumi Cabrera: Annie; Eileen Daly:
Selena; Daniel Figuero: The Teacher; Graham Fletcher-Cook: Mr.
Newman; Kira Hansen: Vampire Woman 4; Isabella Hyams:
Young Girl; Luke Hyams: Young Boy; Daniel Jordan: Dr. Bucher;
Kerry Norton: Erica Steele; Erich Redman: Richard Kurtz; Drew
Rhys-Williams: Alex; Pixie Roscoe: Young Erica; Sue Scadding:
Marilyn; Ric Scadorwa: Disciple 1; Hepzibah Sessa: Vampire
Woman 1; Janine Ulfane: Rosemary; Johnny Vercoutre: Sacrifice
Man
Written by Elisar Cabrera
Produced by Elisar Cabrera (as Elisar C. Kennedy), Matt Devlen,
Gerald Feifer, Daniel Figuero

28. Devi (1960)
India 1960
Genre/keyword: Drama / reincarnation / religion / superstition
Runtime: India:93
Also Known As: Goddess, The (1960)
Directed by Satyajit Ray
Cast: Chhabi Biswas: Kalikinkar Roy; Soumitra Chatterjee:
Umaprasad, Sharmila Tagore: Doyamoyee
Written by Prabhat Mukherjee (story) Satyajit Ray

29. Devil and Max Devlin, The (1981)
USA 1981 Color
Produced by: Walt Disney Productions (aka Walt Disney Pictures)
US
Language: English
Genre/keyword: Comedy / afterlife / deal-with-the-devil / super-
natural

Directed by Steven Hilliard Stern
Cast: Elliott Gould: Max Devlin; Bill Cosby: Barney Satin; Susan
Anspach: Penny Hart
Adam Rich: Toby Hart
Written by (in credits order) Mary Rodgers (I) (story) and Jimmy
Sangster (story) Mary Rodgers (I)
Produced by Jerome Courtland Ron Miller (I) (executive)

30. Eternity (1989)

USA 1989 Color
Produced by: Home Box Office (HBO) US
Language: English
Genre/keyword: Drama
Runtime: USA:110
Directed by Steven Paul
Cast: Jon Voight: James/Edward; Armand Assante: Sean/Roni;
Eileen Davidson: Valerie/Dahlia
Written by Dorothy Koster Paul, Steven Paul, Jon Voight

31. Extraño Retorno de Diana Salazar, El (1988)

Mexico [TV series] 1988
Produced by: Televisa, S.A.
Language: Spanish
Genre/keyword: Romance / Drama / soap / reincarnation /
telekinesis
Runtime: Mexico:60

32. Extreme Ghostbusters (1997)

USA [TV series] 1997 Color
Produced by: Columbia Pictures Television US / Adelaide
Productions, Inc
Language: English
Genre/keyword: Animation / Children's / ghostbusters / based-on-
film / ghost / paranormal / Comedy
Runtime: UK:23
Directed by Chris Berkeley, Alan Caldwell, Chris Dozois, Tim
Eldred, Bob Fuentes, Gloria Jenkins, Sam Liu, Audu Paden, Scott
Wood (II)
Cast: Tara Charendoff: Kylie Griffin (voice); Maurice LaMarche:
Egon Spengler (voice); Jason Marsden: Garrett Miller (voice)

Produced by Monique Beatty (associate) Duane Capizzi, Daniel Goldberg (executive), Jeff Kline (supervising), Joe Medjuck (executive), Audu Paden, Richard Raynis (executive)
Other crew: Dan Aykroyd: characters creator
Fil Barlow: creatures and characters
Spin off from Real Ghostbusters, The (1986)

33. Face of the Screaming Werewolf (1964)
USA 1964 Black and White
Language: English
Genre/keyword: Horror / werewolf
Runtime: USA:60
Directed by Rafael López Portillo
Written by Fernando de Fuentes
Produced by Jerry Warren

34. Fluke (1995)
USA 1995 Color (DeLuxe)
Produced by: Rocket Pictures / MGM (Metro-Goldwyn-Mayer) [aka MGM-UA] US
Language: English
Genre/keyword: Drama / based-on-novel / dog / reincarnation
Runtime: USA:96
Directed by Carlo Carlei
Cast: Samuel L. Jackson: Rumbo (voice); Matthew Modine: Thomas Johnson/Voice of Fluke, Nancy Travis: Carol Johnson
Written by James Herbert (II) (novel), Carlo Carlei & James Carrington
Produced by Tom Coleman (III) (executive), Terri Ferraro (associate), Paul Maslansky, Lata Ryan, Jon Turtle (executive)

35. Ghost (1990)
USA 1990 Color (Technicolor)
Produced by: Paramount Pictures US
Language: English
Genre/keyword: Comedy / Romance / Thriller / love / manhattan / séance / mediums / pottery / new-york / hacker / possession / afterlife / ghost / murder / blockbuster / supernatural
Runtime: USA:128 / Sweden:127

Directed by Jerry Zucker
Cast: Patrick Swayze: Sam Wheat; Demi Moore: Molly Jensen;
Vincent Schiavelli: Subway Ghost; Whoopi Goldberg: Oda Mae
Brown
Written by Bruce Joel Rubin
Produced by Steven-Charles Jaffe (executive), Bruce Joel Rubin
(associate), Lisa Weinstein

36. Goodbye Charlie (1964)
USA 1964 Color
Produced by: 20th Century Fox US
Language: English
Genre/keyword: Comedy / based-on-play / reincarnation / sex-
change
Runtime: USA:116
Directed by Vincente Minnelli
Cast: Pat Boone: Bruce; Ellen Burstyn: Franny; Tony Curtis:
George Tracy
Written by George Axelrod (play)

37. Happy Days (1995)
Sweden 1995 Color
Produced by: Svenska Filminstitutet (SFI) / Göteborg Film
Festival / Sveriges Television
Language: Swedish
Genre/keyword: Drama / afterlife / death / traffic-accident / funer-
al
Runtime: Sweden:12
Directed by Lisa Ohlin
Cast: Jessica Liedberg: Kia; Elisabet Svensson; Mats Flink
Written by Lisa Ohlin / Kjell Sundstedt

38. Heart and Souls (1993)
USA 1993 Color (DeLuxe)
Produced by: Universal Pictures [aka MCA/Universal Pictures]
US / Alphaville Films / Stampede Entertainment
Language: English
Genre/keyword: Comedy / fantasy / life-after-death / reincarnation
Runtime: USA:93
Directed by Ron Underwood
Cast: Robert Downey Jr.: Thomas Reilly; Charles Grodin:
Harrison Winslow; Alfre Woodard: Penny Washington

Written by Gregory Hansen (story), Erik Hansen (story), and
Brent Maddock (story), S.S. Wilson (story), Brent Maddock & S.S.
Wilson and Gregory Hansen & Erik Hansen
Produced by Cari-Esta Albert (executive), Dixie J. Capp (associate), Sean Daniel, Erik Hansen (co-producer), Gregory Hansen
(co-producer), James Jacks (executive), Dirk Petersman (line),
Nancy Roberts

39. Heaven Can Wait (1943)
USA 1943 Color (Technicolor)
Produced by: 20th Century Fox US
Language: English
Genre/keyword: Comedy / Romance / afterlife
Runtime: USA:112
Directed by Ernst Lubitsch
Cast: Gene Tierney: Martha; Don Ameche: Henry Van Cleve;
Charles Coburn: Hugo Van Cleve
Written by Leslie Bush-Fekete (play Birthday) Samson Raphaelson
Produced by Ernst Lubitsch

40. Heaven Can Wait (1978)
USA 1978 Color
Produced by: Paramount Pictures US
Language: English
Genre/keyword: Comedy / based-on-play / reincarnation
Runtime: USA:101
Directed by Warren Beatty / Buck Henry
Cast: Warren Beatty: Joe Pendleton/Leo Farnsworth/Tom Jarrett;
Julie Christie: Betty Logan; James Mason: Mr. Jordan
Written by Warren Beatty, Elaine May, Harry Segall (play),
Robert Towne (uncredited)
Produced by Warren Beatty, Howard W. Koch Jr., Charles
McGuire
Remake of Here Comes Mr. Jordan (1941)

41. Heaven (1987)
USA 1987 Color
Produced by: Columbia Pictures Corporation US
Language: English
Genre/keyword: Documentary
Directed by Diane Keaton
Written by Diane Keaton

42. Oh, Heavenly Dog! (1980)

USA 1980 Color (DeLuxe)
Produced by: 20th Century Fox US / Mulberry Square
Language: English
Genre/keyword: Comedy / Crime / dog / private-detective / reincarnation
Directed by Joe Camp
Cast: Chevy Chase: Browning; Jane Seymour (I): Jackie; Omar Sharif: Bart
Written by Rod Browning
Produced by Joe Camp, Dan Witt (associate)

43. Hi Honey - I'm Dead (1991) (TV)

USA 1991 Color
Produced by: FNM Films
Language: English
Genre/keyword: Comedy / reincarnation
Directed by Alan Myerson
Cast: Curtis Armstrong: Arnold Pischkin; Catherine Hicks: Carol; Kevin Conroy: Brad Stadler
Written by Carl Kleinschmitt
Produced by Paul Rudnick

44. Impure Thoughts (1985)

USA 1985 Color
Language: English
Genre/keyword: Comedy
Runtime: USA:87
Directed by Michael A. Simpson
Cast: Brad Dourif; Stan Wakefield: Quarterback
Produced by Robert F. Phillips (associate), William Vanderkloot

45. Indien (1993)

Austria 1993 Color (Fujicolor)
Produced by: Dor Film AT / DOR FILM Produktionsgesellschaft GmbH
Language: German
Genre/keyword: Comedy / cancer / friendship / reincarnation / road
Runtime: Germany:90
Also Known As: India (1993) (English title)
Directed by Paul Harather

Cast: Josef Hader: Heinzi Bösel; Alfred Dorfer: Kurt Fellner;
Maria Hofstätter: Kirchnerwirtin
Written by Josef Hader (play), and Alfred Dorfer (play), Paul
Harather, Josef Hader, Alfred Dorfer
Produced by Milan Dor, Danny Krausz

46. Kaos (1984)
Italy 1984 Color
Produced by: Filmtre
Language: Italian
Runtime: UK:188
Also Known As: Chaos (1984) (US title)
Directed by Paolo Taviani / Vittorio Taviani
Cast: Margarita Lozano: Maragrazia; Claudio Bigagli: Bata;
Omero Antonutti: Pirandello
Written by Luigi Pirandello (stories), Paolo Taviani, Vittorio
Taviani
Produced by Guiliani G. De Negri

47. Little Buddha (1993)
USA 1993 Color (Technicolor)
Produced by: CiBy 2000
Language: English
Genre/keyword: Drama / buddhism / reincarnation / religion
Runtime: UK:140
Directed by Bernardo Bertolucci
Cast: Keanu Reeves: Siddhartha; Ruocheng Ying: Lama Norbu;
Chris Isaak: Dean Conrad; Bridget Fonda: Lisa Conrad
Written by Bernardo Bertolucci (story), Mark Peploe, Rudy
Wurlitzer
Produced by Francis Bouyges

48. Love of Sunya, The (1927)
USA 1927 Black and White
Produced by: Gloria Swanson Pictures Corporation
Language: English (title cards)
Genre/keyword: Drama / occult / reincarnation
Runtime: USA:78
Directed by Albert Parker
Cast: John Boles: Paul Judson; Pauline Garon: Anna Hagan; Ian
Keith (I): Louis Anthony

Written by Max Marcin (play The Eyes of Youth), Charles
Guernon (play The Eyes of Youth), Earle Browne (adaptation),
Cosmo Hamilton (titles), Lenore J. Coffee (uncredited)
Produced by Gloria Swanson
Remake of Eyes of Youth (1919)

49. Makai tensho (1981)
Japan 1981 Color
Produced by: Toei
Language: Japanese
Genre/keyword: Action / revenge / swordfight / reincarnation /
samurai
Runtime: Japan:122
Also Known As: Samurai Reincarnation (1981)
Directed by Kinji Fukasaku
Written by Futaro Yamada (novel)
Produced by Haruki Kadokawa (executive)

50. Maldición de la momia azteca, La (1957)
Mexico 1957 Black and White
Produced by: Cinematografica Calderon, S.A.
Language: Spanish
Genre/keyword: Horror / mummy
Runtime: Mexico:65
Also Known As: Curse of the Aztec Mummy, The (1957)
Directed by Rafael Portillo
Written by Guillermo Calderón, Alfredo Salazar
Produced by Guillermo Calderón

51. Man from Beyond, The (1922)
USA 1922 Black and White
Produced by: Houdini Picture Corporation
Genre/keyword: Mystery / reincarnation
Directed by Burton L. King
Cast: Harry Houdini: The Man From Beyond; Arthur Maude: Dr.
Gilbert Trent; Albert Tavernier: Dr. Crawford Strange
Written by Harry Houdini (story), Coolidge Streeter (adaptation)

52. Manika, une vie plus tard (1988)
France 1988 Color (Fujicolor)
Produced by: Filmtel, Colombo, Ceylan / Himalaya Productions,
Kathmandu, Nepal / Labrador Film

Language: French
Genre/keyword: catholic / hinduism / reincarnation
Runtime: France:106
Directed by François Villiers
Cast: Ayesha Dharker: Manika Kallatil; Julian Sands: Père Daniel
Mahoney; Stéphane Audran: Soeur Amanda
Written by Jean-Pierre Gibrat, Brian Phelan, François Villiers
Produced by Raoul Katz

53. Manitou, The (1978)
USA 1978 Color
Language: English
Genre/keyword: Horror / supernatural
Directed by William Girdler
Cast: Tony Curtis: Harry Erskine; Susan Strasberg: Karen Tandy;
Michael Ansara: Singing Rock
Written by Jon Cedar, William Girdler, Graham Masterton
(book), Tom Pope

54. Matter of Life and Death, A (1946)
UK 1946 Black and White / Color (Technicolor)
Produced by: J. Arthur Rank Films / The Archers
Language: English
Genre/keyword: Romance / War / camera-obscura / afterlife /
mystical-realism / Drama / surreal / tearjerker / wwii
Runtime: UK:104
Also Known As: Stairway to Heaven (1946) (US title)
Directed by Michael Powell / Emeric Pressburger
Cast: David Niven: Squadron Leader Peter D. Carter; Kim
Hunter (I): June; Robert Coote: Bob Trubshaw; Kathleen Byron:
Angel
Written by Michael Powell, Emeric Pressburger
Produced by George R. Busby (assistant), Michael Powell, Emeric
Pressburger

55. Momia azteca, La (1957)
Mexico 1957 Black and White
Produced by: Cinematografica Calderon, S.A.
Language: Spanish
Genre/keyword: Horror / mummy
Runtime: Mexico:80

Also Known As: Aztec Mummy, The (1957); Attack of the Aztec
Mummy (1957); Momia, La (1957)
Directed by Rafael Portillo
Cast: Ramón Gay: Dr. Almada; Rosa Arenas: Flor; Luis Aceves
Castañeda: Dr. Krup
Written by Guillermo Calderón, Alfredo Salazar
Produced by Guillermo Calderón
Version of Attack of the Mayan Mummy (1964)

56. Mortinho por Chegar a Casa (1996)
Portugal / Netherlands 1996 Color
Produced by: Europa 7 Filme / Dutch Film Fund / European
Script Fund / Instituto Português da Arte
Language: Dutch / Portuguese / English
Genre/keyword: Comedy / afterlife / dreams / ghost
Also Known As: Corvos de São Vicente, Os (1996) (working title);
Dying to Go Home (1996)
Directed by Carlos da Silva / George Sluizer
Cast: Diogo Infante: Manuel Espírito Santo; Maria d'Aires: Júlia
Espírito Santo; Huub Stapel: Joris
Written by Jennifer Field, Carlos da Silva (also story), George
Sluizer (additional dialogue)
Produced by Jennifer Field (associate), Anne Lordon (executive),
Dirk Schreiner (delegate), Carlos da Silva, George Sluizer

57. Mummy, The (1932)
USA 1932 Black and White
Produced by: Universal Pictures [aka MCA/Universal Pictures]
US
Language: English
Genre/keyword: Horror / Romance / classic / mummy / monster /
archaeology / flashback
Runtime: USA:72
Also Known As: Cagliostro (1932); King of the Dead (1932); Im-
Ho-Tep (1932)
Directed by Karl Freund
Cast: Boris Karloff: Imhotep/Ardath Bey; Zita Johann: Helen
Grosvenor/The Princess; David Manners: Frank Whemple
Written by John L. Balderston, Nina Wilcox Putnam (story),
Richard Schayer (story)
Produced by Stanley Bergerman (associate) Carl Laemmle Jr.
Remade as Mummy, The (1998)

58. My Mother the Car (1965)

USA [TV series] 1965-1966
Language: English
Genre/keyword: Comedy / smart-car
Runtime: USA:30
Cast: Cindy Eilbacher: Cindy Crabtree; Maggie Pierce: Barbara Crabtree; Avery Schreiber: Capt. Mancini
No te mueras sin decirme adónde vas (1995)
Argentina 1995 Black and White / Color
Produced by: INCAA Production / ARTEAR
Language: Spanish
Genre/keyword: dreams / Drama / movies / reincarnation / spirituality
Runtime: Argentina:130 / Spain:120
Also Known As: Don't Die Without Telling Me Where You're Going (1995)
Directed by Eliseo Subiela
Cast: Darío Grandinetti: Leopoldo; Mariana Arias: Rachel; Oscar Martinez: Oscar
Written by Eliseo Subiela
Produced by Damian Kirzner (executive), Maria Elena Mitre (associate), Jorge Rocca, Susana Serebrenik (associate)

59. On a Clear Day You Can See Forever (1970)

USA 1970 Color
Produced by: Paramount Pictures US
Language: English
Genre/keyword: Comedy / Musical / hypnotism / psychoanalysis / reincarnation / esp
Runtime: USA:129
Directed by Vincente Minnelli
Cast: Barbra Streisand: Daisy Gamble; Yves Montand: Dr. Marc Chabot; Bob Newhart: Dr. Mason Hume
Written by Alan Jay Lerner (also play)
Produced by Howard W. Koch

60. On Borrowed Time (1939)

USA 1939 Black and White
Produced by: MGM (Metro-Goldwyn-Mayer) [aka MGM-UA] US
Language: English
Genre/keyword: Comedy / Drama / based-on-novel / afterlife / based-on-play / americana / death / fairy-tale / fantasy

Runtime: USA:99
Directed by Harold S. Bucquet
Cast: Lionel Barrymore: Julian Northrup (Gramps); Cedric
Hardwicke: Mr. Brink; Beulah Bondi: Nellie (Granny)
Written by Alice D.G. Miller, Frank O'Neil, Paul Osborn (play),
Lawrence Edward Watkin (novel), Claudine West
Produced by Sidney Franklin (I)

61. Out on a Limb (1987) (TV)
USA 1987 Color
Language: English
Genre/keyword: Drama / based-on-novel / autobiographical /
metaphysics / new-age / reincarnation / peru
Runtime: USA:235
Directed by Robert Butler
Cast: Shirley MacLaine: Shirley MacLaine; Charles Dance: Gerry
Stamford; John Heard: David Manning
Written by Colin Higgins (I), Shirley MacLaine
Produced by Colin Higgins (I), Stan Margulies

62. Reincarnation of Peter Proud, The (1975)
USA 1975 Color
Certification: USA:R / Finland:K-16
Language: English
Genre/keyword: Mystery / Horror / reincarnation
Runtime: 104
Directed by J. Lee Thompson
Cast: Michael Sarrazin: Peter Proud; Jennifer O'Neill (I): Ann
Curtis; Margot Kidder: Marcia Curtis
Written by Max Ehrlich
Produced by Charles A. Pratt (executive), Frank P. Rosenberg

63. Return of Chandu, The (1934/I)
USA 1934 Black and White
Produced by: Principal Pictures Corp.
Language: English
Genre/keyword: Horror / serial / fantasy / based-on-play
Runtime: USA:208 (12 chapter serial)
Also Known As: Return of Chandu the Magician, The (1934)
(video title); Chandu's Return (1934)
Directed by Ray Taylor (I)

Cast: Béla Lugosi: Frank Chandler (Chandu the Magician); Maria
Alba: Princess Nadji; Murdock MacQuarrie: Voice of Ubasti
Written by Barry Barringer, Harry A. Earnshaw (play), R.R.
Morgan (play), Vera M. Oldham (play)
Produced by Sol Lesser
Edited into Return of Chandu, The (1934/II); Chandu on the
Magic Island (1935)

64. Return of Chandu, The (1934/II)
USA 1934 Black and White
Produced by: Principal Pictures Corp.
Language: English
Genre/keyword: Adventure / fantasy
Runtime: USA:65
Directed by Ray Taylor (I)
Cast: Béla Lugosi: Frank Chandler (Chandu); Maria Alba:
Princess Nadji; Lucien Prival: Vindhyan
Written by Barry Barringer
Edited from Return of Chandu, The (1934/I)

65. Return (1985)
Winner of 4 film festival awards
USA 1985 Color
Language: English
Genre/keyword: Thriller / paranormal
Runtime: Germany:78
Also Known As: Return: A Case of Possession (1985)
Directed by Andrew Silver
Written by Andrew Silver
Produced by Yong-Hee Silver / Philip J. Spinelli

66. Riget (1994) (mini)
Denmark / France / Germany / Sweden [TV series] 1994 Color
Produced by: Danmarks Radio (DR)
Genre/keyword: Horror / ghost / hospital / medical / reincarna-
tion / satire
Runtime: Denmark:280 / USA:279
Also Known As: Kingdom, The (1994) (mini)
Directed by Morten Arnfred / Lars von Trier
Cast: Otto Brandenburg: Hansen; Laura Elisabeth Christensen:
Mona; Holger Juul Hansen: Moesgaard

Written by Thomas Gíslason, Lars von Trier, Niels Vørsel
Produced by Sven Abrahamsen, Philippe Bober, Peter Aalbæk
Jensen, Ole Reim, Ib Tardini

67. Sabirni centar (1988)
Yugoslavia 1988 Color
Language: Serbian
Genre/keyword: Comedy / afterlife
Directed by Goran Markovic
Written by Dusan Kovacevic

68. Search for Bridey Murphy, The (1956)
USA 1956 Black and White
Produced by: Paramount Pictures US
Language: English
Genre/keyword: hypnotism / reincarnation
Directed by Noel Langley
Cast: Teresa Wright: Ruth Simmons; Louis Hayward: Morey
Bernstein; Nancy Gates: Hazel Bernstein
Written by Morey Bernstein (book) Noel Langley
Produced by Pat Duggan

69. Seeing Things (1979)
[TV series] 1979 Color
Produced by: Canadian Broadcasting Corporation (CBC) CA
Language: English
Genre/keyword: Mystery / Comedy / psychic

70. Seven Years in Tibet (1997)
USA 1997 Color (Technicolor)
Produced by: TriStar Pictures / Applecross / Reperage &
Vanguard Films / Mandalay Entertainment
Language: English
Genre/keyword: War / Drama / mandala / treason / buddhism /
ice-skating / climbing / egoism / friendship / bonding / culture-
clash / foreigner / historical / divorce / dalai-lama / wwii / violence
/ biographical / teacher-student / food-poisoning / non-violence /
prison-camp / based-on-true-story / escape / religion / political
Runtime: USA:139
Directed by Jean-Jacques Annaud
Cast: Brad Pitt: Heinrich Harrer; David Thewlis: Peter
Aufschnaiter; B.D. Wong: Ngawang Jigme; Mako: Kungo Tsarong

Written by Heinrich Harrer (book) Becky Johnston
Produced by Jean-Jacques Annaud, Michael Besman (executive),
Richard N. Goodwin (executive), David Nichols (executive), Iain
Smith, Alisa Tager (associate), John H. Williams

71. Shades of LA (1990)

USA [TV series] 1990 Color
Language: English
Cast: Warren Berlinger: The Lieutenant; John D'Aquino: Det.
Michael Burton

72. She (1908)

USA 1908 Black and White
Produced by: Edison Company
Language: English
Genre/keyword: fantasy / based-on-novel
Directed by Edwin S. Porter
Written by H. Rider Haggard (novel)
Version of She (1911); She (1916); She (1917); She (1925); She
(1935); She (1965); S*H*E (1980) (TV);
She (1985)

73. She (1911)

USA 1911 Black and White
Language: English
Genre/keyword: fantasy / based-on-novel
Cast: James Cruze; Marguerite Snow
Written by H. Rider Haggard (novel)

74. She (1916)

UK 1916 Black and White
Produced by: Lucoque / Barker Motion Photography
Language: English
Genre/keyword: fantasy / lost-city / based-on-novel
Directed by William G.B. Barker / Horace Lisle Lucoque
Written by H. Rider Haggard (novel), Nellie E. Lucoque
Produced by William G.B. Barker

75. She (1917)

USA 1917 Black and White
Produced by: Fox Film Corporation US
Language: English

Directed by Kenean Buel
Cast: Valeska Surratt
Production Design by Lancelot Speed

76. She (1925)

Germany / UK 1925 Black and White
Genre/keyword: fantasy / based-on-novel
Also Known As: Mirakel der Liebe (1925)
Directed by Leander De Cordova / G.B. Samuelson
Cast: Carlyle Blackwell Sr.; Betty Blythe; Heinrich George; Mary
Odette: She
Written by H. Rider Haggard (novel)
Produced by Arthur A. Lee

77. She (1935)

USA 1935 Black and White
Produced by: RKO Radio Pictures
Language: English
Genre/keyword: Adventure / Romance / arctic / avalanche /
based-on-novel / cannibalism / fantasy / hidden-civilization /
immortality / lost-city / lost-race / reincarnation
Runtime: USA:96
Directed by Lansing C. Holden / Irving Pichel
Cast: Helen Gahagan: Ayesha (She); Randolph Scott: Leo Vincey;
Helen Mack: Tanya Dugmore
Written by H. Rider Haggard (novel), Dudley Nichols (additional
dialogue), Ruth Rose
Produced by Shirley C. Burden (associate), Merian C. Cooper

78. She (1965)

UK 1965 Color (Metrocolor)
Produced by: Hammer Films / MGM (Metro-Goldwyn-Mayer)
[aka MGM-UA] US / Seven Arts Production UK
Language: English
Genre/keyword: Adventure / desert / lost-city / based-on-novel /
reincarnation / fantasy
Runtime: USA:106
Directed by Robert Day (I)
Cast: Ursula Andress: Ayesha (She who must be obeyed); Peter
Cushing: Maj. Horace Holly; Bernard Cribbins: Job

Written by David T. Chantler, Rider Haggard (novel)
Produced by Michael Carreras, Aida Young
Followed by Vengeance of She, The (1968)
Version of She (1908); She (1911); She (1916); She (1917); She
(1925); She (1935); S*H*E (1980) (TV); She (1985)

79. She Creature, The (1957)

USA 1957 Black and White
Produced by: Golden State Productions
Language: English
Genre/keyword: Horror / Sci-Fi / mst3k / hypnotism / reincarnation
Runtime: USA:77
Directed by Edward L. Cahn
Cast: Chester Morris: Dr. Carlo Lombardi; Tom Conway (I):
Timothy Chappel; Cathy Downs: Dorothy Chappel
Written by Lou Rusoff (also story)
Produced by Samuel Z. Arkoff (executive); Israel M. Berman
(associate); Alex Gordon
Remade as Creature of Destruction (1967)

80. Somewhere in Time (1980)

USA 1980 Color
Produced by: Universal City Studios Productions, Inc.
Language: English
Genre/keyword: Drama / Romance / based-on-novel / love / time-travel
Runtime: 108
Directed by Jeannot Szwarc
Cast: Christopher Reeve: Richard Collier; Jane Seymour (I): Elise
McKenna; Christopher Plummer: William Fawcett Robinson;
Teresa Wright: Laura Roberts
Written by Richard Matheson (also novel)
Produced by Stephen Deutsch (II)

81. Sunday at Home (1949)

USA [TV series] 1949 Black and White
Language: English
Genre/keyword: Musical / Mystery / reincarnation / tragedy /
quiz-show
Runtime: USA:15
Cast: Mom Pickard: Regular on autoharp; Obey 'Bud' Pickard Jr.:
Regular; Charlie Pickard: Regular

82. Switch (1991)

USA 1991 Color (Technicolor)
Produced by: Cinema Plus, L.P. / Columbia Pictures Corporation
US / Home Box Office (HBO) US
Language: English
Genre/keyword: Comedy / lesbian-scene / reincarnation / role-reversal / sex-change
Runtime: USA:103
Directed by Blake Edwards
Cast: Ellen Barkin: Amanda Brooks; Jimmy Smits: Walter Stone; JoBeth Williams: Margo Brofman
Written by Blake Edwards
Produced by Tony Adams, Trish Caroselli (associate) (as Trish Caroselli Rintels), Arnon Milchan (executive), Patrick Wachsberger (executive)
Remake of Cleo/Leo (1989)

83. Things to Do in Denver when You're Dead (1995)

USA 1995 Color (CFI)
Produced by: Woods Entertainment / Buena Vista Pictures / Miramax Films
Language: English
Genre/keyword: Drama / Crime / Romance / violence / mafia / vulgarity / paraplegic / prostitution / black-comedy / corpse
Runtime: USA:115 / UK:114
Directed by Gary Fleder
Cast: Andy Garcia: Jimmy "The Saint" Tosnia; Christopher Lloyd: Pieces; William Forsythe: Franchise
Written by Scott Rosenberg
Produced by Marie Cantin (executive), Cathy Konrad (co-producer), Scott Rosenberg (associate), Bob Weinstein (executive), Harvey Weinstein (executive), Cary Woods

84. Three Faces of Eve, The (1957)

USA 1957 Black and White
Produced by: 20th Century Fox US
Language: English
Genre/keyword: Drama
Directed by Nunnally Johnson
Cast: Joanne Woodward: Eve; David Wayne: Ralph White; Lee J. Cobb: Doctor Luther

Written by Corbett Thigpen (book), Hervey M. Cleckley (book),
Nunnally Johnson
Produced by Nunnally Johnson

85. Toothless (1997) (TV)
USA 1997 Color
Produced by: Walt Disney Television US / Mandeville Films
Language: English
Genre/keyword: Romance / Comedy / fantasy / fairy-tale / after-
life
Runtime: UK:82
Directed by Melanie Mayron
Cast: Kirstie Alley: Catherine Lewis; Dale Midkiff: Thomas; Ross
Malinger: Bobby
Written by Mark S. Kaufman
Produced by David Hoberman (executive), Mike Karz (co-produc-
er), Joan Van Horn

86. Twinkle Twinkle Little Star (1996)
Hong Kong 1996 Color
Language: Cantonese
Genre/keyword: Comedy / fantasy / gambling / heaven / hong-
kong / reincarnation / true-love / wrestling
Directed by Jing Wong

87. Two of a Kind (1983)
USA 1983 Color (DeLuxe)
Produced by: 20th Century Fox US / Lamy Films BE / Arsenal
Films ES
Language: English
Genre/keyword: Comedy / Romance / angel / afterlife / love
Directed by John Herzfeld
Cast: John Travolta: Zack Melon; Olivia Newton-John: Debbie
Wylder; Charles Durning: Charlie; Beatrice Straight: Ruth
Written by John Herzfeld
Produced by Joan Edward (associate), Kate Edward (associate),
Michele Panelli-Venetis (associate), Roger M. Rothstein, Joe
Wizan

88. Undead, The (1957)

USA 1957 Black and White
Produced by: American International Pictures (AIP) US / Balboa
Language: English
Genre/keyword: Horror / mad-scientist / medieval / reincarnation / time-travel
Runtime: USA:71
Directed by Roger Corman
Cast: Pamela Duncan: Diana Love/Helen, the witch; Richard Garland: Pendragon; Allison Hayes: Livia
Written by Charles B. Griffith, Mark Hanna
Produced by Samuel Z. Arkoff

89. Yin ji kau (1987)

Hong Kong 1987 Color
Language: Cantonese
Genre/keyword: Romance / Drama / Ghost / Hong Kong / Suicide
Runtime: USA:93
Also Known As: Yan zhi kou (1987) (Mandarin title); Rouge (1987)
Directed by Stanley Kwan
Written by Dai An-Ping Chiu / Bik-Wa Lei
Produced by Jackie Chan

90. You Never Can Tell (1951)

USA 1951 Black and White
Produced by: Universal International
Language: English
Genre/keyword: Comedy / Afterlife / Animals / Fantasy / Private-detective
Runtime: USA:78
Also Known As: One Never Knows (1951); You Never Know (1951)
Directed by Lou Breslow
Cast: Dick Powell: Rex Shepherd; Peggy Dow: Ellen Hathaway; Joyce Holden: Goldie; Charles Drake: Perry Collins
Written by Lou Breslow (also story), David Chandler (III)

91. Yun Pei Dung Lung (1993)

Hong Kong 1993 Color
Produced by: Wong Jing's Workshop Limited

Language: Cantonese
Genre/keyword: Drama / Thriller / Cantonese
Also Known As: All New Human Skin Lanterns (1993); Ghost Lantern (1993); Skinned Girl (1993); New Human Skin Lantern (1993)
Directed by Wai Keung Lau
Cast: Tony Leung Ka Fai: Fai
Produced by Jing Wong

BIBLIOGRAPHY

1. **ALEGRETTI, Wagner;** *Astral Travel: Is It Possible?;* TONE; Ottawa; Canada; Magazine; Monthly; 1997.

2. **ALEGRETTI, Wagner;** *Conscientiology and Projectiology: Two sciences for the Consciousness (Port.:Conscienciologia e Projeciologia: Duas Ciências para a Consciência);* ANO ZERO; Rio de Janeiro, RJ; Monthly Magazine; 21 illus.; March-May, 1992; No. 11: p. 66-71; No. 12: p. 56-62; No. 13: p. 58-65.

3. **ALEGRETTI, Wagner;** *Cosmoethics (Port.:Cosmoética);* Extracurricular course; Miami; Florida; USA; International Institute of Projectiology and Conscientiology; 1996.

4. **ALEGRETTI, Wagner;** *Evolutionary Duos (Port.:Duplas Evolutivas);* BIPRO – BOLETIM INFORMATIVO DE PROJE-CIOLOGIA; Rio de Janeiro, RJ; Brazil; Vol. 5; No. 11; April, 1998.

5. **ALEGRETTI, Wagner;** Editor; *Anals of the I International Congress of Projectiology (Anais do I Congresso Internacional de Projeciologia);* Anthology; I-XI + 208 p.; 8 illus.; 28 x 21 cm; Rio de Janeiro, RJ; International Institute of Projectiology; 1991.

6. **ALEGRETTI, Wagner;** *Out-of-body Experience, Bioenergies and Consciousness Research;* Folheto; Miami; Flórida; USA; International Institute of Projectiology and Conscientiology; 1996.

7. **ALEGRETTI, Wagner;** *Projectiology: A New Approach to an Old Phenomenon;* INSIDER; Atlanta, GA; USA; Newsletter; Vol. 3; No. 1; January, 1994.

8. **ALEGRETTI, Wagner;** *Retrocognition: Recalling Past Lives (Port.: Retrocognição: Lembrando Vivências Passadas;* Extracurricular Course; Miami; Florida; USA; International Institute of Projectiology and Conscientiology; 1995.

9. **ALEGRETTI, Wagner;** *Theorice of Bioenergies (Port.: Teática das Bioenergias);* Extracurricular Course; Rio de Janeiro, RJ; International Institute of Projectiology; 1991.

10. **ALEGRETTI, Wagner;** *A Conscientiological Approach for the Altered States of the Consciousness (Port.: Uma Abordagem Conscienciológica para os Estados Alterados de Consciência);* Conference; I CONBPRO - I Brazilian Congress of Projectiology; Brasília, DF; Brazil; 1991.

11. ALEGRETTI, Wagner; *You and the OBE;* INNER SELF; Hollywood; Florida; USA; Magazine; Monthly; Vol. 11, No. 1; January, 1995.

12. ALEGRETTI, Wagner; & MONTEIRO, Rosália; *Introduction to Projectiology (Port.: Introdução à Projeciologia);* broch.; 22 p.; 2 illus.; Rio de Janeiro, RJ; International Institute of Projectiology; 1990.

13. ALEGRETTI, Wagner; & TRIVELLATO, Nanci; Editors; HOMO PROJECTIUS; Miami; Florida; USA; Newsletter; 1996-1998. (Journal of International Institute of Projectiology and Conscientiology).

14. ANDREWS, Ted; *How to Uncover Your Past Lives* (Llwellyn's How to Series); 198 p.; pb.; Llwellyn Publications; 1997. (ISBN: 0-87542-022-2).

15. ARAÚJO, Luiz; *Extracorporeal Drafts (Port.: Ensaios Extracorpóreos);* 126 p.; pref. Gilson Dimenstein Koatz; Rio de Janeiro, RJ; Brazil; International Institute of Projectiology and Conscientiology; 1998. (ISBN: 85-86019-32-1).

16. BALONA, Málu; & ALEGRETTI, Wagner; *Congress of Projectiology: New Paths for Astral Travel (Port.: Congresso de Projeciologia: Novos Caminhos Para a Viagem Astral);* PLANETA; São Paulo, SP; Magazine; Monthly; No. 217; October, 1990.

17. BOWMAN, Carol; *Children and Their Past Lives (Port.: Crianças e Suas Vidas Passadas);* 312 p.; 1st ed.; Rio de Janeiro, RJ; Brazil; Editora Salamandra; 1997. (ISBN: 85-281-0211-4).

18. CARPENTER, Sue; *Past Lives: True Stories of Reincarnation;* 250 p.; 6.98 x 4.29 x 0.72; pb.; London; Virgin Publishing Ltd.; August, 1995. (ISBN: 0-86369-906-5).

19. CAYCE, Charles Thomas; & SMITH, Robert C.; *Edgar Cayce You Can Remember Your Past Lives;* 274 p.; 6.82 x 4.18 x 0.85; pb.; reedition; New York; Warner Books; 1989. (ISBN: 0-446-34979-8).

20. CERATO, Sonia; *The Conscientiology Science and the Conventional Sciences (Port.: A Ciência Concienciologia e as Ciências Convencionais);* 406 p.; pb.; 1st ed.; Rio de Janeiro, RJ; Brazil; International Institute of Projectiology e Conscientiology; 1998. (ISBN: 85-86019-33-X).

21. CERMINARA, Gina; *Many Lives, Many Loves;* 170 p.; pb.; New York; The New American Library; 1974.

22. CHADWICK, Gloria; Discovering Your Past Lives: The Best Book on Reincarnation You'll Ever Read in this Lifetime!; 216 p.; pb.; Chicago; USA; Contemporary Books; September, 1988. (ISBN: 0-8092-4546-9; LC: BL515.C46 1988; Dewey: 133.9/01/3).

23. EASON, Cassandra; Discover Your Past Lives; 154 p.; 9.16 x 5.97 x 0.62; pb.; England; Foulsham and Co. Ltd.; January, 1996. (ISBN: 0-572-02198-4).

24. FINKELSTEIN, Adrian; Your Past Lives and the Healing Process: a Psychiatrist Looks at Reincarnation and Spiritual Healing; 195 p.; pb.; 2ª. ed.; Malibu; California; USA; 50 Gates Publishing Co.; January, 1996. (ISBN: 0-9647831-1-8; LC: BL515 .F55 1996; Dewey: 615.8/52).

25. FIORE, Edith; You have been Here Before: a Psychologist Looks at Past Lives; 242 p.; New York; Ballantine Books; 1978. (ISBN: 0-345-42022-5; LC: RC489.R43 F56 1978; Dewey: 616.8/916/2).

26. GOLDBERG, Bruce; Past Lives, Future Lives; 276 p.; pb.; USA; Ballantine Books; October, 1997. (ISBN: 0-345-42023-3).

27. GUIRDHAM, Arthur; We are One Another: Astounding Evidence of Group Reincarnation; 228 p.; England; The C. W. Daniel Co.; 1991. (ISBN: 0-85207-248-1).

28. GULLO, Carla; PEREIRA, Cilene; & PROPATO, Valéria; The Music of the Souls (Port.: A Ciranda das Almas); ISTO É; São Paulo, SP; Magazine; Weekly; No. 1453; 2, april, 1997.

29. HALL, Judy; Principles of Past Life Therapy; 138 p.; pb.; San Francisco, CA; USA; Thorsons Publishing; 1996. (ISBN: 0-7225-3353-5).

30. LEARNING COMPANY; Compton's Interactive World Atlas; USA; 1997. (CD-ROM).

31. LINN, Denise; Past Lives, Present Dreams: How to Use Reincarnation for Personal Growth; 178 p.; pb.; reprint; New York; Ballantine Books; March, 1997. (ISBN: 0-345-40002-X; LC: BP573.R5 L56 1997; Dewey: 133.9/01/35).

32. McCLAIN, Florence Wagner; Practical Guide to Past Life Regression; 148 p.; pb.; Llewellyn Publications; December, 1997. (ISBN: 0-87542-510-0).

33. MICROSOFT CORPORATION; Encarta 97 Encyclopedia; USA; 1997. (CD-ROM).

34. MISHLOVE, Jeffrey; *The Roots of Consciousness: The Classic Encyclopedia of Consciousness Studies;* ed. rev.; Tulsa; Oklahoma; USA; Council Oak Books; 1993. (ISBN 0-933031-70-x).

35. NEWTON, Michael; *Journey of Souls: Case Studies of Life Between Lives;* 288 p.; pb.; St. Paul; Minn.; USA; Llewellyn; July, 1994. (ISBN: 1-56718-485-5; LC: BF1275.D2 N48 1994; Dewey: 133.9/01/3).

36. O'CONNELL, Loraine; *A Return to the Past;* THE ORLANDO SENTINEL; Orlando, FL; USA; Newspaper; Daily; November 23, 1993; p. E1.

37. PAULSON, Genevieve Lewis; & PAULSON, Stephen J.; *Reincarnation: Remembering Past Lives;* 194 p.; pb.; St. Paul; Minn.; USA; Llewellyn Publications; October, 1997. (ISBN: 1-56718-511-8; LC: BL515.P38 1997; Dewey: 133.9/01/35).

38. PERES, Maria Júlia P. Moraes Prieto; *TRVP – Regressive Experimental Peres Therapy (Port.: Terapia Regressiva Vivencial Peres);* broch.; 44 p.; São Paulo, SP; Instituto Nacional de Terapia de Vivências Passadas; Novembro, 1996.

39. SCHLOTTERBECK, Karl; *Living Your Past Lives: The Psychology of Past Life Regression;* 319 p.; pb.; New York; Ballantine Books; 1987. (ISBN: 0-345-34028-0).

40. SQUIRE, Larry R.; & LINDENLAUB, Elke; *The Biology of Memory;* Symposia Medica Hoechst; 670 p.; Vol. 23; Stuttgart; Germany; F. K. Schattauer Verlag; 1990. (ISBN: 3-7945-1387-8).

41. STEIGER, Brad; & STEIGER, Francie; *Discover Your Past Lives;* 260 p.; pb.; Atglen, PA; USA; Schiffer Publishing Ltd.; September, 1987. (ISBN: 0-914918-76-1).

42. STEIGER, Brad; *You Will Live Again: Dramatic Case Histories of Reincarnation;* 238 p.; Nevada City, CA; USA; Blue Dolphin; 1996. (ISBN: 0-931892-29-5; LC: BL515 .S734 1996; Dewey: 133.9/01/3).

43. STEINER, Rudolf; *A Western Approach to Reincarnation and Karma: Selected Lectures and Writings;* ed. e int. Rene Querido; 154 p.; Hudson, NY; USA; Anthroposophic Press; 1997. (ISBN: 0-88010-399-x; LC: BP596.R44 S74213 1997; Dewey: 299/.935).

44. STEINER, Rudolf; *Reincarnation and Karma: Two Fundamental Truths of Human Existence;* trad. D. S. Osmond, C. Davy, S. e E. F. Derry; 104 p.; Hudson, NY; USA; Anthroposophic Press; 1992. (LC: BP595.S894 W4713 1992; Dewey: 299/.935).

45. STEVENSON, Ian; *Twenty Cases Suggestive of Reincarnation;* 396 p.; Charlottesville; University Press of Virginia; 1974. (ISBN: 0-8139-0872-8; LC: BL515.S75 1974; Dewey: 133.9/013).

46. SUTPHEN, Dick; *Past Lives, Future Loves;* 254 p.; 6.73 x 4.11 x 0.72; pb.; New York; Pocket Books; 1978. (ISBN: 0-671-70828-7).

47. TALBOT, Michael; *Your Past Lives: A Reincarnation Handbook;* 178 p.; 6.89 x 4.19 x 0.54; pb.; reprint; New York; Fawcett Crest Books; May, 1989. (ISBN: 0-449-21679-9).

48. TOBEN, Robert; & WOLF, Alfred Alan; *Space-Time and Beyond (Port.: Espaço-Tempo e Além);* 192 p.; trad. Hernani Guimarães Andrade e Newton Roberval Eichenberg; 4ª. ed.; São Paulo, SP; Brazil; Editora Cultrix; 1995.

49. TRIVELLATO, Nanci; & ALEGRETTI, Wagner; *An Overview of the Consciousness (Port.: Panorâmica de la Conciencia);* broch.; Miami; Florida; USA; International Institute of Projectiology and Conscientiology; 1996.

50. TRIVELLATO, Nanci; & ALEGRETTI, Wagner; *Dynamics of the Evolutionary Duo,* JOURNAL OF CONSCIENTIOLOGY; Miami, FL; USA; Quarterly; Vol. 5; No. 20; April, 2003. (Journal of International Academy of Consciousness).

51. TRIVELLATO, Nanci; & ALEGRETTI, Wagner; *Evolutionary Duo in Practice (Port.: A Dupla Evolutiva na Prática);* ANAIS DO I CONGRESSO INTERNACIONAL DE INVERSÃO EXISTENCIAL; Florianópolis, SC; Brazil; Janeiro, 1998.

52. TRIVELLATO, Nanci; & ALEGRETTI, Wagner; *Out-of-Body Experience - A Natural Phenomena;* Namasté Magazine, South Africa; pp 22-23; September-October 1999.

53. TRIVELLATO, Nanci; & ALEGRETTI, Wagner; *Quantitative and Qualitative Analysis of Experimental Research Project into Out-of-Body Experience Part 1;* ITC Journal; No. 15; pp 18-35; September 2003.

54. TRIVELLATO, Nanci; & ALEGRETTI, Wagner; *Quantitative and Qualitative Analysis of Experimental Research Project into Out-of-Body Experience Part 2;* ITC Journal; No. 16; pp 52-61; December 2003.

55. VIEIRA, Waldo; *100 Tests of Conscienciometry (Port.: 100 Testes da Conscienciometria);* 232 p.; 100 chaps.; 14 refs.; 21 x 14 cm; pb.; 1st ed.; Rio de Janeiro, RJ; International Institute of Projectiology and Conscientiology; 1997. (ISBN: 85-86019-26-7).

56. VIEIRA, Waldo; *200 Theorices of Conscientiology (Port.: Teáticas da Conscienciologia);* 260 p.; 200 chaps.; 13 refs.; alph.; 21 x 14 cm; pb.; 1st ed.; Rio de Janeiro, RJ; International Institute of Projectiology and Conscientiology; 1997. (ISBN: 85-86019-24-0).

57. VIEIRA, Waldo; *700 Experiments of Conscientiology (Port.: 700 Experimentos da Conscienciologia);* 1058 p.; 700 chaps.; 300 tests; 8 indexes; 2 tabs.; 600 enu.; ono.; 5.116 refs.; geo.; glos. 280 terms; 147 abbrev.; alph.; 28,5 x 21,5 x 7 cm; enc.; 1st edition; Rio de Janeiro, RJ; International Institute of Projectiology; 1994.

58. VIEIRA, Waldo; *Conscientiogram: Technique for the Integral Evaluation of the Consciousness (Port.: Conscienciograma: Técnica de Avaliação da Consciência Integral);* 344 p.; 100 pages of evaluation; 2.000 items; 4 indexes; 11 enu.; 7 refs.; glos. 282 terms; 150 abbrev.; alph.; 21 x 14 cm; 1st edition; Rio de Janeiro, RJ; International Institute of Projectiology; 1996. (ISBN: 85-86019-15-1).

59. VIEIRA, Waldo; *Evolutionary Duo Manual (Port.: Manual da Dupla Evolutiva);* 212 p.; 40 chaps.; 16 refs.; alph.; 21 x 14 cm; pb.; 1st ed.; Rio de Janeiro, RJ; International Institute of Projectiology and Conscientiology; 1997. (ISBN: 85-86019-27-5).

60. VIEIRA, Waldo; *Existential Program Manual (Port.: Manual da Proéxis: Programação Existencial);* 164 p.; 40 chaps.; 10 refs.; alph.; 21 x 14 cm; pb.; 1st ed.; Rio de Janeiro, RJ; International Institute of Projectiology and Conscientiology; 1997. (ISBN: 85-86019-19-4).

61. VIEIRA, Waldo; *Penta Manual: Personal Energetic Task (Port.: Manual da Tenepes: Tarefa Energética Pessoal)*; 138 p.; 34 chaps.; 5 refs.; glos. 282 terms; 147 abbrev.; alph.; 21 x 14 cm; pb.; 1st edition; Rio de Janeiro, RJ; International Institute of Projectiology; 1995.

62. VIEIRA, Waldo; *Manual of Conscientiological Redaction (Port.: Manual de Redação da Conscienciologia)*; 272 p.; 21 x 28 cm; 1st ed.; Rio de Janeiro, RJ; International Institute of Projectiology and Conscientiology; 1997. (ISBN: 85-86019-22-4).

63. VIEIRA, Waldo; *Our Evolution (Port.: Nossa Evolução)*; 168 p.; 15 chaps.; 6 refs.; glos. 282 terms; 149 abbrev.; alph.; 21 x 14 cm; pb.; 1st edition; Rio de Janeiro, RJ; International Institute of Projectiology; 1996. (ISBN: 85-86019-08-9).

64. VIEIRA, Waldo; *What is Conscientiology (Port.: O Que é a Conscienciologia)*; 180 p.; 100 chaps.; 3 refs.; glos. 280 terms; alph.; 21 x 14 cm; pb.; 1st edition; Rio de Janeiro, RJ; International Institute of Projectiology; 1994.

65. VIEIRA, Waldo; *Projectiology: An Overview of Experiences of the Consciousness outside the Human Body (Port.: Projeciologia: Panorama das Experiências da Consciência Fora do Corpo Humano)*; XXVIII + 900 p.; 475 chaps.; 40 illus.; 1.907 refs.; glos. 15 terms; 58 abbrev.; ono.; geo.; alph.; 27 x 18.5 x 5 cm; enc.; 3rd edition; Londrina; Paraná; Brasil; Livraria e Editora Universalista; 1990.

66. VIEIRA, Waldo; *Conscientiology Themes (Port.: Temas da Conscienciologia)*; 232 p.; 90 chaps.; 16 refs.; alph.; 21 x 14 cm; pb.; 1st ed.; Rio de Janeiro, RJ; International Institute of Projectiology and Conscientiology; 1997. (ISBN: 85-86019-28-3).

67. WEISS, Brian L.; *Many Lives, Many Masters (Port.: Muchas Vidas, Muchos Sábios)*; 220 p.; trad. Edith Zilli; Buenos Aires; Argentina; Javier Vergara Editor; 1989. (ISBN: 954-15-0958-3).

68. WEISS, Brian L.; *Only Love Is Real: A Story of Soulmates Reunited*; 176 p.; pb.; reedition.; New York; Warner Books; March, 1997. (ISBN: 0-446-67265-3).

69. WHITTON, Joel L.; & FISHER, Joe; *Life Between Life*; 220 p.; 6.77 x 4.13 x 0.69; pb.; re-issue; New York; Warner Books; January, 1988. (ISBN: 0-446-34762-0).

HOW TO ACCESS AN
ADDITIONAL BIBLIOGRAPHY

The author has compiled an additional bibliography that can be accessed through the Web Site: www.iacworld.org, in the Resources section. That bibliography was not consulted during the preparation of this work, and its primary objective is to help those who wish to research the subjects at hand more deeply.

This auxiliary bibliography propitiates a better overall vision and illustrates the universalistic character of the themes of this book. Many people, for lack of information, think that regression therapies to past lives were recently created by one or another famous contemporary author, or that the seriality theory was discovered by Allan Kardec.

This compilation is the result of an extensive search through the Internet. Several sources were explored and the results gathered, cross-referenced and standardized; eliminating duplicated references and confirming the respective information. The main sources consulted were: Amazon (www.amazon.com), Barnes & Noble (www.barnesandnoble.com) and, mainly, the database of the American Library of Congress (lcweb.loc.gov). The main keywords used in the search mechanisms (search engines) were: reincarnation, past life, regression and its variations.

This bibliography can be summarized or illustrated by the following statistics:

- References: 1157
- Languages: 26 – German, Arabic, Burmese, Chinese, Danish, Spanish, Finnish, French, Greek, Hindu (India), Dutch, Hungarian, Indonesian, English, Icelandic, Italian, Polish, Portuguese, Russian, Sanskrit (India), Singhalese (Sri Lanka), Swedish, Thai, Telugu (India), Tibetan, Urdu (India)
- Countries: 32 – South Africa, Germany, Argentina, Brazil, Burma, Canada, China, South Korea, Denmark, Spain, USA, Finland, France, Greece, Holland, Hungary, India, Indonesia, England, Iceland, Israel, Italy, Lebanon, Monaco, Nigeria, Poland, Russia, Sweden, Switzerland, Thailand, Taiwan, Tibet.
- Medias: 6 – Book, Audiocassette, Audio-CD, Vinyl Disc, Film, Video VHS.
- Year of the oldest reference: 1692

ABOUT THE AUTHOR

Born in 1961 in São Paulo, Brazil, Wagner Alegretti graduated as an electronic engineer before embarking on a career in engineering fields including electricity generation, biomedical equipment and software development. In 1988 Alegretti chose to forego his career in favour of full-time teaching and research into the consciousness and its manifestations.

Alegretti's interest in the non-physical manifestations of the consciousness, including the phenomenon of retrocognition, started at an early age, resulting from his experiences of spontaneous conscious projections starting at the age of ten.

By 1980, Alegretti had developed the ability to produce lucid out-of-body experiences largely at will, and his research into the projection and its associated phenomena and implications has been continuous since that time. Meeting Dr. Waldo Vieira in 1982, Alegretti was part of the group that founded both the International Institute of Projectiology and Conscientiology (IIPC) in 1988 and the International Academy of Consciousness (IAC) in 2000.

Administrative Director of the IIPC in Brazil for five years, Alegretti was also instrumental in the expansion of the IIPC into the international arena with its Miami office in 1995, a milestone in the establishment of the sciences of projectiology and conscientiology. Continuing in this principal role, Alegretti went on to establish the IIPC's London offices before being elected President of the IAC in 2000, a position he still holds today. He now continues his work as a researcher, instructor and writer in Lisbon, Portugal, where he currently resides.

Alegretti's research experience includes field investigations into poltergeists and this has given rise to a special interest in the field of bioenergies. He has worked to develop prototype devices designed to detect and meausre this subtle form of energy with some success.

Since 1985, Alegretti has delivered lectures on a diverse subjects within the remit of the sciences of projectiology and conscientiology at numerous universities and international fora, and at the majority of international conscientiological events around the world. Alegretti delivered a keynote presentation at the International Earth Summit in 1992 (Rio de Janeiro), and has given projectiology classes at the Miami Dade Community College. He has participated in numerous international media programs and presentations, and has had articles published around the world.

Alegretti has made many television appearances including 'Eye Witness News,' Atlanta (Fox TV, Georgia-US); 'Cristina TV show' (broadcast to 17 countries including the US); 'The Scene' (CBS TV, Florida-US); 'Globo News' (Brazil); and 'Enterese' (Educational TV-US). He has also featured in publications such as: 'Lo Insólito' (Mexico); 'Cristina magazine' (US); 'The Miami Herald' (Florida-US); 'Revista Planeta' (Brazil); and given numerous radio interviews worldwide, most recently on the James Whale Show in London (UK).

Alegretti has given courses and lectures in English, Spanish, and Portuguese in many cities globally, including: Miami, New York, Los Angeles & Atlanta (USA); Madrid, Barcelona & Seville (Spain); Lisbon, Porto & Coimbra (Portugal); Amsterdam & Rotterdam (Holland); London & Cambridge (United Kingdom); Helsinki (Finland); Ottawa (Canada); Buenos Aires (Argentina); Tokyo (Japan); Brisbane (Australia); and all the major cities of Brazil.

As co-editor of the Journal of Conscientiology, Alegretti works closely with Nanci Trivellato, fellow researcher and co-editor, and is responsible for independent research into the out-of-body experience, bioenergetics, cosmoethics and conscientiometry. Together with Ms. Trivellato, he is conducting an ongoing worldwide survey related to the out-of-body experience, and experimental research into non-physical perceptions.

INDEX

IAC – INTERNATIONAL ACADEMY OF CONSCIOUSNESS

The IAC is a non-profit, multinational, multicultural, and universalistic organization dedicated to the research of conscientiology and its subdisciplines and giving educational activities related to these areas.

The objective of the IAC is to catalyze evolution through clarifying about the multidimensional nature of the consciousness and the implications arising from that. The Academy stimulates expanded awareness through the dissemination of pragmatic information, employing logic, discernment, and the highest principles of cosmoethics. The work of the IAC is founded on updated scientific precepts and aims to further human knowledge based on the consciential paradigm. Information offered by the IAC is a result of the accumulation of decades of investigation and is a consensus of numerous personal experiences. It is also grounded in both historical and current investigations into these subjects.

The IAC was founded in October 2000 as the first conscientiological research campus in Europe. In the first two years of its existence the IAC hosted two conferences, performed three large research experiments under controlled conditions, and developed and implemented a series of new and unique courses. During this period the Academy also began the construction of its campus in Évora (Alentejo, Portugal). Ongoing and completed research projects were also published in periodicals and on the IAC's website.

In May 2002, all of the IIPC offices outside of Brazil were transferred to the IAC, including research, educational programs, human resources and scientific publications. The IAC inherited the historical experience and the accomplishments realized through the efforts of the IIPC team that had worked internationally since 1994. As of April 2004, the Academy has organized and given events in 13 countries, taking the materthosene of conscientiology to: Canada, Finland, France, Holland, Italy, Mexico, New Zealand, Portugal,

Spain, Switzerland, the United Kingdom, the USA, and Venezuela.

IAC courses emphasize the practical experience of multidimensionality and parapsychism. In the organization's curriculum of courses there is a accreditation program in the foundations of conscientiology, which is awarded to participants who accumulate the required number of points from compulsory and elective courses taken within a four-year time frame. Among these courses is *The Projective Field*, an immersion course for inducing out-of-body experiences, and a one-year course called *Objective: Intrusionlessness*, focused on developing freedom from intrusion.

The research campus being constructed on approximately 25 acres of wooded land will provide an environment optimized for both formal research and self-experimentation. A key feature of the campus is the series of consciential laboratories - purpose-built environments that combine physical, non-physical and bioenergetic elements to create multidimensional chambers for self-experimentation. Among the laboratories is the world's first *Projectarium*, a spherical structure 10m (32.8ft) in diameter whose design encompasses key characteristics known to facilitate out-of-body experiences. Other laboratories will include: cosmoconsciousness, existential inversion, assistantiology, interconsciential recycling, intermissive course, neothosenes, multidimensional self-awareness, holochakralogy, universalism, macrosoma, holokarma, conviviology, recuperation of cons, self-conscientiotherapy, holosomatics, paratechnology, communicology, and waking physical immobility.

The *Journal of Conscientiology* is published by the IAC and is the official vehicle through which the scientific study of conscientiology is disseminated. It offers an open forum for the presentation and scientific debate of consciousness studies, and is comprised of articles from researchers affiliated with different organizations from all over the world. The Journal is distributed to individuals and organizations from 21 countries.

www.iacworld.org

MAIN OFFICES

Portugal - Lisbon
Lisboa@iacworld.org
Phone: +351 21 386 8008 / 09
Fax: +351 21 386 8033
Avenida Ressano Garcia, 39 - 5 Ft
1070-234 Lisbon

Portugal - Oporto
Porto@iacworld.org
Phone/Fax: +351 22 606 4025
Rua Julio Dinis, 880 - 5 Ft
4050-322 Oporto

Spain - Barcelona
Barcelona@iacworld.org
Phone/Fax: +34 93 232 8008
C/Ausias Marc, 49 - 5° despacho 30
08010 Barcelona

Spain - Madrid
Madrid@iacworld.org
Phone/Fax: +34 91 591 2587
Calle Rodríguez San Pedro, 2
Despacho 902
28015 Madrid

Spain - Seville
Sevilla@iacworld.org
Phone: +34 954 921 891
Avda. San Francisco Javier, 9
Pl. 10, Mod. 14
41018 Seville

United Kingdom - London
London@iacworld.org
Phone/Fax: +44 (0) 20 7723 0544
3rd Floor, 45 Great Cumberland Pl.
Marble Arch
London W1H 7LH

USA - Los Angeles
California@iacworld.org
Phone: +1 310 482 0000
Phone/Fax: +1 310 482 0001
Toll Free: (1) 877 IAC 4OBE
3961 Sepulveda Blvd, Suite 207
Culver City, CA 90230-4600

USA - Miami
Florida@iacworld.org
Phone: +1 305 668 4668
Fax: +1 305 668 4663
Toll free: (1) 888 234 4472
7800 SW 57th Ave, Suites 207-C & D
Miami, FL 33143

USA - New York
NewYork@iacworld.org
Phone: +1 212 867 0807
Fax: +1 212 867 0875
Toll Free: (1) 800 778 3778
51 East 42nd Street, Suite 419
New York, NY 10017

ASSOCIATE OFFICES

Australia – Sydney
Australia@iacworld.org

Brazil – Iguassu Falls
Brasil@iacworld.org
or contact the London office

Helsinki – Finland
Suomi@iacworld.org
or contact the London office

Holland – Rotterdam
Nederland@iacworld.org
Phone: +31 (0) 87 190 2110

Italy – Bergamo
Bergamo@iacworld.org
Phone: +39 340 731 4195
or contact the Barcelona office

Mexico – Mexico City
Mexico@iacworld.org
Phone: +52 (55) 52 07 46 70
or contact the Miami office

New Zealand – Dunedin
NewZealand@iacworld.org
or contact the Sydney office

ARACE – THE INTERNATIONAL ASSOCIATION FOR THE EVOLUTION OF CONSCIOUSNESS

ARACE is an institution that approaches consciousness research with a focus on groupal evolution. It acts in the spheres of education, research and the extension and development of activities that intend to promote consciential holomaturity, having as a foundation the application of the science of Conscientiology.

ARACE promotes courses, lectures and workshops, open to the community, in the States of Espirito Santo, Minas Gerais, Paraná, Rio de Janeiro, Rio Grande do Sul, São Paulo and Santa Catarina. The institution has support teams in Cachoeiro de Itapemirim, Belo Horizonte, Curitiba, Foz do Iguaçu, Florianópolis, Porto Alegre, Ribeirão Preto, Rio de Janeiro, São Paulo, Uberaba and Vitória.

The activities are realized by a multidisciplinary team of volunteer-researchers specialized in the areas of architecture, administration, education, engineering, philosophy, journalism, marketing, medicine, psychology, information technology and tourism.

The research Campus headquarters is located in Venda Nova do Imigrante – ES, 25 kilometers from the city of Domingos Martins.

CAMPUS

ARACE's research Campus is situated on land that has a large amount of phytoenergy and geoenergy, in a place optimized for the realization of events and immersions. There are four halls with a spherical architecture called assemblies, plus a support area with a snack bar, store- room and bathrooms. For the lodging of researchers a Village exists, made up of eight apartments designed as mini-lofts.

FUNCTIONAL LINES

Applied Conscientiology

The Association offers courses regulated by the exemplarism of its researchers and contextually by the presupposed theories of the science of conscientiology. The set of themes are related to the self-research of the teachers and systemized from the theory-practice binomial (theorice).

The Applied Conscientiology (APC) course is taught over 2 basic years – which is composed of Multidimensional Self-Conscientization (MDS) and two more specialties, optional in nature, each lasting a further 2 years: the Pluri-Existential Self-Conscientization (PLS) course and the Teacher Self-Researcher (TES) course.

The team is also dedicated to the provision of original self-research laboratories. The first one developed is the Radical Heuristic Laboratory - Serenarium, whose basic proposal is 3 days of isolation to develop personal heuristics. ARACE also edits publications for the divulgation of its activities and research.

Conscientiological Organization

The set of themes concerning administrative-organization issues is one of the focuses of the performance of ARACE. The institution researches organizational and financial alternatives, in order to propose new administrative models to society that are based on the science of conscientiology.

Feasibility Projects Program in Conscientiology - FPPC

FPPC is one of the principal programs of ARACE, created for the establishment of partnerships with other conscientiocentric organizations in order to make projects in conscientiology possible. The program is open to all COs (conscientiological organizations) interested in materializing specific or supra-institutional projects. In order to establish a joint initiative, it is sufficient for the CO to submit a project, which could be implemented as long as it is coherent with the technical conditions expected by the FPPC.

The first partnerships have been agreed with the International Association of the Center for Higher Studies of Conscientiology (CHSC), which proposes the publication of works from the Encyclopedia of Conscientiology; and with the International Institute of Projectiology and Conscientiology (IIPC), to direct resources to a specific project of the institution.

ARACE - International Association for the
Evolution of the Consciousness
Rua Goiás, 67 B - Vila da Mata - Venda Nova do Imigrante – ES
– Brasil. CEP: 29375-000 – Telefax: +55 28 3546 2769
Site: www.arace.com.br
Site: www.conscienciologiaaplicada.com.br

CAMPUS OF THE INTERNATIONAL ASSOCIATION OF THE
CHSC – CENTER FOR HIGHER STUDIES OF CONSCIENTIOLOGY
1ST CONSCIENTIOLOGY CAMPUS SINCE 1995

CHSC (CEAEC in Portuguese) is the 1ˢᵀ Conscientiology Campus, established by volunteers of the IIPC in 1995. CHSC is located in Iguassu Falls (PR), the second most popular destination for international tourists in Brazil. The city is also characterized by the existence of 54 different ethnic groups and the border with Argentina and Paraguay.

This campus is coordinated by an international association of volunteers specialized in conscientiology. It is a non-profit organization that is maintained through courses and the periodic publication of technical books that divulge the results of conscientiological researches. Those interested can subscribe to or acquire the magazine Conscientia, a technical-scientific publication of conscientiology, created by the CHSC publishing company, where among others works research projects, original articles, results of work realized in Conscientiocentric Institutions, stories from the self-research laboratories, and reviews are divulgated.

CHSC aims to supply the conscientiology researcher an environment optimized for self-research and intraconsciential recycling. To this end, it provides an infrastructure favorable to updating volunteers, instructors, researchers, authors of books and those generally interested, in conscientiology:

• Bioenergetic Spa: an environment that predisposes the lucid utilization of consciential energies and the development of mentalsomatic attributes due to the ecological wealth of the campus. At least 4 types of immanent energies are able to be distinguished - geoenergy, aeroenergy, hydroenergy, and phytoenergy.

• 16 self-research laboratories: Self-organization, Cosmoethics, Cosmogram, Petifreeology, Evolutionary Duo, Vibrational State, Evolutiology, Waking Physical Immobility, Mentalsomatics, Paragenetics, Thosenology,

Proexis, Retrocognitions, Energetic Signals, Projective Techniques, and Penta.

• Acoplamentarium: the 1st laboratory of groupal self-research in the history of humanity, whose purpose is the development of lucid parapsychism through facial clairvoyance, energetic coupling and other techniques

• Village with a capacity to accommodate 48 researchers and a spacious dining hall

• Holotheca (collection of artifacts of knowledge): characterized by a library with about 40,000 items, books and periodicals from 54 countries, the majority specialized in parapsychism; the Comictheca, one of the biggest comic collections in Latin America, with more than 30,000 examples from 22 countries, in 16 languages; the Malacotheca possesses 9,000 shells

• Holocycle: the work area where the first *Encyclopedia of Conscientiology* and other scientific treatises - *Homo bellicosus* and *Homo neonatus*, are being produced.

The *Encyclopedia of Conscientiology* is a supra-institutional project, headquartered today at CHSC, which assembles more than 100 volunteers, under the coordination of Dr. Waldo Vieira, the propounder of conscientiology. The objective is to compile the main theories, techniques and research that clarifies, based on facts, the microuniverse of the consciousness with greater logic and rationality.

INTERNATIONAL ASSOCIATION OF THE
CENTER FOR HIGHER STUDIES
OF CONSCIENTIOLOGY −
CHSC
Rua da Cosmoética, 11, Região do Tamanduazinho
Caixa Postal 921, Centro, Foz do Iguaçu, PR, Brasil,
85851-000
Tel.: 55 45 525-2652 / Fax: 55 45 525-5511
Email: ceaec@ceaec.org
Site: www.ceaec.org

IIPC – INTERNATIONAL INSTITUTE OF PROJECTIOLOGY AND CONSCIENTIOLOGY

IIPC. The International Institute of Projectiology and Conscientiology - IIPC - is a research and education institution, established in 1988, that is dedicated to the development and divulgation of the sciences of projectiology and conscientiology.

Volunteer. It operates as a non-profit organization, through the activities of volunteers, and has maintained the title of a federal public utility since 1998.

Purpose. It has the purpose of being a cosmoethical transforming agent of intra and extraphysical societies, with increasing excellence in education, research and the application of conscientiology.

Mission. Its mission is defined as the collaboration with consciousnesses through technological, business enterprises and cosmoethical solutions, adding multifaceted values to their consciential gestations, with the intention to dynamise the evolution of all.

Materthosene. It has parapedagogy as an institutional materthosene - or main philosophy of work – defined as the specialty of conscientiology that studies the philosophy of education and pedagogy beyond the resources of intraphysicality, through lucid multidimensionality, the projectability of human consciousness, and its consequences in human life (Vieira, 1999).

Performance. Since its foundation, IIPC has continuously operated in Brazil, and the rest of the world, through scientific and didactic-pedagogic activities, in a total of nearly 130 cities in 16 countries, reaching more than 150,000 students. In May of 2002 IIPC transferred the administration of international units to the International Academy of Consciousness - IAC.

Formation. The IIPC has until now trained a total of 410 teachers of conscientiology and projectiology, nowadays IIPC possess a faculty of 230 teachers (October 2003).

Publishing company. The IIPC has, also since its foundation, operated a publishing company for the technical publications from the area of conscientiology and its specialties. As of October 2003 51 titles had been published, with a total of 176,000 books printed.

Campus IIPC - Saquarema. Situated in an area of 320,000 square meters, in the city of Saquarema, State of Rio de Janeiro, the IIPC Campus was inaugurated in March 2002 with the objective of being a complex for IIPC research and events. A scientific, cultural, assistential and universalistic reference in the consolidation of the leading-edge ideas of the sciences of projectiology and conscientiology. Nestled on land rich in immanent energies, located between the sea and the mountains, with landscaped terrain, a forest reserve, and the Roncador River, the Campus optimizes intraconsciential recycling, the development of bioenergetic and parapsychic potentialities and the healthy conviviality of people interested and motivated to dynamise their evolutionary process. The objective is to provide ideal conditions to all that are disposed to deepen their self-knowledge. Currently facilities available include chalets for lodging, an events hall, a restaurant, and an administrative centre. The first technical laboratories for Consciousness self-research are already being constructed.

IIPC Research Complex - Brasilia. Situated in the Federal Capital of Brazil - Brasilia - DF, the IIPC Research Complex is an international point of reference in the research of projectiology and conscientiology. It contains the first section of a Public Library specialized in parapsychic subjects and scientific self-research, whose initial objective is to make available the bibliography of the treatise Projectiology. Beyond the official research centre, the Complex houses the historical records of the IIPC. Possessing a specialized bookshop, video library, an event hall for debates and, in the future, a large laboratorial complex destined to contribute to the expansion of knowledge about conscientiology in society.

CONTACTS:

WORLD-WIDE HEADQUARTERS
Av. Das Américas, 500, bloco 2, salas 216 e 224
Barra da Tijuca, CEP 22631-000 –   Rio de Janeiro, RJ
Tel.: 55 21 3153-7575 / Fax: 55 21 3153-7941
E-mail: iipc@iipc.org.br / Home page: www.iipc.org

IIPC CAMPUS: (22) 2654-1186
E-mail: campusiipc@iipc.org.br

IIPC RESEARCH CENTRE: (61) 346-5573
E-mail: poloiipc@brturbo.com

BELO HORIZONTE: (31) 3241-1358
E-mail: iipcbh@task.com.br

CAMPO GRANDE: (67) 349-0123
E-mail: iipccgd@ig.com.br

CURITIBA: (41) 233-5736
E-mail: iipcctb@mps.com.br

FLORIANÓPOLIS: (48) 224-3446
E-mail: iipcfln@yatech.net

FOZ DO IGUAÇU: (45) 527-0798
E-mail: iipcfoz@ig.com.br

MANAUS: (92) 232-4291
E-mail: iipcman@argo.com.br

NATAL: (84) 234-3818
E-mail: unipcnatal@ig.com.br

PORTO ALEGRE: (51) 3224-0707
E-mail: iipcpoa@terra.com.br

RIO DE JANEIRO: (21) 3153-7574
E-mail: iipc.rj@iipc.org.br

SALVADOR: (71) 450-0628
E-mail: iipcsdr@ufba.br

SÃO PAULO: (11) 287-9705
E-mail: iipcsp@terra.com.br

IOC – INTERNATIONAL ORGANIZATION OF CONSCIENTIOTHERAPY

The International Organization of Conscientiotherapy - IOC is a conscientiocentric organization specializing in conscientiotherapy. Its objective is the establishment, development and maintenance of this specialty.

Founded on the 6th of September 2003, in the city of Iguassu Falls, Parana, Brazil, the International Organization of Conscientiotherapy is a non-profit institution, directed toward the practice of re-education in individual and groupal health.

The institution aims to be a multidimensional organization of excellence in conscientiotherapy, being a reference in the training and improvement of conscientiotherapists, acting in the establishment of the holothosene of health on the planet.

Conscientiotherapy studies the treatment, relief and remission of disturbances of the consciousness, executed through technical resources and derived from the approach of the "integral" consciousness, in its healthy, homeostatic, pathological and parapathological condition. It is one of the 70 specialties of conscientiology.

The term conscientiotherapy and its basic techniques were proposed in 1988 by doctor and researcher Prof. Waldo Vieira. The author based his studies in more than 20 years of experience in medicine and odontology, and more than 40 years of theorical (theoretical and practical) research of parapsychism.

Conscientiotherapy is based in the Consciential Paradigm and as a method of research and assistance looks to approach the human being in an integral way.

Its foundations have been established over 11 years of research, since the first CRG - Consciousness Research Group - in October 1992, during which conscientiotherapy was founded. In addition, through its volunteers in the area of health, the International Institute of Projectiology and Conscientiology (IIPC), was responsible for the establishment of experimental clinics of conscientiotherapy: the first one being founded at São Bernardo do Campo, São Paulo, in 1993; and the second in Rio de Janeiro, in 1995.

The Rio de Janeiro clinic was the starting point, in 1996, of the Centre of Integral Assistance to the Consciousness - CIAC (NAIC in Portuguese) which was responsible for the theorical activities of conscientiotherapy until September 2003.

NAIC, besides having attended more than 500 people since its founding, has trained 30 conscientiotherapists and organized the following:

- I Symposium of Conscientiotherapy (Iguassu Falls - PR, 1996);
- I Consciential Health Meeting (Rio de Janeiro - RJ, 2000);
- II Consciential Health Meeting (Rio de Janeiro - RJ, 2001);
- III Consciential Health Meeting (Iguassu Falls - PR, 2003).

It has also participated in other research events, such as:

- I Brazilian Congress of Psychotherapies (Belém - PA, 1996);
- II National Forum of Consciential Quality (Curitiba, PR - 1996);
- III International Congress of Projectiology (New York, USA - 2002).

The basic principle of conscientiotherapy is self-cure, or in other words, the relief or remission of pathologies and parapathologies through the will and action of the individual's own consciousness. As a result the individuals are called evolutients and not patients. Each one can, and must, be the agent of its own evolution and not a passive patient in relation to integral health. Self-cure is relative and demands constant investment and self-research on behalf of the individuals.

The term self-conscientiotherapy denotes a set of techniques utilized by the evolutient, when interested in promoting its self-cure, thus being the therapist of itself.

The International Organization of Conscientiotherapy is a center for the development of conscientiotherapy, where professionals in the area of health, acting as volunteers, systemize the techniques and research in this area.

IOC offers a series of conscientiotherapeutic activities available to interested people: individual, couples, family and group sessions (intensive or biweekly); and courses with a conscientiotherapeutic approach. Also there is already a program to train conscientiotherapists for those that want to be a volunteer of the institution.

INTERNATIONAL ORGANIZATION
OF CONSCIENTIOTHERAPY - IOC
Rua Rui Barbosa, 820, conjunto 506
Bairro Centro, Foz do Iguaçu, PR, Brasil,
CEP 85851-170
Tel / Fax: 55 45 3025-1404
E-mail: oic@consciencioterapia.org.br
Site: www.consciencioterapia.org

This book studies mnemosomatics, a subspecialty of conscientiology